DDR – Das Ende eines Staates

Reviews of previous volumes in the series

Unvollendete Geschichte

I find Hollis's work a model of its kind: challenging as well as reassuring, scholarly as well as 'consumer-oriented' … it should have no difficulty in cornering the market **German Teaching**

*With Andy Hollis's accomplished edition of Volker Braun's **Unvollendete Geschichte** the series has got off to an excellent start and set a high standard for future volumes …* **Modern Language Review**

Der Aufmacher

A feature of this edition which I find particularly valuable is its open-endedness. In his zeal to 'categorise and classify' Sandford does not treat the reader as a passive recipient of knowledge; this is a 'hands-on' edition for a fellow worker, for those who want, like Sandford, to get behind the enigma that is Wallraff **German Teaching**

Berlin seit dem Kriegsende

… the anthology is a useful foundation for courses combining language, literature and Landeskunde **Forum for Modern Language Studies**

DDR – Das Ende eines Staates

edited with introduction and notes by

Paul Jackson
University of Mannheim

943.087
DDR

1118996 /7

Permission to reproduce the German texts and extracts was
kindly granted by the following copyright holders:
Text 1, *Die Morgenpost*; Text 2, *Die Welt*; Texts 3, 46, *Junge
Welt*; Texts 7, 8, 11, 35, 42, *Neues Deutschland*; Text 10, *Neue
Ruhr-Zeitung*; Texts 13, 17, Quell Verlag; Texts 16, 24, Peter
Hammer Verlag; Texts 18, 34, 51, 65, *Der Spiegel*; Texts 21, 26, 64,
Frankfurter Rundschau; Text 31, *Stern*; Texts 32, 33, 36, *Die
Tageszeitung*; Text 38, Bundeszentrale für politische Bildung;
Texts 39, 43, Schroedel Verlag; Texts 44, 47, 49, *Süddeutsche
Zeitung*; Texts 52, 59, Knaur; Texts 54, 56, Elefanten Press;
Text 57, *Die Zeit*; Text 61, *Leipziger Volkszeitung*; Text 66,
Luchterhand

Published by Manchester University Press
Oxford Road, Manchester M13 9NR, UK
and Room 400, 175 Fifth Avenue,
New York, NY 10010, USA

*Distributed exclusively in the USA and Canada
by* St. Martin's Press, Inc.,
175 Fifth Avenue, New York, NY 10010, USA

British Library Cataloguing-in-Publication Data
A catalogue record for this book is available from the British Library

Library of Congress Cataloging-in-Publication Data
DDR, Das Ende eines Staates / edited with an introduction and
    notes by Paul Jackson.
        p. cm. — (Manchester German texts)
    Includes bibliographical references.
    ISBN 0-7190-3818-9 (pbk.)
    1. Germany (East) — Politics and government — 1989–1990 —
Sources.   2. Socialism — Germany (East) — History — Sources.
3. Germany — History — Unification, 1990.   4. Opposition
(Political science) — Germany (East) — History — Sources.
5. Social movements — Germany (East) — History — Sources.
I. Jackson, Paul, 1944– . II. Series.
DD289.D348   1995
943.1087'8—dc20   93-50586

ISBN 0 7190 3818 9 *paperback*

Typeset in Great Britain
by Williams Graphics, Llanddulas, North Wales
Printed in Great Britain
by Bell & Bain Ltd, Glasgow

26.07.96

Contents

Illustrations

Acknowledgements

My thanks to Juanita Bullough, Andy Hollis and, above all, Steve Parker for invaluable editorial assistance. My debt to Petra Hachenburger for her work on the typescript is immeasurable.

Map of the GDR

Introduction

These texts deal with the collapse of the German Democratic Republic. They treat German aspects of larger-scale European events at the end of the 1980s which were rapid, complex and interrelated in their development.

In summer 1989, in the weeks leading up to its fortieth anniversary, the GDR was shaken, as scores of its citizens began to escape across the Hungarian border into Austria and West Germany, followed later by hundreds and thousands.

Others occupied the West German embassies in Prague and Budapest and the Permanent Mission in East Berlin during the summer, until securing the right to leave as citizens of the Federal Republic.

During the autumn protests in Leipzig and other East German cities swelled into massive demonstrations for the right to travel, for democratic freedoms and against the power of the ruling SED and the *Stasi* security force.

On 9 November, as a result of popular pressure, the Berlin Wall and then the German–German borders were opened. Millions of East Germans were able to cross unhindered on sight-seeing and shopping trips to West Germany.

With calls for an end to the division of Germany growing, free elections were held in the GDR in March 1990, followed by negotiations on unification. The GDR became part of the Federal Republic on 3 October 1990.

The German Democratic Republic was a state of manifest achievements, which disintegrated as a result of its even more manifest failures. These were rooted in the GDR's specific geopolitical situation, adjacent and rival to the strongest economy in Western Europe. But its collapse was also systemic – a chapter in the rapid downfall of socialism throughout Eastern Europe at the end of the 1980s. In Poland the power of the Communist Party had been slowly eroded since the formation of the trade-union opposition movement Solidarity in 1980. In December 1989 the leading role of the Communist Party was removed from the Polish Constitution. In Hungary the Communist Party accepted the principle of multi-party democracy in February 1989. In May 1989 Hungary dismantled the border fencing with Austria (the Iron Curtain), setting in train the mass exodus from the GDR. In spring 1990 free elections were held. In Czechoslovakia ever-increasing popular pressure during November and December 1989 forced the Jakes government and the Communist Party Politburo to resign. In December the former dissident

1

and reformist figurehead Vaclav Havel was elected President. In Bulgaria the Communist Party leader Todor Zhivkov was ousted from office by his own party and later prosecuted for corruption and abuse of office. In Romania, after a bloody civil war between popular forces and the *securitate* secret police, the Communist Party autocrat Nicolai Ceausescu was captured and executed by firing-squad in December 1989. In Albania the authority of the Communist Party crumbled within a year despite electoral support from the peasantry. Yugoslavia imploded as a state and descended into civil war and the most appalling ethnic conflict and slaughter to occur in Europe since the war years. The Soviet Union finally broke up under the weight of nationalist movements in the Baltic region, in Georgia and other parts of the USSR. Following the failure of a coup against Mikhail Gorbachev in 1991 the Soviet Communist Party was declared illegal. The USSR was transformed into the loosely constructed CIS.

These events marked not just the end of the Cold War between East and West, but, in the opinion of some observers, the true end of the Second World War. We cannot understand the creation, development and decline of the GDR without seeing it as a direct outcome of this conflict (with 40 million Soviet war dead) and the political thinking which it produced.

East Germany after the Second World War

The situation in the Soviet Zone of Occupation in Germany from 1945 onwards was characterised by post-war chaos and the hostility between East and West, already developing into the Cold War.[1] There was a strong wish to overcome the deep historical fissure between German Communists and Social Democrats, which had been a substantial factor during the Weimar Republic, contributing to the rise of National Socialism.[2] The shared fate of German Communists and Social Democrats in Nazi prisons and concentration camps led to a strong desire in 1945 to collaborate in creating a democratic and anti-fascist Germany. But, despite broad co-operation between Communists and Social Democrats in the *Antifa* committees in the Soviet Zone and throughout Germany, the KPD (Ost) was initially opposed to any premature fusion with the SPD (Ost).

The amalgamation of the SPD (Ost) and the KPD and the formation of the *Sozialistische Einheitspartei Deutschlands* (SED) was carried out under Soviet pressure in April 1946, with the sharpening of East–West tensions and the rift developing between Stalin and Tito in Yugoslavia. There was also, however, strong rank and file support for popular front

2

unity in all four zones of occupation. The joint chairmen of the SED were the Communist, Wilhelm Pieck, who was to become the first President of the German Democratic Republic in 1949, and the Social Democrat, Otto Grotewohl, who became the first Minister President of the GDR. Grotewohl's deputy as head of the SED was Walter Ulbricht, who had been in exile in the Soviet Union since 1933. Ulbricht was to become the dominant political figure in the GDR for the first twenty years.

The evidence is that well into the 1950s the Soviet Union hoped to see a unified, demilitarised and neutralised Germany at the centre of Europe. In the early 1950s East German Communists were obliged to remain spokespeople for a united Germany. The founding of the GDR as a separate state was largely a reaction to initiatives taken by the West, in particular the United States. In contravention of the Big Four Potsdam Agreement of 1945 the economic unity of Germany was terminated by the Currency Reform in the Western Zones of Occupation in July 1948. The introduction of the D-Mark effectively put an end to Germany as an economic entity. In response the Ostmark was issued in the Soviet Zone four days later. Soviet pressure to prevent Berlin – with its special four-power status – from being included in the new western economic sphere led to the Berlin Blockade from June 1948 to May 1949. This was a major early confrontation in the evolving four-decade drama of the Cold War.

The Federal Republic was founded in September 1949, setting the seal on the division of Germany and anchoring West Germany in the western camp in the geopolitical stand-off with the Soviet Union. The German Democratic Republic was founded in October of the same year. The economic and political absorption of the two German states into separate blocs was followed by military integration. The West German Chancellor Adenauer campaigned long and hard for the rearmament of West Germany despite popular opposition in East and West. On 9 May 1955 the Federal Republic became a member of NATO (established in 1949). The Warsaw Pact alliance was founded five days later (East Germany joining in January 1956) to counter what the Soviet Union saw as military encirclement in Europe and beyond, part of a US roll-back strategy, using a 'revanchist' West Germany bent on regaining territories 'lost' in the East.[3] Strategically the GDR became an integral part of a *cordon sanitaire* erected and rigorously maintained by the Soviet Union for forty years to prevent a third invasion of its territory in this century. Depending on Cold War perspectives the GDR was depicted either as a forward base for Communist Aggression or as a bulwark against Imperialist Adventurism.[4] Pointing to the re-emergence of industrial, military and political groups in the Federal Republic who had played a leading role in the Third Reich, the GDR based its legitimacy on the elimination of those who had prosecuted Hitler's war. Its aim was the construction of the 'first Workers' and Peasants' State on German soil'. For forty years, by means of coercion, planned effort and economic achievement, the GDR survived the political and military polarisation which divided Europe and proved ruinous even to the superpower economies of the USSR and the United States.[5]

It is likely that East German leaders long saw themselves as a possibly expendable pawn in a larger geopolitical game. The events of 1989 and 1990 suggest that that, indeed, is what they were in the long term, as the USSR finally traded off its strategic defensive perimeter in Eastern Europe for the prospect of economic co-operation with the West. In the 1950s Soviet leaders had held out hopes that a united but neutral Germany – a much larger territorial version of Austria[6] – would be loosely socialist or social democratic in orientation and might thus be a factor for stability in Central Europe. The Stalin Note of 10 March 1952[7] offered German unification and a withdrawal of troops of occupation in return for German neutrality. This was a Soviet attempt to prevent the United States from using the territory and economic potential of West Germany in its conflict with communism. In western interpretations it was a ploy to prise Germany out of the western camp. It was clear to all sides that without a remilitarised West Germany in the western political bloc NATO would not have been viable.

The 1950s saw several East German *démarches* proposing to hold free elections in the whole of Germany, or to take part in an all-German conference on reunification. The offers, including plans for a confederation, were rejected by Bonn. The West German government refused to give recognition to an SED government of dubious democratic legitimacy, which it regarded as a Soviet puppet. It consistently demanded free elections in East Germany before negotiations could take place. Adenauer is said to have had little real interest in a reunited Germany with a probable Social Democratic electorate and hence a loss of CDU control. The Federal Republic refused to recognise the GDR as anything other than the 'Soviet Zone of Occupation'. The calls for German reunification became central to Western rhetoric. The GDR for its part now dismissed such demands and held out for recognition as a separate German state.

The SED State

Political pluralism was brought to an end and a Stalinist brand of Marxism–Leninism was imposed in East Germany with the onset of the Cold War.[8] From 1948 the Communists in the SED had begun to purge the party of Social Democratic elements, accusing them of collusion with the West and being instruments of imperialism. The SED leadership came to consist for the most part of Communists who had survived the anti-fascist struggle, many in prisons and concentration camps, or those who had spent the period since the rise of Nazism in exile in Moscow. Typical of the Moscow groups were those around Walter Ulbricht, whose experience in the Weimar Republic, the Spanish Civil War and under Stalin had taught them to be as hard with deviation within their own ranks as with the class enemy. The bitterness of imprisonment proved the formative experience of many other anti-fascists. Some, such as Erich Honecker, Horst Sindermann and Hermann Axen, were still members of the GDR's ruling gerontocracy in its final days. The years in Nazi prisons and concentration camps produced a mixture of anxiety, paranoia and a retributive sense of justice towards their fellow-countrymen. A further factor was the conspiratorial tightness inherited from the early days of the Bolsheviki in Russia, which reproduced itself in the inner-circle structures of the SED Politburo. Persecution under the Nazis not only depleted the German working-class movement of people of ability, but left a legacy of dogmatic inflexibility in the survivors which discredited the socialist cause they served. The SED came to define itself as a Leninist vanguard party, an instrument of proletarian dictatorship. Ulbricht and other opponents of Nazism regarded themselves as a select group whose record of resistance qualified them to lead a nation of fascist collaborators into a socialist future. Claiming a lineage with the revolutionary, progressive and humanist traditions of German history, they used the repressive methods of a Stalinist 'educational dictatorship'. Their revolution-from-above employed forms of coercion which ran counter to the widespread desire for a democratic and non-capitalist Germany. The methods, aimed to combat Cold War subversion from the West, formed a fateful symbiosis with the repressive authoritarianism recently employed by the Nazis.[9] But the notions of discipline, leadership and loyalty were linked to the Leninist principles of Democratic Centralism, exemplified by the rule of the Soviet Communist Party. A quasi-synthesis of democratic accountability and military command structures, Democratic Centralism was a form of political control suited to revolution in its first phase of consolidation, to combat factionalism and counter-revolutionary aggression. It was not, however, a basis for a modern, complex civil society and proved more amenable to creating bureaucratic totalitarianism than to harnessing popular will.

The military victory of the Soviet Union over the might of Hitler's Germany was thought to have demonstrated the superiority of centralised economic planning. After 1948 the Soviet Union became the model upon which East German socialism was to be based. The slogan was *'Von der Sowjetunion lernen, heißt siegen lernen!'* Although at a slower pace than other East European countries, the GDR nationalised and concentrated industries. It confiscated the property and land belonging to those inplicated with Nazism. Key industrial areas were taken into public ownership. A land reform was carried out, in which the property of the 7,000 largest landowners and *Junkers* was reallocated into small holdings and co-operatives before being reorganized into collective farms (LPGs, or *landwirtschaftliche Produktionsgenossenschaften*). Production indicators were worked out for factories by central planning authorities. The gratitude towards the Soviet liberators and the legacy of guilt for the USSR's 40 million war dead became the moral and political basis for the SED's subservience to the methods of Stalinism. The Stalinist brand of bureaucratic command socialism was typified by the total authority of the Party and the cult-of-personality. It was the political counterpart to Soviet War Communism[10] during its armed struggle against outside aggression and during the period of forced industrialisation. It carried over into the post-war period in Eastern Europe under conditions partly analogous – the industrialisation of predominantly agrarian economies, the 'purging' of bourgeois (or Nazi) elements and the maintenance of armed readiness against the real or imagined threat of aggression from the West. The main characteristics of Stalinism, in East Germany, as in most of Eastern Europe, were one-party rule, central administrative planning and the suppression of political opposition. The political primacy of the SED was written into the East German Constitution, the removal of this Article being one of the first demands of the demonstrators in autumn 1989. The SED Party apparatus and the state apparatus ran in tandem through a parallel hierarchy operative in all areas of society. SED control was ensured by an interlocking tenure of key posts in the Party, state institutions and mass organisations.

As in the Soviet Union, public political activity consisted of congresses, rallies, slogans popularising Party resolutions and productivity drives. Political schooling in Marxism–Leninism, declarations of international friendship, parades and awards were intended to raise popular political awareness. The display of portraits of Party functionaries, small-scale personality cults, were early attempts to produce the façade of popular support. Disaffection, controversy and democratic debate were stifled beneath displays of unanimity, support for congress resolutions and SED directives, commitments to implement five-year plans and to exceed production targets. Society was mobilised by SED cadres and mass membership of the SED as well as by the many organisations whose prime task it was was to act as 'transmission belts' for SED decisions.

Among the most important were the trade union *FDGB* (*Freier Deutscher Gewerkschaftsbund*), the youth movement *FDJ* (*Freie Deutsche Jugend*), the *Gesellschaft für Deutsch-Sowjetische Freundschaft*, the *Gesellschaft für Sport und Technik*, and the *Demokratischer Frauenbund Deutschlands*. The media and cultural activity were strictly controlled. Intellectual, educational and scientific work were subject to a stifling dogmatism. Creative and artistic projects followed the fluctuations of SED directives, sometimes strict, sometimes liberal. Literary modernism was rejected in favour of socialist realism. Up until the 1960s western culture, the formalism or nihilism of the avant-garde, jazz, pop music and western fashion were regarded as subversive influences. For many years watching western television was illegal, a ban which, however, it proved impossible to uphold.

The SED's adherence to constitutionality and legality was often a formality rather than a reality. Real power resided not with the state institutions of the *Volkskammer* or *Ministerrat*,[11] but with the Central Committee of the SED and the inner circle of the Politburo.[12] Parties other than the SED, the 'Allied Bloc' of the CDU (*Christlich-Demokratische Union*), LDPD (*Liberal-Demokratische Partei Deutschlands*), NDPD (*Nationaldemokratische Partei Deutschlands*) and DBD (*Demokratische Bauernpartei Deutschlands*) were organised into the National Front to create the semblance of political pluralism. Although the questioning, approval or rejection of candidates on the National Front Unity Lists was permitted, elections always became ritualistic demonstrations of support for SED-led policies. Participation in elections was compulsory. The use of the constitutional right to vote in secret and thus vote against the Unity Lists was enough to arouse suspicion and invite reprisals. Although occupying only a minority of seats in the *Volkskammer*, the SED kept a tight control through the representatives of the mass organisations which it dominated. The *Volkskammer* met only briefly each year. Its function was not to debate but to give the seal of approval to Politburo decisions with a unanimous vote.

Deriding what it regarded as the charade nature of bourgeois parliamentary democracy, with its sham choices, susceptibility to lobby influence, media manipulation and ultimate subservience to monopolies, the GDR redefined democracy in its own terms. For the SED this involved policies in the 'objective interests' of the working class (the vast majority of the population) and active participation in mass organisations. In reality democratic ownership of the means of production meant control by state bureaucracies, while mass participation subordinated individual action to group initiatives. In later years a large number of East Germans were involved in one representative body or another – works committees,

7

collectives, brigades – but few of these wielded any direct political influence. Political dissent, both inside and outside the SED, was rigorously prosecuted up until the 1960s and 1970s,[13] with more sophisticated methods being used later.

East Germany's economic and social development

The GDR faced a threefold task: making restitution to the Soviet Union for the ravages of the war, the maintenance of the *Nationale Volksarmee* (NVA) to oppose perceived western hostility, and the establishment of a new economic, social and political order. Political and civil rights and a popular, libertarian socialism throughout Eastern Europe were always contingent on achieving economic parity with the West with its domination of the global economy and world trade. As a result, 'socialism with a human face' was destined to remain an ever-receding prospect. After the war the US military governor in Germany, General Clay, forced the Soviet Union to draw its reparations exclusively from its own Zone of Occupation. There is agreement that the Soviet Zone bore the overwhelming burden of the reparations due to the Soviet Union, paying the economic price which was originally to have been extracted from Germany as a whole. This included requisitions, the dismantling and transfer of industrial plant, compulsory exports, and, until 1958, maintenance costs for Soviet troops. The division of Germany effectively absolved the Federal Republic from reparations payments to the countries of Eastern Europe.[14] Meanwhile US policy was to rebuild West Germany by means of Marshall Aid. The Federal Republic, with its social market economy, became a key trading partner and market for US imports and was established as a stable capitalist front-line state during the Cold War period.

Before the war the territory of East Germany had had largely light industry; it was predominantly agrarian and poor in natural resources. Economic policy was thus geared to making massive investments in heavy industry at the expense of improving living standards to match those in the West. The prevailing image of the GDR for many years was that of grim and oppressive drabness, as resources were poured into reparations and industrial investment. The collectivisation of agriculture led to an exodus of farmers and acute food shortages. Austerity measures and the decision by the SED to increase working norms and production quotas provoked unrest. Protests by building workers in Berlin in June 1953 escalated into an uprising with rioting in many parts of the GDR. Only the intervention of Soviet tanks was able to restore the situation. The evidence of western provocation did not obscure the fact that there was

8

little popular support for the SED state. Together with the Hungarian Uprising of 1956, the Polish October of 1956, the Prague Spring of 1968, the food riots in 1970 and strikes in 1980 in Poland, the repressive nature of SED rule served to discredit Eastern European socialism, despite its subsequent economic and social achievements. The GDR's greatest economic weakness was the constant drain of the population, as workers, artisans, farmers, technical workers and scientists left for the West. In the 1950s up to 200,000 were crossing East Berlin's open border to West Berlin each year, seeking both the greater affluence of the West and freedom from political constraints.

Ideological dependability as much as ability was the key to success in East Germany. Conformity[15] was largely ensured by SED control in all walks of life, in factories, in schools and universities, and in the local community. Social provisions, educational opportunities and promotion prospects were conditional on toeing the social and political line or at least the avoidance of anything that could be construed as detrimental to socialism. Political criticism could be − and was − seen in terms of an attack on Party office-holders; this, in turn, was interpreted as a breach of loyalty to the SED. Even changes in policy were tantamount to admissions of mistakes; such a confession of error undermined the Party's monopoly of wisdom and truth and cast doubt on the SED's entitlement to be the leading party of the working class and its monopoly on power. Debate was occasionally tolerated, then stifled. Reform was carried out from above in fits and starts. Mirroring the anti-communist hysteria in the West at the height of the Cold War, dissidence was branded as 'anti-Soviet', 'bourgeois' or 'CIA-inspired'. Criticism of the GDR from the left was 'Social Democratic', 'revisionist', 'Trotskyist' or 'left−utopian' in character. The threat of subversion from the West was countered by oppressive security and the omnipresence of the *Ministerium für Staatssicherheit (Stasi)*. The activities of the *MfS* were partly directed at the identification of troublemakers and the early control of unrest, but they were also those of surveillance and information-gathering. This later involved huge numbers of agents, informants and 'unofficial collaborators'. Although mostly covert, much of the work of the SED's 'Shield and Sword' was deliberately conspicuous, producing the collective 'surveillance trauma', to which, it was reported, even top Politburo members succumbed. The many arrests and show trials of the 1950s produced a stifling, repressive climate. Later, critics who were not actually prosecuted were frequently forbidden from working or publishing. Before the building of the Berlin Wall some left for the West; others were exposed to continuous bureaucratic harrassment or placed under house arrest.

Nonetheless, by the mid-1950s significant economic growth had been achieved in the GDR with claims of growth rates of up to 13 per cent per annum, as investments in basic industries began to pay off. Despite political disaffection and continued problems in economic planning the GDR established a leading position in the Eastern bloc. It gained a measure of support from the population by guaranteeing employment, housing at low rents and cheap food; it provided generous education and training opportunities, giving working-class children preferential admission to higher education and offering career prospects to workers. The abolition of old structures after the war, the establishment of a new state and administrative apparatus and rapid industrialisation created new openings for thousands of East Germans. The replacement of older elites – those with a Nazi record or those who left for the West – secured career opportunities and a sense of allegiance to the GDR. For a new generation, upward social mobility provided rewards which compensated for any political frustrations or desire for the luxuries of the richer West German state.

In February 1956 the repressive character of Stalinism and the crimes for which the Soviet leader was responsible were condemned by Khrushchev at the Twentieth Congress of the Soviet Communist Party. This was the signal for at least a verbal retraction of the methods of Stalinism in East Germany as well. But Ulbricht survived the discrediting of Stalinism. He was saved from replacement by the more liberal Karl Schirdewan by the need to counter unrest in the Soviet bloc after the Hungarian Uprising in 1956.

Attracted by the Western economic boom fuelled by the Korean War (1950–53) and the growing affluence of the Federal Republic, the flow of skilled workers from East Germany contributed to the West German *Wirtschaftswunder* in the 1950s. Despite attempts to catch up with West German living standards the GDR was unable to stop the economic haemorrhaging caused by the flight of thousands to the West. To prevent imminent economic collapse the border between East and West Berlin was closed on 13 August 1961. Work began on the Berlin Wall, which was to divide the city until 9 November 1989.

A total of 200 people were killed by gunfire or mines while trying to cross the Berlin Wall or the border to West Germany. The East German population as a whole became resigned to being cut off from the West. With the building of the Berlin Wall, however, the recurring East–West confrontations over the city ended. The international situation was stabilised. The Federal Republic maintained its claim to represent *all* Germans (*Alleinvertretungsanspruch*). It isolated the GDR from countries outside the Eastern bloc with the *Hallsteindoktrin*, threatening to break off diplomatic and trading links with countries which recognised the GDR. Nevertheless, it became apparent in time that the building of the Berlin Wall had enabled the GDR to consolidate and develop its economy. It achieved considerable growth rates in the 1960s and 1970s. Consumer goods were more widely available. Leisure time increased. Social benefits became more generous. Economic reforms reduced the role of centralised planning and allowed the GDR's economy to grow into the strongest in Eastern Europe. East Germany, however, could not free itself from the image of a country which protected its citizens with barbed-wire fencing, watchtowers, mined land-strips and self-triggering automatic guns.

As a result of fundamental weaknesses in its methods of economic management the GDR was never able to catch up with the Federal Republic. Inflexible planning and the concentration on quantitative targets led to repeated shortages or wasteful overproduction. Attention to quality was neglected, often resulting in shoddy goods or items which remained unsellable. People complained about the unavailability of products or long waiting-periods. Frequently there were large-scale deliveries of items which were not needed or which entered the shops at the wrong time of the year. A poor infrastructure and cumbersome distribution often resulted in local shortages. Products available in Leipzig might be in short supply in Rostock. There were campaigns to eliminate wastefulness and inefficiency or to introduce modern methods. But socialist competition between *Volkseigene Betriebe* (*VEB*) did not raise productivity or yield the expected benefits. Over-centralised planning proved to be a brake on innovation and initiative. This became all the more serious the more the economy needed to move from the first phase of extensive growth to a phase of intensive growth requiring a more sophisticated and flexible mode of production. Planning often degenerated into a charade. For example, workers and plants submitted low planning targets to the central authorities in the ministries in order to be able to claim bonuses for exceeding targets. Regular shortages obliged firms to submit exaggerated orders for raw materials or components. Cheap basics, including energy, encouraged wastefulness and provided no incentive to increase productivity. The massive resources required for subsidies on food and housing became a drain on the economy, preventing the necessary reinvestment in capital stock. Pricing methods made any reliable system of cost-accounting difficult to achieve. Labour productivity was about only one-third of that in West Germany. People were free to come and go from work, for instance to consult the works' doctor – or to go shopping. But the relatively relaxed work-discipline was outweighed by the grinding search for essentials or queueing in shops, or by moonlighting on other jobs outside hours. The regular announcement in the media of

11

victories on the production front and the exceeding of planning targets met with unamused popular cynicism.

The normalisation of East and West German relations

Economically and politically, the West maintained a propaganda advantage over socialist states such as the GDR. While exercising their own post-colonial forms of domination, draining Third World economies through interest payments on credit and doing business with repressive dictators and racist regimes, western leaders championed the cause of liberal democracy in the politically and economically un-free states of Eastern Europe. But by the 1960s the GDR was coming to be generally perceived as an economic and political fact of life. It became conventional wisdom in East and West that in the age of nuclear weapons any disturbance of the status quo could have serious and unforeseen consequences. The pragmatics of peaceful coexistence came to displace the hostility of the Cold War. The apparently stable political division of Europe, including the existence of the GDR, became accepted realities. In the late 1960s the GDR benefited from the fundamental shift from the Cold-War attitudes of the CDU-led administrations in West Germany. During the period of the CDU–SPD Grand Coalition (1966–69) and in the era of the Social–Liberal Coalition governments under the SPD Chancellors Willy Brandt and Helmut Schmidt (1969–82) the two German states worked towards a *modus vivendi*. Brandt's *Ostpolitik* paved the way for a series of agreements between East and West which scaled down the level of Cold War confrontation.[16]

In May 1971 Erich Honecker was elected Walter Ulbricht's successor as First Secretary of the SED. Honecker became as central a figure in the next eighteen years of the GDR's history as Ulbricht had been in the first two decades. Other powerful members of the Politburo were Willi Stoph, Kurt Hager, Egon Krenz and Erich Mielke. Whereas Ulbricht had laid emphasis on the development of the industrial base after the war, Honecker's domestic policies were aimed at increasing living standards. He also held out the promise of greater liberalisation, although the SED's control over all aspects of economic and political life was strengthened under the impact of the Prague Spring in Czechoslovakia in 1968 and social and political unrest in Poland in 1970.

In 1972 the *Grundlagenvertrag* was negotiated between the two German states. The agreement fell short of a full recognition of GDR statehood. Permanent diplomatic missions, not embassies, were established in Bonn and East Berlin. But the treaty marked the end of the Hallstein Doctrine and ended the diplomatic isolation of the GDR by the West. A key factor in the process of detente, it provided a basis for economic co-operation between East and West Germany in the next two decades. The SPD approach of 'change through *rapprochement*' (*Wandel durch Annäherung*) meant that in return for *de facto* recognition and economic co-operation the GDR was prepared to allow its citizens greater contact with the West. In 1973 the GDR became a member of the UN together with the Federal Republic. By 1975 it had been recognised by 115 countries. It was also earning widespread international acclaim and domestic legitimacy from its own people through its phenomenal successes in sport, in particular athletics. In 1975 both Germanies signed the Final Act of the Conference on Security and Co-operation in Europe. The Helsinki Agreements met eastern demands to guarantee the inviolability of existing borders in Europe and western demands to commit all nations to observe basic human and civil rights, including the right to emigrate. *Ostpolitik*, the *Grundlagenvertrag* and the Helsinki Agreements were to open up East German society to western influences and oppositional social pressures which in the end proved subversive and impossible to control.[17]

Upon assuming office in 1971 Honecker declared that taboos were a thing of the past in intellectual life. He initiated a period of cultural openness during which novels, plays and films criticising aspects of life in the GDR were tolerated.[18] Living standards were improved. An impressive housing programme was carried out. Spending on the building of flats tripled in the 1970s. This allowed millions of East Germans to move into modern, though somewhat cramped apartments, with an improved range of furnishings and consumer goods. The 1970s was also a period in which the GDR developed a more relaxed attitude to western popular culture. Long hair, jeans, rock music and fashion were no longer regarded as features of terminal decadence. As a result of the process of normalisation with the Federal Republic the number of visitors from the West increased. Arrangements on cross-border travel (*Grenzverkehr*) and family visits to the Federal Republic made for improved contacts between East and West. More and more East Germans learned at first hand about the higher living standards in the West.

The policy of co-operation with the West in economic and technical fields was flanked by a policy of 'demarcation' (*Abgrenzung*) in the hope of inoculating East Germany against western values and ideas. The GDR authorities tried to limit the number of western visitors at times of heightened political tension by increasing the amount of money visitors had to exchange (*Zwangsumtausch*). Two million state employees were forbidden from personal contact with western visitors. A clampdown was imposed on the GDR's own critics on the Marxist left, which hit particularly those who published in the West. A key figure for many years was the scientist Robert Havemann, who called for political pluralism and an end to Soviet hegemony in Eastern Europe but who also criticised the slavish imitations of western consumerism. He anticipated the Eurocommunist line advocated in the 1970s and 1980s in Spain, Italy and France. One of the SED's most formidable critics, Havemann was kept under constant observation and placed under house arrest in his final years. The writer Stefan Heym, who was to be styled the 'Nestor' of the Autumn Revolution of 1989, was obliged to publish most of his work in the West. Although a defiant critic of the SED, Heym maintained his commitment to socialism in the GDR, refusing to leave for the Federal Republic, as other writers did. The controversies around the work of GDR writers such as Heiner Müller, Volker Braun, Christa Wolf, Ulrich Plenzdorf and Günter Kunert also signalled the broader degree of opposition among East German authors and intellectuals. Some of it emerged from the ranks of the SED itself. Rudolf Bahro, for instance, was a former SED technocrat, who published *Die Alternative*, a Marxist critique of centralist Stalinist structures and dictatorial bureaucracy. Sentenced to eight years in prison, he was expelled to the West in 1979. Wolf Biermann, the critical *Liedermacher* and friend of Havemann's, was banned in 1965 from performing in the GDR owing to his bitter songs on the SED perversion of socialism. His expulsion in 1976 marked the end of the liberal phase of the early Honecker years and generated a rift between the SED and many leading GDR writers.[19]

The view of East German socialism as monolithic and closed to debate is misleading. It can be assumed that internal SED criticism and debate was widespread. What was disapproved of was not criticism but *open* criticism, always seen as exposing a flank to the Cold War enemy. In 1978 the West German *Spiegel* published a *Manifest der Opposition*. This radical criticism of SED orthodoxy and demands for reform were thought to reflect not only popular feeling, but to have been formulated by high-ranking members of the SED. The question of the precise authorship of the *Manifest* became as hot an issue as the critique itself. Although the GDR found ways of dealing with challenges from its internal critics, they represented subversive currents which were to survive and re-emerge prior to the collapse of the SED state in 1989. Rolf Henrich's *Der vormundschaftliche Staat* (1989) was a final comprehensive rejection of SED socialism by a former communist and founding member of the opposition group Neues Forum in 1989.

Symptomatic though they were of wider dissatisfaction, the GDR's own critics remained relatively isolated figures. The SED was able to buy off political disaffection with improved levels of affluence and the introduction of privileges for those who accommodated themselves to the system. *Intershops, Delikat* and *Exquisit* shops provided western and luxury items for those granted access or for those who had western currency. Membership of the political, managerial, scientific or artistic and sports elite made it easier to get hold of western currency and to travel to the West. Loyalty was secured in return for privileges in obtaining holidays, hospital treatment, shorter waiting-periods for cars and consumer durables. This did not necessarily mean that Party and state officials automatically enjoyed privileges denied to the rest of the population. Anyone with western contacts or those sent D-Marks by relations in West Germany could buy quality products. This, in turn, fuelled resentment among those with no access to western currency. It became possible, however, for most East Germans to develop a domestic life-style using the 'second economy' based on the D-Mark, or by resorting to alternative sources of income. What evolved was a shadow economy with barter, under-the-counter sales, black-market goods, petty theft, and also large-scale corruption. These arrangements, to which the authorities turned a blind eye, were a constant source of frustration, but they also provided a means of living tolerably on a day-to-day basis. Those who chose to evade political pressures or not to be involved in social or political work developed a comfortable life-style in what became a characteristic feature of the GDR – the 'niche' society, the withdrawal into privacy, the escape to the allotment and the *dacha* on the outskirts of the city at the weekend.

The Façade of Stability

It is a mistake to believe that the GDR was a chronically unstable state throughout its history, held together by *Volkspolizei* and *Stasi*. Over a limited period it was not unsuccessful in creating a separate GDR national identity. What emerged was less a commitment to a socialism which always appeared to be lagging behind the *soziale Marktwirtschaft* of West Germany, but more a sense of egalitarian social justice mixed with a sense of national pride. This evolved out of an awareness of East German economic and social achievements in the face of great difficulties. It was also partly a response to the overbearing and patronising attitudes of West Germans visiting the GDR. Even allowing for its collapse in 1989, the view of the GDR as a social and economic disaster needs qualification. In view of the catastrophic conditions from which it started out, its achievements were considerable. With few natural resources in the less industrialised area of Germany, it carried the burden of the enormous reparation payments due to the Soviet Union. As a non-recipient of Marshall Aid and only later profiting from co-operation with West

Germany, it carried out a reindustrialisation programme on its own, developing heavy industry, engineering, textiles, chemical products and electrical goods. While regularly losing skilled workers, engineers, scientists and technicians to the West, it grew into one of the world's leading industrial nations. In its final years, it was also building up an advanced electronics industry. Despite oil price explosions in the 1970s, its living standards rivalled those in many areas of Western Europe. By the 1980s it was claiming a higher per capita gross national product than Britain and Italy. It had a skilled and well trained work force. General levels of education were high, and a growing proportion of the population had university or technical college qualifications. This in itself produced resistance to SED controls on intellectual activity and thought. A socially more egalitarian society than in the West, the GDR avoided major disparities in private wealth, notwithstanding privileged access to luxury goods and the emergence of an East German *Schickeria*. Its polytechnic system of education, aimed at eliminating the distinction between academic and vocational training, had its admirers in the West, as did the polyclinics, offering a comprehensive level of free medical provision in most areas. It boasted cheap subsidised food and basics, low rents, minimal charges for energy and public transport. It offered job security, protection from social marginalisation and the avoidance of an 'underclass' such as was re-emerging in the West. Women had a high degree of financial and social independence and professional opportunities, although, as in the West, they were conspicuously absent from top administrative or political posts. Childcare provisions – kindergartens, crèches – were generous, enabling both parents to go out to work, although male attitudes in the GDR, as elsewhere, remained slow to change. Maternity leave involved a full year at home on full pay. Crime rates were low and right-wing and racist extremism was kept in check. East Germans were well-dressed and their homes, though sometimes providing only limited space, were better furnished and equipped with consumer goods than their run-down façades often suggested. Life remained circumscribed by bureaucracy. East German public servants learned nothing of the civility of their western counterparts. The inability to travel to the West remained people's major grievance, particularly as fewer and fewer intended to use the chance to emigrate. The pace of life and discipline of work was more relaxed than in the competitive West. The GDR embarked slowly on the renovation of old historical areas and the modernisation of dilapidated housing stock. The pouring of resources into prestige projects produced civic pride but also resentment. Music and the theatre were heavily subsidised. Visits to museums, art galleries, theatres and concerts were encouraged. Cheap editions of the world's classics were made available; the GDR had a flourishing literary culture, although reading was widely regarded as a substitute for more direct experience of the world outside. The work of its writers and artists was as interesting as much of what was available in the Federal Republic, and its theatrical and musical performers were increasingly invited to work in the West. The GDR's standing in science was internationally recognised. A more sophisticated Marxist approach to the humanities, history, literary studies and philosophy, produced work of high quality.

Despite seeking peaceful coexistence with the West, the GDR maintained its ideological hostility to capitalism. Any claim which the GDR had to being a revolutionary and socialist society lay − *ex negativo* − in the absence of those features which it saw as characteristic of the West: the inherited influence of social elites, the uncontrollable power of speculators, monopolies and multinationals, the recurrence of unemployment, crises and slumps, control of the world economic order, exploitation of the Third World and support for dictators and military juntas. The GDR came to play a limited but significant role in the Third World and in Arab countries. It gave support to anti-imperialist liberation movements in southern Africa. It assisted post-colonial countries such as Angola, Mozambique, Ethiopia, Guinea-Bissau, Cuba and Vietnam, providing skilled labour, know-how, medical help and technical and military support.

Most areas of the GDR were able to receive West German television. While filtering out the tedious optimism of SED propaganda, East Germans obtained information and a reading of world events in their own media not generally available in the West. This combination produced a population which was politically literate and at least as well-informed as much of the media audience in the West, entertained to death and narcotised by trivia. But the long-term, cumulative influence of West German television stimulated a desire for western living standards, an appetite for consumer goods of a better quality than the shoddy domestic products, a wittier, more libertarian and laid-back youth culture, and a more open and pluralistic type of public discourse. In their perception of their western neighbours they were torn between images of a shopping-complex cornucopia and a cold and competitive *Ellenbogengesellschaft.*

Tensions between the USA and the USSR increased again during the 1980s during what came to be called the 'Second Cold War'.[20] But, as far as their bloc commitments would allow, the two German states worked to sustain their closer co-operation and to reduce tensions to a minimum. In December 1981 SPD Chancellor Helmut Schmidt conferred with Honecker outside Berlin. The result was an increase in the number of East Germans allowed to visit the Federal Republic. The effort to maintain constructive relations continued after the Social−Liberal coalition of

Schmidt in Bonn was replaced by the CDU–FDP government of Helmut Kohl in October 1982. The process of normalisation even survived the tensions over the stationing of Soviet and American medium-range missiles in central Europe. There were few, even in West Germany, who doubted the GDR's commitment to peace and military disengagement. If East German socialism was militarised, it was not militaristic.

In July 1983 the West German cold warrior, the CSU leader Franz Josef Strauss, visited the GDR. He took the world and his own conservative supporters by surprise by arranging a government-backed loan of DM1 billion to the GDR, outwardly, at least, an acknowledgement of the stability of the East German state.

An ever-increasing number of East Germans below retirement age were allowed to visit the Federal Republic on urgent family business – by 1985 up to 200,000 per year. The GDR also began to allow its citizens to emigrate to the West. In 1984, however, prefiguring events in 1989, several hundred East Germans occupied the West German diplomatic mission in East Berlin, demanding asylum. Others entered the West German Embassy in Prague, also demanding permission to emigrate to the West. The crisis was resolved by the GDR promise to process their applications for legal emigration. While West Germany continued to guarantee further loans, upon which the GDR economy was becoming increasingly dependent to finance imports, East Germany reduced its currency exchange requirements, which had discouraged large numbers of West Germans from travelling to East Germany. The East–West confrontation threatened to come to a head again, as NATO carried out 'modernisation' of its missile programme, claimed to be a response to the stationing of SS20 missiles by the Soviet Union. As a result of Soviet pressure, Honecker's planned visit to the Federal Republic was postponed twice. Meanwhile, on a party level, the West German SPD and the SED worked on joint proposals for non-provocative defence strategies and plans for an atom-free zone in central Europe. The culmination of German–German detente was when Honecker finally paid his official visit to Bonn in September 1987. Though the Federal government still paid lip service to the constitutional aim of German unification, Honecker's trip appeared to mark the normalisation of relations and the acceptance of the GDR as an equal partner.

In the 1980s income levels in East Germany reached 75 per cent of average levels in the European Community. Increasing living standards and the drop in the number of East German visitors who opted to stay in West Germany suggested to the SED a degree of social stability in the GDR that made political liberalisation unnecessary. The overall economic situation, however, began to deteriorate, producing both immediate and longer-term causes for growing political unrest.[21] While incomes increased by 4 per cent annually, the gross economic output only increased by an average of 2 per cent between 1981 and 1987. The failure of output to meet rises in demand led to bottlenecks in supply, which the State tried to meet by importing from the West. The outlay on improved living standards meant a lack of investment in the modernisation of the GDR's productive capacity. This resulted in a further drop in productivity and a reduction in the attractiveness of GDR products in the West. The value of GDR exports to western countries dropped by 50 per cent in the 1980s, aggravating the shortage of convertible currency. The gross national product doubled in the 1980s but the outlay for subsidies more than trebled, and in the case of foodstuffs rose fourfold. This was covered by draining further capital resources from industry, which reduced even further the scope for investment and modernisation. By the 1980s defence expenditure was rising at double the rate of national income growth. This placed a further intolerable burden on a system of socialism which – in the Soviet Union and Eastern Europe as a whole – was defending itself to the point of economic self-destruction.[22]

The industrialised world was moving from conventional 'extensive' economic growth into an era of 'intensive' growth technologies, where Eastern Europe lagged behind not only the West but also Pacific-rim countries. The SED was more than aware of the need to keep up with the 'technical–scientific revolution' both to survive competitively and in order not to fall into total technological dependence on the West. Honecker declared the GDR's aim of playing a central role in the micro-electronic future. Massive resources were directed into the development of semiconductors, robotics, CAD/CAM and the technology of flexible automation. But not even the high-tech products which GDR technology produced at crippling expense were able to compete in a global market in which even West European and American companies were falling behind. Investment in high-tech prestige projects such as the *Kombinat Robotron* meant neglect of other strategic areas. The result was further shortages, massive under-investment in energy, communications, construction, the infrastructure and a scandalous failure to deal with environmental and pollution problems that were among the worst in Europe. Discontent mounted.

Like most other East European countries, the GDR became dependent upon credit from the West to resolve its internal difficulties. It required loans, which the West was eager to give, to finance trade, to meet consumer needs, to keep up with rises in world commodity prices, to import western technology and to service its own mounting debts to the West. East Germany became caught in the credit trap, which not only placed a stranglehold on the economies of Eastern Europe and the Third World, but also led to massive levels of private, corporate and government indebtedness in the West.[23] The GDR's currency debt increased sevenfold between the late 1970s and late 1980s. The logical outcome of this growing dependence on the West was either to push the economy to the point of collapse or to sacrifice economic sovereignty, dragging the GDR into an effective economic community with West Germany. Seen in this light, the huge loan to the GDR negotiated by Franz Josef Strauss, which shocked many in his own party, was not only consistent with detente and a new era of economic co-operation; it was also part of a long-term strategy whose resolution Strauss did not live to see — the irrestistible gravitational pull of an insolvent GDR into the orbit of the West.

The run-down condition of much industrial plant and housing stock in the GDR, which only became known to a wider public after the Autumn Revolution of 1989, was an indication of the extent to which the GDR had been living beyond its means. The SED Politburo member responsible for economic planning, Günter Mittag, is said to have concealed the gravity of the situation with rigged balance-sheets. The statistical authorities were forbidden from issuing reliable figures. Honecker's only elementary grasp of economics led to a further neglect of the crisis despite the growing complaints. Nevertheless, it seems implausible in retrospect that the true scale of the GDR's long-term predicament was unknown - either in the Politburo or in the inner circles of Bonn. What was conventionally described as the 'surprise' nature of the GDR's collapse in 1989 was, on the contrary, all too predictable for those with inside information. In 1992 the CDU politician Wolfgang Schäuble conceded that the GDR's trouble-shooter on matters of currency and trade, with close intelligence links in the West, Alexander Schalck-Golodkowski, had told him about the real condition of the East German economy in 1986. It was not only far worse than official figures suggested, but also more precarious than even intelligence reports indicated.

Protest comes to a head

The signing of the Helsinki Agreements in 1975 had put human and civil rights on the agenda in the countries of the Soviet bloc and had given encouragement to opposition groups and civil rights campaigners throughout Eastern Europe, including the GDR.[24] A political counter-culture emerged developing the necessary survival skills to deal with harassment and *Stasi* surveillance. Most of the groups were devoted to single-issue campaigns and they coalesced only briefly during the peaceful revolution. Some were pacifists, like the *Schwerter zu Pflugscharen* movement. They protested against *Wehrkunde*, the preparatory military instruction in schools and the hostile propaganda still aimed at the West, increasingly anachronistic in the age of detente. A major issue was the failure of the GDR to provide a non-military option for conscientious objectors. Refusal to do military service usually put an end to a young person's further-education prospects; pupils who wore the Swords-into-Ploughshares badge at school were subject to reprisals. A grass-roots peace movement grew up in the GDR parallel to that in the Federal Republic, protesting against the stationing of Cruise and Pershing missiles and the growing threat of a nuclear holocaust. This campaign had the benevolent support of the authorities; the SED government conspicuously dragged its feet on the stationing of Soviet SS20s. Peace forums, peace weeks and workshops in the early 1980s attracted thousands of young East Germans, providing embryonic forms of grass-roots political activity on other issues. Peace and civil rights provided a platform for an East–West dialogue between activist groups.

Ecology became another focus for protest, as the catastrophic damage of the GDR's heavy industry to the environment became evident. Half the river mileage was unsuitable for bathing in, let alone for drinking. Many lakes were biologically dead. Permanent smog conditions blighted the industrial area around Leipzig, Bitterfeld and Halle. The use of brown coal for heating and electricity generation produced sulphur dioxide emissions three times higher than that of the much larger Federal Republic. Forty per cent of the forests were affected by *Waldsterben*. Asthma and lung cancer were widespread in industrial regions. The incidence of respiratory ailments and skin diseases was high among children. The figures on real pollution levels and life expectancy in industrial areas, still unpublished in a secretive society, made a mockery of the GDR's claims of an exemplary health system.

The Evangelical (Lutheran) Church acquired the role of a sanctuary for many of the dispersed opposition groups, for dissent and counter-culture protest. It provided a forum for alternative values and discussion[25] and became a training ground in the methods of non-violent resistance. The Church had achieved a basis of reciprocal tolerance with the SED state by defining itself as a 'church-in-socialism'. It accepted the principles of East German society, Christians and socialists finding common moral ground on issues of peace and social equality. But the Church was also a focus for the autonomy of individual conscience and free judgement – its Protestant legacy – particularly in matters leading to conflict between the individual and authority. The church was a moral safety-valve for dissent, but, as became evident only after German unification, it also served as a listening-post for the *Stasi*, which was able to use church groups as a base for monitoring opposition.

As observers have commented, the ranks of dissidents and protesters were full of those who had been members of socially or politically active organisations in the cause of socialism. In some cases they were the daughters and sons of party cadres, whose thwarted idealism turned towards peace, ecology, civil rights and alternative life-styles. They were largely the men and women who were to take a lead in the early days of the Autumn Revolution. There were approximately 160 groups of about 25,000 activists, with a hard core of only 60, according to *Stasi* estimates.

Greater tolerance began to be demanded even by those writers[26] who remained loyal to the GDR. This had been evident at the time of Biermann's expatriation in 1976, but also from calls for greater openness at the conference of East and West German writers organised by Stephan Hermlin in 1981. Writers and artists started to focus on individual and subjective problems rather than on social and political issues. The idea was challenged publicly that under GDR socialism the interests of the individual and those of the State were congruent. Women writers were now questioning the notion that socialist emancipation lay alone in the right of women to work, at least given the prevailing conditions and the slow change in attitude among East German men.[27]

The counter-culture which emerged in all Eastern European countries in the 1970s and 1980s in response to western influences became a school for *Zivilcourage*. It was partly an underground scene, partly a fringe culture tolerated on the margins of society. The counter-culture evolved values, an aesthetic of insubordination and a philosophy of life which conflicted with the clean-scrubbed ideals of the FDJ and SED. Individuals either pursued socialist ideals to a more logical limit or imitated the recalcitrant style and streetwise manner of punks and skinheads. Although GDR youth culture made a fetish out of western merchandise, jeans, Coke, Walkmen and western rock, it also gave young East Germans the confidence to mock official rituals, cope with intimidation and push back the limits of official tolerance. At their re-election in 1986 eight members of the Politburo were in their seventies. This was a gerontocracy ill-equipped to deal with insolence. More people were beginning to be bored by ageing SED authority than those who were afraid of it. A growing number of people, wishing to see the wider world and to escape from the claustrophobia of the GDR, set about applying for exit permits. They suffered discrimination at work, forfeited claims to social benefits and their applications were processed only very slowly. Applications which were rejected were not accompanied by any explanation. The right to travel and to emigrate became the most provocative issue in the GDR, emerging as the prime focus for protest during the 1980s. The authorities issued an increasing number of permits, but were not able or willing to keep pace with the growing number of applications. The issue came to a head in 1989.

Hopes for political reform in Eastern Europe lay in the prospect of the older generation of 'hard-liners' being replaced by more open-minded technocrats, less burdened by dogma or memories of the war. But these reformers, for their part, were suspected of wanting to open socialism too much to influences from the West. Mikhail Gorbachev's elevation to the leadership of the Soviet Communist Party in 1985 signalled the radical break with the structures of Stalinism. Gorbachev's aim was to create a more open and democratic society (*Glasnost*) and less rigid forms of government and management (*Perestroika*). Gorbachev realised that without radical reform socialism could not challenge liberal democracy, whose welfare policies were sustained by modernising, global capitalism. To all outward appearances immune to crisis and able to contain social and political turbulence, western capitalism seemed to East European reformers strong enough to sustain affluence, welfare policies and technological modernisation. At the same time, in terms of military technology, it was beginning to pull away from the Soviet bloc, which would only be able to keep pace again by diverting even vaster economic resources away from civil into military projects. Gorbachev abandoned the assumptions underlying East–West confrontation. He resolved to overcome the obsolete political, ideological and military divide and propagated the 'common European home'. This involved forgoing the use of force in defence of the Soviet *cordon sanitaire* and abandoning the doctrine of the 'limited sovereignty' of allied socialist states. The strategic importance of countries such as the GDR against West German territorial claims in the East or against NATO aggression became a secondary consideration in view of the critical need for western credit and know-how and the urgency of cutting military budgets.

This political reorientation went back to the fundamental reassessment of Soviet military policy in the mid-1980s, when it was evidently decided that East Germany and Czechoslovakia were no longer essential parts of the Soviet glacis. The new thinking became more explicit in the statement of Warsaw Pact doctrine in 1987 and in Gorbachev's announcement before the UN in 1988 of massive unilateral cuts in troops. The changes in Soviet position were carried out in the face of resistance from sections of the military. But since 1985 Gorbachev had worked with considerable room to manoeuvre in the field of foreign affairs, subsequently with Foreign Minister Eduard Shevardnaze and a new generation of reformist advisers. The military had no vote in the Politburo and the Communist Party played no significant role in the reformulation of foreign policy. What appears to have emerged were reformist scenarios of a group of neutral socialist states – Poland, Hungary and East Germany and possibly even independent Baltic states – establishing close economic ties with the West while maintaining political ties with the Soviet Union. This may have suggested considerable potential economic advantages for the Soviet Union itself. But it also indicated, if not political *naïveté*, then a readiness to take risks born of desperation. In any event, for several years there were clear signs that the Soviet Union would not intervene to prop up forms of socialism in Eastern Europe which could not command popular support. Any western doubts about Soviet intentions arose only from lingering uncertainty about the power relations within the Soviet political and military hierarchy.

The advent of *Glasnost* and *Perestroika* in the Soviet Union was a clear sign to many in East Germany and elsewhere that reform was possible in the system of Eastern European communism. There were hopes that some Gorbachev-type figure might emerge to lead the SED. But the East German party leadership denied the need for the GDR to follow the Soviet example. The SED's unwillingness to adapt to *Perestroika* became all too evident in a growing rift between the GDR and its Soviet ally. A number of events underlined the SED's determination to follow its old course, generating profound disappointment among those hoping for change.

– In November 1987 the *Stasi* raided the 'Environmental Library' housed in a church building in East Berlin, arresting members of peace and environmental groups.
– The awarding of the *Karl-Marx-Orden* to Nicolae Ceausescu, the brutal Communist Party despot in Romania, in 1988 was regarded as a moral affront and a political provocation to all hopes of liberal reform.
– In January 1989 the official gathering to commemorate the socialists Liebknecht and Luxemburg, murdered in 1919, was used by the *Initiative für Frieden und Menschenrechte* as an occasion to protest for greater freedoms. There were many arrests.

The SED maintained the optimistic picture of East German society and economic strategy; they pointed to a standard of living that was two to three times higher than in those countries which had taken a reformist course. The split with the Soviet leadership became public.

– Relations were strained when the Soviet journal *Sputnik* was banned in the GDR for a critical article on the history of German socialism.
– In autumn 1988 the authorities refused to allow the release of the sensational Soviet anti-Stalin film *Repentance*, which had been running to full houses in the USSR.

24

− SED disapproval of the Gorbachev reforms was voiced at the Seventh Congress of the SED Central Committee in December 1988.
− In April 1988 the SED published the attack on Gorbachev and defence of Bolshevik principles by Nina Andreyeva.
− A graphic rejection of reformist ideas came from Politburo member Kurt Hager, who said that if one's neighbours were decorating their house, this did not mean that one had to change one's own wallpaper.

The protests by civil rights groups and the spreading unrest among ordinary members of the SED about the lack of reforms also reflected unease among senior SED functionaries. They chose to remain silent as the fortieth anniversary of the founding of the GDR approached. Could the reformist groups in the SED have salvaged socialism if they had moved earlier against the ailing Honecker? Would a spread of reform and democracy at this late stage − or, indeed, at *any* stage in the GDR's history − have opened the way to a democratic and popular socialism? Or would a loosening of the Party's grip on society and the state have led to western destabilisation, as happened in Chile and Nicaragua? Would liberalisation have inevitably led to political collapse, as the example of the Soviet Union in 1991 came to demonstrate? Was Honecker's evaluation of the risks of liberalisation and subsequent disintegration − in its own terms − more realistic than the aspirations of reformers? Whether out of a blindness to realities or out of an all too accurate awareness of political realities, Honecker's thwarting of reformist hopes triggered frustration, disillusionment and even despair. These were major psychological factors leading to the outbreak of popular discontent in autumn 1989.

The immediate cause of protest was the failure to satisfy the growing demand for permission to emigrate, although the authorities issued larger numbers of exit permits in 1989 − about 60,000 by September as against a total of 35,000 the previous year. Pent-up frustration and the suspicion of bureaucratic foot-dragging grew in response to the failure to keep up with an estimated 700,000 applications on behalf of a total of 2 million people − 12 per cent of the East German population. Prayers for Peace, which had been held regularly in the Nikolaikirche in Leipzig, became one of the rallying points for those demonstrating for their right to emigrate. Leipzig emerged as the focal point for the growing protest movement. There were a number of reasons for this. The Leipzig shops were inadequately stocked with basic commodities compared with its rival East Berlin. There was bitterness about the rapidly declining state of the old housing stock in the city, as more and more resources and building workers were transferred to East Berlin to complete projects in time for the anniversary celebrations. The pollution rates in the Leipzig area were among the worst in Eastern Europe. Leipzig lacked a responsive SED leadership such as emerged with Modrow and Berghofer in Dresden, who were prepared to listen to people's grievances. Protesters used the presence of the international media at the time of the industrial fair to draw attention to their grievances. Reformist hopes received their greatest setback in May 1989. The municipal elections were held with the usual single Unity Front candidates, although Moscow had hinted that it was time to introduce the principle of competing candidates. The blatant falsification of the election results which produced the usual near-unanimity for SED and Block parties was challenged by civil rights and church groups, who had evidence of a large number of no-votes cast.

The mass exodus and demonstrations

On 2 May 1989 Hungary began to dismantle the barbed-wire fencing along the border with Austria (**Text 1**). This marked the first breach in the Iron Curtain which had separated the two blocs for four decades. It opened the way for the mass defections of East Germans to the West. Hungarian border patrols were initially strengthened. Would-be defectors who were caught were returned to the GDR to face prosecution in accordance with an agreement between the two allied states. Nevertheless, the opening of the Iron Curtain was the clearest sign so far that the Hungarian party and government leadership Nyers, Pozsgay and Horn were looking to the West. During the summer months East Germans on holiday began to occupy the West German embassies in Budapest and Prague, as well as the Permanent Mission back in East Berlin, demanding citizenship and the right to emigrate to West Germany.

In June there was alarm in East Germany as the media described the pro-democracy demonstration of students in Tianenmen Square in Beijing, at the time of Gorbachev's visit to China, as 'a counter-revolutionary insurrection' and sanctioned the bloody restoration of law and order. In July Honecker announced defiantly that the Berlin Wall would stand for another hundred years. The shoot-to-kill policy on the German–German border, however, was amended and promises were given that applications to emigrate would be treated less bureaucratically.

A 'picnic' for European Integration organised by the Conservative Pan-European Union close to the Hungarian border provided an opportunity for several hundred East Germans to rush the border and cross into Austria (**Text 2**). At first a trickle, then a flood of people made a sharp dash over the Hungarian–Austrian border in the coming weeks. Many used the opportunity to travel from the GDR to Czechoslovakia without a visa in order to cross the Czech–Hungarian border at night and from there to Austria and the West. Conditions in the overcrowded embassies became intolerable. The numbers increased as many left East Germany, hoping to forestall an expected clampdown by the SED. They profited from the inactivity of the Politburo, which was paralysed and unable to respond to the growing crisis during Honecker's absence in hospital until September 1989. In early September some from among the first wave of refugees occupying the embassies returned to East Germany in return for promises that their applications for exit visas would receive early attention. But in Prague and Warsaw many held out, insisting on the right to leave as West German citizens.

The pre-revolutionary phase in the GDR at the beginning of September was signalled by the resumption of the demonstrations in Leipzig. The numbers assembling to protest after the Monday Prayers for Peace in the Nikolaikirche were considerably larger than in June, rising to about 1,500. They received coverage from the international media, gathering in East Germany for the Leipzig Fair and the fortieth anniversary celebrations, but also sensing unrest in the country. In place of the call '*Wir wollen raus*' from earlier in the year came the even more provocative '*Wir bleiben hier*' – a challenge to the authorities in East Germany. The growing number of demonstrators and the brutal reaction of the security forces increased fears that they might ultimately resort to the 'Chinese Solution' of Tianenmen Square. The SED ignored calls from figures both inside and outside their ranks to enter into a dialogue with protesters and those wishing to leave to discuss the reasons for the obvious disaffection. The Embassy occupiers, the East Germans crossing the borders and the demonstrators in East German cities were becoming a humiliating embarrassment, as the GDR prepared to celebrate forty years of socialist achievement. The East German media, unable to ignore the problem, tried to discredit the demonstrators (**Text 3**). The GDR was one of the depleted number of hard-line states, including Czechoslovakia, Romania and Bulgaria, trying to ride out unrest in the Warsaw Pact alliance. How can the intransigence of the SED, the Politburo and Honecker be accounted for? Did their privileged isolation make them blind to what was happening internationally and in their own country despite *Stasi* intelligence (**Text 4**)? Evidence suggests that Honecker may not have fully grasped the fact that the GDR was on the brink of insolvency and that discontent could no longer be bought off. The SED may have been disastrously inclined to believe their own propaganda and the hopelessly over-optimistic picture of the economy painted by Günter Mittag. A further factor may have been the communist inclination to think historically, in the long term, to regard immediate difficulties as transitory, a difficult phase like others in the past, which the GDR could ride out in a climate of detente. Honecker may have believed that further economic growth would enable the GDR to catch up with its western neighbours, making it possible to reintroduce the liberalisation he had once attempted. We might also speculate as to whether Honecker anticipated a move against Gorbachev by Soviet Party and military hard-liners and was unwilling to be trapped in a replay of the Prague Spring in East Berlin. Gorbachev was known to command a majority in the Soviet Politburo though not in the Central Committee. The balance of power in the Defence Council was not known to outsiders. The SED leadership is likely to have maintained contacts with other groupings in the Soviet hierarchy for whom the Gorbachev line was ultimately a sell-out of socialism and of Soviet strategic interests. The unquantifiable constellation of forces in the Soviet Union may have made it seem safer to Honecker to hold on to power, expecting that the more orthodox forces would not allow the GDR the risk of reform followed by collapse. Was Honecker the last of the obdurate Old Guard or was he a realist who might have risked reform, had he had any confidence in Gorbachev's chances of surviving? The failed coup against Gorbachev in Moscow in 1991 indicated the presence of forces against whom any premature reform might have found itself historically wrong-footed in 1989.

Invoking the UN convention prohibiting political refugees from being returned to their home countries to face punishment, Hungary opened its border to those wishing to cross to Austria on 10 September. Within hours 20,000 East Germans entered Austria, going from there to reception camps in Bavaria. East Germany responded by suspending travel agreements with Hungary. The opening by Hungary of its border was a gesture towards the Federal Republic of historic proportions, which was reciprocated by generous credit and economic assistance. The Hungarians' action was bitterly criticised in East Berlin and in other Warsaw Pact countries with the notable exceptions of Poland and the Soviet Union. The lack of critical comment from Moscow was a signal of unequivocal clarity that it would not intervene in events in Eastern Europe.

On 10 September Neues Forum was constituted as the first national platform for critical dissent in the GDR (Text 5). A loose group of civil rights activists, intellectuals and artists, including Bärbel Bohley, Jens Reich and Rolf Henrich, Neues Forum aimed for a strategy of controlled reform within the framework of a democratic, socialist GDR. Reflecting the spectrum of opposition groups, it consisted of a mixture of campaigners for legal reform, ecology and peace activists, left-wing protestants, Social Democrats, a solid contingent of Marxist reformers and disaffected members of the SED. With a conscious avoidance of anything that constituted a challenge to the authority of the SED, Neues Forum called for a dialogue between the leadership and the people. The wording of the declaration '*Die Zeit ist reif*' was so reasonable that even members of the SED felt able to give their support. Within a few days 25,000 signatures were collected. The demand for the legalisation of Neues Forum, which the authorities classified as *staatsfeindlich*, became a rallying-call in subsequent demonstrations as reformist demands became more insistent (**Text 6**). The personal courage and integrity of the demonstrators and Neues Forum was unquestionable. But the deeper question which their reformist–socialist idealism raised was that of their political judgement. Did their wishes reflect those of the majority of East Germans? The examples of Poland and later of the Soviet Union showed that any popular challenge to the discredited authority of the Party was bound to culminate in its loss of power and the abandonment of socialism in whatever form.

On 30 September the GDR authorities capitulated and allowed the refugees in the Prague (5,500) and Warsaw (800) embassies to emigrate. The proviso negotiated with West German officials was that they leave via the territory of the GDR so that, in formal terms, they could be expelled. East Germany's decision to allow the East Germans in Prague to leave was probably also due to pressure from the Czech government. The political mood in Czechoslovakia was turning volatile, too, with growing support for the civil rights groups Charter 77 and Civic Forum. There was the fear that the example of the embassy refugees might prove contagious. The announcement by the German Foreign Minister Hans-Dietrich Genscher to the refugees, assembled in squalid conditions in the grounds of the Prague Embassy, that they would be permitted to travel to the West led to scenes of jubilation, repeated as they arrived in East German *Reichsbahn* trains in Hof in Bavaria (**Text 10**). By 3 October the number of refugees crowding again into the Prague Embassy in a second wave had risen to 5,000. Once more the GDR allowed them to depart for West Germany in trains to avoid further embarrassment before the fortieth anniversary celebrations. Crowds assembled in Dresden, some attempting to jump on the trains as they passed through. While the police used water cannons in Dresden to drive back the crowds, a demonstration of several thousand in Leipzig calling for democratic reform was broken up. Further demonstrations during the next few days in Erfurt, Magdeburg and East Berlin also met with a brutal police reaction.

Neues Deutschland published articles accusing the West German media of complicity in luring East Germans over the border (**Text 7**). The Bonn government was identified as being at the centre of a concerted campaign (**Text 8**). A critical comment, said to have been inserted by Honecker himself, suggesting that those leaving were no loss to the country, caused outrage, even in his own party. Doubts grew as to whether someone of such embittered intransigence was capable of dealing with the growing crisis. An estimated 25,000 people demonstrated on 2 October in Leipzig. They were dispersed by security forces and works' militia. Public calls for dialogue increased (**Texts 12, 15**). Tension mounted, as the possibility of violent clashes between the authorities and demonstrators grew (**Text 13**). As communist heads of state and the world's media assembled in East Berlin for the fortieth anniversary celebrations, there were demonstrations for *Perestroika*-type reforms, signalled by the calls '*Gorbi, Gorbi*'. The groups of demonstrators were herded together, beaten, detained or imprisoned. The prevailing tone of the official celebrations from 6 to 8 October was one of over-wrought self-congratulation, with parades and FDJ rallies. Honecker's address was stridently defiant (**Text 14**). Gorbachev is reported to have reacted with audible disbelief to the complacency of Honecker's report to the Politburo. The Soviet leader indicated to senior members of the Politburo that he did not think that Honecker's poor health would allow him to continue running the country. He issued a clear warning that 'those who delay are punished by life itself', to which Honecker's rejoinder was that 'those who are declared dead usually live a long time'. After the official celebrations the Autumn Revolution erupted with demonstrations across the GDR — in East Berlin, Leipzig, Karl-Marx-Stadt and Potsdam. The security forces tried to nip the protest movement in the bud. The eyewitness reports of police brutality, intimidation and ill-treatment of demonstrators (**Text 17**) prompted further protest, calls for investigation and the punishment of those responsible. After the brutal reaction to the wave of protests in early October no one knew what to expect at the planned Monday demonstration on 9 October in Leipzig. Readers' letters to the press were intended to suggest enough public indignation at the disturbances to justify a tough line against troublemakers. A letter in the *Leipziger Volkszeitung* from a commander of the works' militia warned that order would be maintained, if necessary, by force of arms. Riot police were strengthened by the works' militia and military units. Hospitals were warned to have enough empty beds and to lay on extra blood supplies. It was later reported that the security forces had been put on emergency stand-by, issued with live ammunition and told that they might have to shoot at civilians. Though later denied, the order is said to have been issued with Honecker's full knowledge. Another version was that Egon Krenz had rescinded the order.

Despite the threats and fears and the fresh memory of events on the Square of Heavenly Peace in Beijing, an unprecedentedly large crowd, estimated at 70,000, took to the streets in Leipzig on 9 October (**Texts 18,**

19). The refusal of the security forces to move against the demonstrators was probably due to two factors − the absence of any signal from the Soviet military authorities sanctioning the use of force or guaranteeing support, and a large measure of recalcitrance among men and officers unwilling to move in against fellow-citizens. A deciding factor was the enormous self-control on the part of the crowd, as in all subsequent demonstrations, and a refusal to be provoked. A joint public appeal to avoid violence by personalities from cultural life, including the conductor Kurt Masur, and by local SED officials underlined what was to remain the main characteristic of the overthrow of the SED − its peaceful character.

As people's fears dissipated, the demonstrations grew **(Text 20)**. By the time the Politburo (enlarged to include the Central Committee) met in crisis session on 11 October it had changed its position. Contradicting what Honecker had written into the editorial in *Neues Deutschland* on 2 October, a communiqué declared that it was not immaterial that young people were turning their backs in ever-increasing numbers on the GDR. Honecker himself shifted his position minimally, calling for dialogue and debate to make socialism even more attractive. But on 18 October he was pressured into resigning − for reasons of 'poor health' **(Text 21)**. The motion proposing his resignation was formulated by Egon Krenz, Honecker's erstwhile protégé and Günter Schabowski, but moved by the older Politburo member Willi Stoph. The proposal only obtained a majority when linked to the choice of Krenz as Honecker's successor to guarantee a measure of continuity.[28]

Honecker's earlier doubts about Krenz's reliability had surfaced when he appointed Günter Mittag, not Krenz to deputise for him at Politburo meetings while he was in hospital. A previous head of the FDJ and the Politburo member responsible for the Stasi, Krenz was closely implicated in the rigging of the May elections. He had caused widespread outrage in June 1989 by apparently approving of the Beijing leadership's decision to crush the democracy movement. The classic *Wendehals*, or opportunist, who with some agility tried to move with the wave of reform, Krenz began a new, short-lived career as the embodiment of East German *Perestroika*. Promising open dialogue and reforms **(Text 22)**, he conceded that the SED had made serious mistakes, but he continued to ignore Neues Forum. He insisted on the irreconcilability of socialism and capitalism. His nomination to the offices held by Honecker was confirmed on 24 October in the *Volkskammer*, but with 24 votes against and 26 abstentions. While promising dialogue and reform, his constant warning to his fellow East Germans was that the eyes of their allies and neighbours were on them. The paramount importance of stability and the avoidance of anarchy and international turmoil were axiomatic to Krenz's brief hold on power. Whatever his illusions about the SED's ability to stay in control, he remained acutely aware of the international dangers involved in a collapse of the GDR and in an over-hasty dash for German unification. Social unrest, strikes, bloody ethnic and national conflict were already rife in the disintegrating Soviet Union. In East and West attitudes to events in the streets of Leipzig, Dresden and East Berlin were tempered by anxieties. It was clear that provocation of or by the authorities, bloodshed and the involvement of Soviet troops in East Germany could trigger off a diplomatic or even military stand-off between East and West. During his forty days in office Krenz allowed anger and frustration to find outlets in dialogue and plans for reform. The suspicion hardened, however, that the SED was simply trying to find ways of hanging on to its control of the country.

The demonstrations calling for reforms and then for free elections increased in number and size, spreading all over the GDR. In Leipzig 300,000 turned out on 23 October for the regular Monday demonstration (**Text 23**). The Autumn Revolution has been described as a *Feierabend-revolution*. People went about their daily business and assembled in the evening to make ever more radical demands. The much-mocked German instinct for orderliness and self-discipline was now a widely admired curb on violence. Apart from sporadic abuse and outbursts of anger there was little active aggression towards SED functionaries or *Stasi*. Declarations and programmatic statements were issued by factories, theatres, rock musicians, lawyers and academics.[29] The East German revolution was a movement without leaders. In Czechoslovakia the playwright and dissident Vaclav Havel and in Poland the Solidarity founder Lech Walesa emerged as figureheads around whom opposition crystallised. In East Germany popular pressure was generated by ordinary people, as protesters witnessed their own growing courage on television. The Church remained a moderating force. During demonstrations young people and members of Neues Forum sought to prevent violence by cordoning off buildings such as *Stasi* headquarters. Vigils with candles became emblematic forms of protest. State authority, though flouted, was not provoked.

A number of new opposition groupings emerged in addition to Neues Forum – Demokratischer Aufbruch, Demokratie Jetzt and a reconstituted grouping of East German Social Democrats, the SDP,[30] founded on 7 October in Schwante in Oranienburg. On 3 November there were further resignations from the ranks of the Politburo: Kurt Hager, Erich Mielke, Herman Axen, Alfred Neumann and Erich Mückenburg, all of whom had been central and powerful SED figures for decades. Protesters continued to demonstrate for free elections, the right to travel, an end of the SED's monopoly on power, investigations of police brutality and, above all, the disbanding of the *Stasi*. The unpopularity of Mielke, the head of the *Stasi* and of Günter Mittag, held responsible for the economic ruin of the GDR, rivalled that of Honecker. Grass-roots anger erupted in the SED and in the Block Parties, leading to rapid resignations. Self-criticism became the order of the day, as the media, trade-union representatives,[31] youth organisations and cultural bodies called for a policy of openness. East German television[32] reversed its policy by broadcasting critical debate between activists, reporters, SED representatives and academics. Public discussions were held (**Text 24**) and police brutality was investigated. On 4 November more than one million people assembled in East Berlin for the largest demonstration in the GDR's history. At a mammoth gathering on the Alexanderplatz, broadcast on television, crowds listened to calls for a renewal of political and social life from intellectuals, civil rights activists, from Markus Wolf, the former head of GDR espionage, and from leading East German writers (**Texts 26–29**).

By November plans were emerging for a reformed and democratic socialism, while others began to advocate the virtues of market-driven economies. Reformist–socialist SED theorists called for a synthesis of socialist planning and direct democracy, the conversion of state-owned property into socially-owned property, competition between co-operatives, collectives and shareholder companies to be owned by workers and freely elected councils to represent public interest against the dictates of economic planning. More market-oriented proposals called for price-reforms, the dismantling of subsidies, the reduction of planning to a minimum, the introduction of more market factors into economic regulation, the decentralisation of the *Kombinate*, private initiative in industry, the craft and service sectors and the gradual adjustment of the GDR economy to the conditions of the world economy and the convertibility of the East German Mark. There appeared to be no strong desire to introduce full-blooded capitalism in the GDR, let alone to restore the old pre-war forms of ownership. If a 'third way' between socialism and capitalism was at all diffusely present in reformers' minds, it was for the security and egalitarianism of welfare planning paired with the amenities and luxuries of the free market.

The government submitted to the *Volkskammer* a draft reform on travel, providing for thirty days' travel to the West every year, subject to police approval. Such half-hearted concessions were greeted with contempt and rejected by the *Volkskammer*. In response the entire GDR government under Willi Stoph resigned. On 8 November, the entire Politburo of the SED also resigned, its authority in pieces.

The newly-formed SED Politburo included the reformer Hans Modrow, the Party Secretary from Dresden, hitherto an outsider to the inner circles of power. The protesters and burgeoning citizens' groups clearly had no desire to take over control. They were cautious or shrewd enough not to be seen reaching for power for fear of what this might provoke from the SED, the security forces, or the military, but also because power lay beyond their personal ambition. They were split into too many diverse camps to find a common basis. Those campaigning for a reform of socialism were largely concentrated in Berlin. They had little impact, in Leipzig for example, where protest largely took the form of demonstrations on the streets. There was talk of two revolutions – a liberal, middle-class movement in Berlin, Erfurt and Weimar, and a working-class movement in the industrial areas in the south of East Germany, more aggressive in tone. It is a measure, ultimately, of the political innocence of the reformist-socialist groups that spearheaded the revolution that they were unaware that the working-class majority was at best indifferent and, in the end, hostile to the prospect of further socialist 'experimentation'.

From the opening of the Wall to unification

On 9 November the post-war period came to an abrupt end. History moved into fast-forward, as it was announced that the Berlin Wall was to be opened and East Germans were to be allowed to cross freely to the West. At the end of a press conference, after shuffling some papers, SED spokesman Günter Schabowski announced that visa requirements would no longer be required. What ensued has been described as 'the greatest street-party in the history of the world', as East Germans flooded across the open crossing-points (**Tests 31–34**). Having collected their DM 100 'greetings money', East German couples and families strolled around West Berlin, most of the them for the first time in their lives. They flocked along the shopping malls and crowded into department stores before returning home with plastic bags full of shopping – coffee, bananas, toys and video cassettes. They were offered free transport in West Berlin, free concerts and tickets to watch soccer. The reception for the East German crowds and their Trabi cars was warm. Even for those whose definition of liberty and social justice transcended the freedom to shop it was difficult to begrudge the modest pleasures. Though most East Germans returned home, or in time for the night-shift, as *Neues Deutschland* was eager to point out (**Text 35**), there was a sense that more than a wall had been breached. In the next few days and weeks East Germans streamed over the borders to West German towns and cities – Lübeck, Göttingen, Hof, Hanover, Hamburg – to taste the experience of free travel and the intoxication of shopping in what seemed to be the ultimate consumers' paradise. East German cities became ghost-towns, as cars queued up to 30 miles at the newly established crossing-points.

It was a subject of puzzlement, even mystery, as to whether the SED really intended the Wall to be opened to unrestricted travel on 9 November. It is not clear whether, at that moment in history, anyone was really in control at all. Was the opening of the Wall a calculated step or an act of desperation? Did the GDR authorities have any choice, in view of the thousands of East Germans now crossing to the West via Czechoslovakia and Hungary? One interpretation was that the move would force the West German government, desperate to staunch the unmanageable influx of refugees, into offering rapid economic aid to stave off economic collapse, enabling the SED to cling to power. Whether such was the gamble or not, it was based on a misinterpretation of the Bonn position. While sharing the East German wish to prevent the situation getting out of hand, there is little reason to assume that ruling circles in West Germany would forego the historical chance of reunification. A striking feature of the strategy was the great care that both the Bonn government and the conservative media took in forestalling accusations of interference, let alone of steering events towards unification. Many opinion leaders were categorical in rejecting the idea of unification, trying to dampen premature hopes. Beyond humanitarian help and appeals for democratic reform West Germany took care not to be seen to be interfering – at least on any visible level – in events in East Germany. Yet, to believe that the West should have remained completely passive at its moment of triumph in the Cold War is at best ingenuous.

On 13 November Hans Modrow was elected *Ministerpräsident* (**Text 38**) in the *Volkskammer*. He rejected the idea of reunification, describing speculation as 'unrealistic and dangerous'. He came to advocate a fusion of market and planning principles for the economy, co-operation with the West, including the European Community, reforms in administration, legal and constitutional structures and education. Modrow's temporising proposal was for a *Vertragsgemeinschaft*, a contractual community, in which East and West Germany would share key institutions, co-operate economically, but remain separate sovereign states. A central consideration was the continued security interests of the Soviet Union and the effort to keep a unified Germany from entering the western military alliance. The GDR's residual hopes for survival lay with resistance to unification from abroad, from the Soviet Union, from Poland, with its lingering doubts about Bonn's recognition of its borders, also, indeed, from

Western Europe. Britain and France issued early warnings against any prospects for German unification. Western countries were not only aware of the defence requirements of Poland and the Soviet Union at a critical stage in history but also conscious of the alarming prospects of a powerful and dominant Germany.

The main concern of the opposition groups was to dismantle the concentration of SED power in the organs of state and administration (**Text 39**). The establishment of the Round Table[33] on 7 December provided a point of contact and coordination between the SED and opposition groups. The Round Table consisted of fifteen members of the SED and Block Parties, fifteen representatives of activist groups and three church representatives to arbitrate. It was to be the guarantor of the achievements of the Revolution and a counterweight to the still powerful apparatus of the SED. The Round Table agreed on free elections to the *Volkskammer* on 6 May 1990. Although lacking power, the Round Table became for a brief period the highest moral authority in East Germany, supervising the dismantling of the SED state and co-ordinating the local citizens' committees which began to guard the files of the now disarmed *Stasi*. In 1990 it produced a Social Charter and a draft constitution, with which, prior to unification, it hoped to salvage elements of the GDR's social order.

Initially there had been few discernible calls for German unification. The first elements of nationalism appeared with the transformation of the slogan '*Wir sind das Volk*' into '*Wir sind ein Volk*' and the chanting of the unsung lines from the GDR national anthem '*Deutschland einig Vaterland*', dating from a time when a unified Germany had still been a declared East German aim. But in December there were the first threats of a general strike if the government did not call a referendum on unification. The increasing nationalist element in demonstrations gave rise to renewed anxieties. Chancellor Kohl judged and exploited public pressure in East Germany with considerable skill. Keeping a low profile on the very idea of unification, he awaited the growing vocal support for the notion before launching his Ten-Point Plan on 28 November. The points included:

– immediate humanitarian and financial assistance for the GDR conditional on political and economic reform
– democratic elections in the GDR
– joint commissions on practical forms of co-operation between the two countries
– confederative structures linking the two states
– the aim of an eventual unitary federal state

Kohl was careful to place the idea of German unification in the context of a long-term strategy, subject to the security needs of Germany's neighbours and safely embedded in the machinery of military disengagement by the two rival blocs and of European integration. The prospect of the GDR losing its sovereignty mobilised opposition among leading GDR figures (**Text 42**). The principle of German self-determination, however, became something that few wished to challenge. Protest from abroad to Kohl's Ten-Point Plan remained ineffective in the face of popular pressure in Germany, which threatened to become a dangerous historical force, if thwarted.

On 3 December Krenz resigned as First Secretary of the SED, together with the entire Politburo and Central Committee. Three days later he also resigned as *Staatsratsvorsitzender*. The SED forfeited much of its political control to the Round Table, the citizens' committees and the *Volkskammer* (**Text 43**). But the old SED was seen to still retain much of its power locally, in administration, in factories and in management. Its moral collapse came with the disclosures of corruption and abuse of office on the part of many leading SED figures. These disclosures grew apace as the media produced reports on the luxury ghetto of SED functionaries in Wandlitz and as the *Volkskammer* committees began to open the books. Wandlitz became a byword for privileged enjoyment of western luxuries, although by western standards it was a down-market *dolce vita*. Outrage was caused by the disclosure of holiday homes, hunting lodges, private access to fleets of cars, sanatoria, bank accounts abroad and the liberal availability of western products siphoned off by the *Stasi* from postal deliveries from West Germany. Popular rumour gave rise to even wilder speculation. A key figure in dubious SED business was Alexander Schalck-Golodkowski, a secretary of state with *Stasi* connections and links with West German intelligence and the CIA. The FDGB was disgraced by reports of donations for Nicaragua being squandered on parades. Widespread protests flared up across the country (**Text 44**). There were mass resignations and cases of suicide among SED officials. The SED purged itself of its old leaders — Honecker, Krenz, Schabowski, Hager. It changed its name to the SED–PDS (*Partei des demokratischen Sozialismus*) — and then simply to PDS. It elected as chairman the lawyer Gregor Gysi, who had established a reputation defending political dissidents.

Together with early neo-Nazi outrages and attacks on foreign workers in East German cities growing nationalism began to arouse unease and even fear among those campaigning for the survival of the GDR (**Texts 46, 47**). Having taken enormous personal risks in the early days, Neues Forum and civil rights activists found themselves shouted down as they tried to argue against unification (**Texts 46, 47**). Black, red and gold flags with the central GDR emblem cut out of the middle signalled the appearance of nationalist sentiment at the Leipzig demonstrations from 11 December onwards (**Text 48**). The cues for unification may have been provided by elements filtering across from West Germany, but these merely served to prompt those now joining the Monday demonstrations, following the courageous lead of the civil rights activists.

The prevailing impression during the final weeks of 1989 and the early months of the following year was that political initiatives by politicians and governments were repeatedly overtaken by the tide of events and popular pressure. East Germans were abandoning their country in their thousands (**Text 49**). Calls were made on the West German government to assist in making conditions in the GDR sufficiently attractive for them to stay. An overriding consideration was not to strengthen the position of Gorbachev's opponents in the Soviet Union by seeming to want to reverse the outcome of the Second World War in an uncontrolled dash for unification. On 19 December Hans Modrow and Helmut Kohl met in Dresden for consultations on a planned German–German contractual community. Kohl spoke to enthusiastic crowds (**Text 50**), warning against any precipitate move towards unification.

On 22 December the Brandenburg Gate in the centre of Berlin was opened jointly by the *Bürgermeister* of West and East Berlin and West Germans were allowed to cross freely into the GDR, opening up an already shaky economy (**Text 51**) to economic predators from the West. The demonstrations, which continued into January 1990, were directed at the SED hold on power and the massive scale of *Stasi* surveillance (**Text 52**). The foundations of the GDR were crumbling.

The ever louder calls for unification[34] had a number of causes, among others the sudden exposure through unrestricted travel to the opulence of West. More important, however, was the realisation that the SED regime was no longer in a position to impose a clampdown as a result of its loss of political will-power and the disintegration of morale in the security forces. The calls for unification were economic as much as political, expedient rather than chauvinistic. The desire for the amenities of the D-Mark and the evident collapse of the East German economy[35] impelled many thousands to leave their jobs and homes. The flood of between 2,000 and 3,000 each day across the now open borders at the beginning of 1990 rendered all action plans and timetables in East and West obsolete as soon as they were drafted. Most of those leaving were young couples, skilled workers or academically trained professionals. A commonly voiced opinion was that they did not intend to waste their lives waiting for reform in the GDR, as their parents had. Hospitals, factories and administration were affected. Building sites came to a standstill, production plans were jeopardised, both by the migration of workers and by strikes, walk-outs and go-slows in protest against the continued influence of SED cadres.

The loss of pride and self-respect and the capitulation to the D-Mark **(Text 54)** was widely criticised in East and West as mere consumerism, a sell-out of identity for the tinsel of the West. But the urgency of demands stemmed from the feeling that the opportunity provided by Soviet acquiescence was only as secure as Gorbachev's hold on power. The subsequent failed coup of August 1991, which attempted to salvage the Soviet Union and heralded the end of Gorbachev's power, confirmed East German suspicions of how narrow the window of opportunity was. After visiting Gorbachev on 30 January 1990 it became clear to Modrow that the Soviet leader had accepted the inevitability of German unification. On 1 February Modrow produced a blueprint for a united German fatherland **(Text 53)**. This was to be a step-by-step process with no firm timetable. But the idea of neutrality which Modrow's and Gorbachev's proposals involved was dismissed by the West as an attempt to detach Germany from the Atlantic Alliance. At a meeting between Helmut Kohl and Gorbachev on 10 February the Soviet leader conceded the right of the German people to decide themselves on the speed and character of unification **(Text 55)**.

Kohl refused to grant any major economic assistance to the GDR until *Volkskammer* elections had been held **(Text 56)**. The momentum towards a rapid rather than gradual move towards unification was skilfully exploited by the West German Chancellor, even though this opened East Germany to the shock therapy of over-sudden exposure to competitive market conditions **(Text 57)**. The approaching *Bundestag* elections in December 1990, which a few months previously he had looked in danger of losing to the SPD, offered him an opportunity – which he took – of presenting himself as the architect of German unification. In its own terms Kohl's policy could hardly be faulted. It steered a course between the exploitation of popular pressures and diplomatic caution. In addition there was an unspoken awareness of the underlying weakness of the Soviet hand and, in the final analysis, western reluctance to hold back the tide of German unification.

In February 1990 the Foreign Ministers of the Warsaw Pact countries and of NATO met at a conference in Ottawa, where negotiations between the German states and the four Allied Powers were agreed (the 2 + 4 talks) to settle foreign policy and security issues connected with Germany. At the same time the USA and the USSR agreed on substantial troop reductions, improving the prospects for cuts in the numbers of middle-range and strategic missiles.

West German political parties provided financial and logistical help in the *Volkskammer* elections, brought forward to March 1990 to deal with the growing crisis in the GDR.[36] Although early surveys pointed to an SPD lead, the Social Democrats lost support. Their position on immediate unification was perceived to be equivocal, subject to internal controversy and hedged with caution. The CDU-led *'Allianz für Deutschland'* won with the promise of early unification, an exchange rate of 1:1 and the rapid growth of prosperity. Kohl made the pledge, later to be held against him, that no one would suffer economically from unification and that no extra sacrifices would be called for. In reality the costs of unification were to have serious repercussions for Germany and the economies of Western Europe as a whole.

A coalition government led by the newly elected CDU (Ost) chairman Lothar de Maizière was sworn into office on 12 April (**Text 60**), its main task being to negotiate monetary union and the process of political unification. The threat to abandon the GDR if monetary and national unification were not introduced forthwith was the bargaining pressure exerted by ordinary East Germans: *'Kommt die D-Mark, bleiben wir, kommt sie nicht, gehen wir zu ihr!'* Although the Bundesbank argued strongly for an exchange rate of DM 1 for 2 East German Marks, contradicting Kohl's promise of a 1:1, a compromise arrangement was found.[37] Monetary union, which effectively wound up the GDR as a sovereign state, was rapidly negotiated. The treaty of Economic and Monetary Union was signed on 18 May 1990 (**Texts 61−64**), coming into operation on 1 July. While the 2 + 4 talks progressed, Gorbachev and Scheverdnaze forcefully rejected the idea of united Germany remaining a member of NATO. But the Soviet leadership gradually scaled down its demands. One fall-back proposal was that Germany could belong to both NATO and the Warsaw Pact for a transitional period. The progressive withdrawal of Soviet positions was evidence of both what one observer called the unprofessional dilettantism and *ad hoc* nature of Soviet policy, and a fundamentally weak bargaining position. Gorbachev's critics in the USSR, however, seemed to be disarmed or paralysed by the speed of events.

At the meeting in the Caucasus in July 1990 Gorbachev and Kohl achieved a breakthrough in their negotiations. Kohl committed Germany to reducing its military from 650,000 to 370,000 and to giving the Soviet Union wide-ranging technological, economic and infrastructural assistance in dealing with its mounting problems. At the completion of the 2 + 4 talks and the signing of the treaty in Moscow it was agreed that the 360,000 Soviet troops in East Germany would be given until 1994 to withdraw. Germany promised to meet the cost of maintaining, moving and housing them back in the USSR − a total amounting to $7.5 billion. Kohl achieved his aims by eschewing triumphalism, by giving reassurances to the West and to Poland, by close personal contacts with Gorbachev, by repeatedly voiced gratitude towards the USSR, backed up by generous economic assistance. Unification was to be accompanied by a balanced withdrawal of Soviet and NATO troops. The competing military blocs were transformed into co-operating military alliances before the Warsaw Pact was completely disbanded in July 1991. The fears of a hegemonial 'German Europe' were allayed by the prospect of a Germany embedded within the European Community. Did Gorbachev make a decision to abandon the GDR at some earlier stage in the 1980s, or did he think that the socialist state was politically stable enough to survive the withdrawal of the Soviet umbrella and the test of free elections? If German unification was regarded from the very outset as an inevitability, then initial Soviet intransigence in negotiations must be seen merely as an attempt to extract as high an economic price as possible. If Gorbachev believed that a reform of 'real existing socialism' in the GDR could carry popular support, then German unification is a direct outcome of one of the most momentous miscalculations in modern history.

On 23 August 1990 the *Volkskammer* voted to accede to the Federal Republic. After the signing of the 2 + 4 Agreement Germany regained its full sovereignty. The *Bundestag* and *Volkskammer* passed the *Einigungsvertrag* on 20 September 1990. The German Democratic Republic ceased to exist with the unification of the two German states on 3 October 1990.

Hermann Weber's verdict is that the collapse of 'real existing socialism' in East Germany represents not the victory of capitalism over socialism but of democracy over dictatorship.[38] The GDR based its legitimation on the past – its anti-fascism – and on the future – the hope of socialism. By the 1980s, however, the past was fading for a generation of East Germans and the prospect of a reformed socialism was receding into a future beyond anyone's imaginable lifetime. The resulting upheavals of 1989 and 1990 in East Germany have been exhaustively chronicled[39] and narrated in the larger Eastern European context.[40] Politicians centrally involved in the collapse of the GDR have given their version of events.[41] The texts selected here can only touch on aspects of what was a watershed in European history. An analysis of events and their background remains to be written.

Vocabulary
Antifa anti-fascism
Junkers (Prussian) land-owners
landwirtschaftliche Produktionsgenossenschaft agricultural co-operative
Freier Deutscher Gewerkschaftsbund (FDGB) Confederation of Free German
    Trade Unions

Freie Deutsche Jugend (FDJ) Free German Youth
Gesellschaft für Deutsch—Sowjetische Freundschaft Society for German—Soviet Friendship
Gesellschaft für Sport und Technik Society for Sport and Technology
Demokratischer Frauenbund Deutschlands Democratic Women's Association of Germany
die Volkskammer People's Chamber
der Ministerrat Council of Ministers
die Nachfolgestaaten successor states
die Reparationen reparations
die Siegermächte bei Berücksichtigung der Zinsen victorious (allied) powers taking account of interest payments
das Ministerium für Staatssicherheit Ministry for State Security
das Wirtschaftswunder economic miracle
der Alleinvertretungsanspruch claim to exclusive diplomatic representation
Volkseigene Betriebe nationally owned companies
die Ostpolitik Eastern Policy
der Grundlagenvertrag basic treaty
der Grenzverkehr cross-border traffic
die Abgrenzung demarcation
der Zwangsumtausch compulsory currency exchange
der Liedermacher balladeer
das Manifest der Opposition manifesto of the opposition
der vormundschaftliche Staat state tutelage
Neues Forum New Forum
die Volkspolizei People's Police
die soziale Marktwirtschaft social market economy
die Schickeria smart set
die Ellenbogengesellschaft pushy, competitive society
das Kombinat combine
Schwerter zu Pflugscharen swords into ploughshares
die Wehrkunde military instruction
das Waldsterben the dying of the forests
die Zivilcourage civic courage
Glasnost openness
Perestroika restructuring
staatsfeindlich hostile to the State
die Reichsbahn East German railway
der Wendehals wry-neck duck, turncoat
die Feierabendrevolution the revolution after work
Demokratischer Aufbruch New Democratic Beginning
Demokratie Jetzt Democracy Now
die Vertragsgemeinschaft contractual community
der Staatsratsvorsitzende Chairman of the State Council
der Einigungsvertrag Treaty of Unification

Notes

1 For introductory reading on the Cold War see Carlton and Levin (1988), Fleming (1961) and Kaldor (1990).

2 The left socialist minority in the *Reichstag* led by Karl Liebknecht and Rosa Luxemburg broke with the Social Democratic majority in 1914, who closed ranks with Wilhelmenian Imperialism and voted for war credits. In 1918/19, when revolution broke out in Germany, Social Democratic leaders (Ebert and Noske) allowed the *Reichswehr* and the right-wing *Freikorps* to fire on Spartakist revolutionaries, ending the prospect of revolution in an advanced industrial country. The use of the *Reichswehr* again by Social Democrats in 1920 and 1923 to put down strikes in the Ruhr deepened the schism between the two working-class parties. The KPD condemnation of the SPD as Social Fascists put an end to attempts to build Popular Front solidarity against the Nazis' seizure of power.

3 East Prussia, Silesia and Pomerania.

4 Most of the proliferating theories of the Cold War, in which Germany was always central, confer a historical continuity and consistency of aim upon the political, military and undercover agencies of East and West. Mutual suspicion, however, is likely to have thrived on unclear perceptions of true intent arising from incongruencies and inconsistencies on both sides. These, whether deliberate or not, stemmed from tensions between military and political establishments in each camp, but also from discrepancies between diplomatic rhetoric and game-plan belligerency, where German territory was always of key importance. The West regularly dismissed the security preoccupations of the military in the USSR – with its 40 million war dead – as 'defensive paranoia'. If this was the case, it was a paranoia in the Soviet military establishment constantly nourished by the West's economic superiority and its lead in arms race technology.

5 Cf. Paul Kennedy, *The Rise and Fall of the Great Powers. Economic Change and Military Conflict*, London, 1988, p. 644 ff.

6 Soviet and Allied troops withdrew from Austria after the signing of the State Treaty in 1956, in which Austria committed itself to neutrality.

7 Cf. Rolf Steininger, *Eine Chance zur Wiedervereinigung? Die Stalin-Note vom 10. März 1952*, Bonn, 1986.

8 Cf. Weber (1991).

9 Most writers are emphatic in dismissing any basis for comparing the SED regime to the unique barbarity of the Nazis.

10 Kaldor (1990), p. 55.

11 For studies of the GDR state apparatus and system of government cf. Henrich (1989), Neumann (1991), Spittmann (1987) and Starrel and Mallinckrodt (1975).

12 For reading on the Politburo cf. Schabowski (1990), Neumann (1991) and Przybylski (1991).

13 Early victims of Ulbricht's brand of Stalinism were SED reformers such as Wilhelm Zaisser and Rudolf Herrenstadt, who advocated new economic policies, integrating market elements into the centrally planned economy. The group around the SED academic Wolfgang Harich was prosecuted and imprisoned in 1956 for advocating workers' councils, the abolition of collective farms and profit-sharing schemes. Karl Schirdewan, the second man in the GDR after Ulbricht, and Ernst Wollweber lost their positions in 1958 for advocating de-Stalinisation and improved relations with the West.

14 'Die meisten Bundesbürger ... wissen bis heute nicht – oder wollen es nicht wissen –, in welchem Maße die BRD ihre Wirtschaftskraft und ihre

Reichtumsproduktion auf Kosten der DDR entwickelt hat. Die beiden deutschen Nachfolgestaaten des Dritten Reiches haben zur Reparation der Schäden insgesamt 101 Milliarden DM (zum Wert von 1953) an die Siegermächte bezahlt; davon die BRD zwei Milliarden, die DDR 99 Milliarden. Der Bremer Historiker Arno Peters hat errechnet, was die BRD demnach der DDR schuldet – in Preisen von 1989. Heraus kommt, bei Berücksichtigung der Zinsen, eine Summe von über 700 Milliarden DM' Schneider (1990), p. 57.

15 For a study of psychological effects of conformist pressures on people in the GDR cf. Maaz (1990).

16 The most important were the Moscow Treaty (1970), the Warsaw Treaty (1970), the Four-Power Agreement on Berlin (1971) and the *Grundlagenvertrag*, settling diplomatic relations between the two German states (1972/3).

17 On opposition groups in the GDR cf. Bohley *et al.* (1989), Knabe (1990), Kroh (1988), Tismanenau (1989) and Woods (1986).

18 Symptomatic were Volker Braun's *Die Kipper*, Ulrich Plenzdorf's *Die neuen Leiden des jungen W.* and the film *Die Legende von Paul und Paula*.

19 Criticism of Biermann's expatriation was voiced among others by Christa Wolf, Jurek Becker, Rolf Schneider and Erich Loest. A number of writers chose to move to the West: Reiner Kunze, Jürgen Fuchs, Sarah Kirsch and Günter Kunert.

20 Cf. Fred Halliday, *The Making of the Second Cold War*, London, 1983.

21 For studies of the GDR's economic difficulties, cf. Barthel (1979), Bryson and Melzer (1991), Hertle (1991), Kusch *et al.* (1991), Luft (1991), Mittag (1991), Schwärzel (1990), Voskamp and Wittke (1990), Land (1990) and Lipschitz and McDonald (1990).

22 The military always had a prior claim upon the resources of socialist societies in Eastern Europe. Both eastern and western intelligence agencies had a common interest in concealing the drain of military expenditure on socialist economies. The GDR's position was inextricably linked to that of the USSR, both failing to satisfy the requirements of their people in the civilian economy. Western intelligence achieved the remarkable double of both overstating Soviet military strength and grossly underestimating the real GNP outlay on defence. Some estimates now go as high as 30 per cent. Cf. Henry S. Rowen and Charles Wolf, jun. (eds.), *The Impoverished Superpower. Perestroika and the Soviet Military Burden*, San Francisco, 1989.

23 Cf. Andreas Köves, 'Problems and prospects of East–West Economic Cooperation. An East European view', in Mary Kaldor *et al.* (eds.), *The New Detente. Rethinking East–West Relations*, London, 1989, pp. 253–72.

24 On civil rights groups in the GDR cf. Gesamtdeutsches Institut (1990), Grabner *et al.* (1990), Herles und Rose (1990), Knabe (1990), Müller-Enbergs *et al.* (1991), Probst (1991), Rein (1989), Bohley (1989), European Nuclear Disarmament (1978), Kroh (1988) and Woods (1986).

25 On the role of the Church in the GDR cf. Cordell (1990), Motschmann (1990), Neubert (1991), Sandford (1989) and Tismaneanu (1989).

26 Studies of East German literature and society include Dennis Tate, *The East German Novel: Identity, Community, Continuity*, New York, 1984; Ian Wallace (ed.), *The Writer and Society in the GDR*, Tayport, 1984; Gisela Helwig (ed.), *Die DDR-Gesellschaft im Spiegel ihrer Literatur*, Köln, 1986; J. H. Reid, *Writing without Taboos, The New East German Literature*, New York, Oxford and Munich (1989).

27 Among leading GDR women writers, Christa Wolf, Irmtraud Morgner, Maxie Wander and Helga Königsdorf.

28 For coverage of the crisis in the Politburo leading to Honecker's resignation cf. *Spiegel* no. 16, 16 April 1990; no. 17, 23 April 1990; no. 18, 30 April 1990.

29 Cf. Schüddekopf (1990).

30 The *Sozialdemokratische Partei in der DDR* (SDP) was founded in early October by Ibrahim Böhme (later accused of having *Stasi* connections), Angelika Barbe, Markus Meckel, Wolfgang Thierse and others. It called for an all-German council to work out a new German Constitution, a federal structure for a new Germany, and it opposed membership of NATO. The SDP later changed its name to SPD (*Sozialdemokratische Partei Deutschlands*), fusing with the West German SPD. Neues Forum remained a loose coalition of reformers and civil rights activists, later divided between groups opposing and those supporting unification, those wishing to form a political party and those wanting to remain an extra-parliamentary group. Demokratie Jetzt, formed by left–liberal activists close to the Church and civil rights protesters, called for reforms leading to a social and ecological market economy and a confederal solution to German unification. The centre–right group Demokratischer Aufbruch was founded predominantly by church ministers – Rainer Eppelmann, Minister of Defence and Disarmament in the de Maizière government, Friedrich Schorlemmer and Wolfgang Schnur (later accused of having links with the *Stasi*). Supporting the idea of a social–ecological market economy, DA entered the electoral Allianz Für Deutschland with the East German CDU and DSU (a parallel grouping to the conservative Bavarian CSU).

31 Cf. Müller, in Löw, 1991.

32 On developments in the GDR media during the revolution cf. Grimme (1990), Hoff (1991), Holzschuh (1990) and Holzweißig (1990).

33 On the Round Table cf. Herles and Rose (1990) and Thaysen (1990).

34 On shifts in public opinion in the GDR during the revolution cf. Infratest Kommunikationsforschung (1990) and Schierholz and Tschicke (1990). See also Carr *et al.* (1991).

35 Roesler, contrary to the dominant view, argues that 'the planned economy of the GDR was not necessarily finished at the end of the 1980s'. Cf. Jörg Roesler, 'The Rise and Fall of the Planned Economy in the German Democratic Republic, 1945–89' in *German History*, Vol. 9 (1990), No. 1, 46–61.

36 For studies of the *Volkskammer* elections cf. Fitzmaurice (1990), Hamilton (1990) and Veen *et al.* (1990).

37 Wages, salaries and rent were converted at a rate of 1:1. Personal savings were exchanged at a 1:1 rate up to a top limit of DM 6,000 and for higher deposits at a rate of 2:1.

38 Weber (1991), p. 202.

39 Cf. Bahr (1990), Bahrmann and Links (1990), Spittmann and Helwig (1989), *die Tageszeitung* (1990), Wimmer *et al.* (1990) and Weiland *et al.* (1990).

40 Ash (1990), Brown (1991), East (1992), Frankland (1990), the *Observer* (1990), Prins (1990) and Selbourne (1990).

41 Krenz (1990), Luft (1991), Mittag (1991), Modrow (1991), Schabowski (1990), Schäuble (1991), Stolpe (1992) and Teltschik (1991).

I. The final years of the GDR

21 December 1972. The *Grundlagenvertrag* is signed, normalising relations between the German Democratic Republic and the Federal Republic of Germany.

18 September 1973. The GDR and the Federal Republic become members of the United Nations.

1970s – 1980s. The GDR wins widespread international recognition.

7 – 11 September 1987. Erich Honecker visits the Federal Republic. The long-planned but frequently postponed visit represents the high point in diplomatic relations between the two German states.

25 November 1987. The *Stasi* searches the rooms of the Zion Congregation in East Berlin. Material and documents from the 'Environmental Library' with data on pollution in the GDR are confiscated. Members of the church peace and environmental groups are arrested.

15 August 1988. The GDR and the European Community establish diplomatic relations.

15 January 1989. On the seventieth anniversary of the murder of the socialists Rosa Luxemburg and Karl Liebknecht in 1919 150 members of peace, environmental and civil rights groups are arrested in Leipzig for calling for freedom of opinion and assembly and a free press. Fifty-four are expelled to West Germany.

12 March 1989. There are demonstrations of several hundred East Germans in Leipzig who have applied for official emigration papers.

2 May 1989. Hungary begins to dismantle the barbed-wire fence along its border with Austria, part of the 'Iron Curtain' dividing East and West Europe.

II. The mass exodus begins

1. The 'Iron Curtain' is breached

Mit Unterstützung der Bevölkerung haben gestern ungarische Grenzbeamte damit begonnen, den 'Eisernen Vorhang' an der Grenze zu Österreich niederzureißen. Auf mehreren Kilometern Länge wurden bei den Ortschaften Köszeg, Sopron und Hegyeshalom Signalanlagen und Stacheldrahtverhaue abgebaut.

Bis Ende 1990 soll der gesamte Grenzzaun auf einer Länge von 354 Kilometern abgebaut sein. Andras Koevari vom Innenministerium sprach vom 'Ende einer Epoche'.

Vor rund 100 in- und ausländischen Journalisten betonte der Oberst der Grenzwache, Balasz Novaky, nach dem 'historischen Augenblick' würden je Woche bis zu fünf Kilometer Grenzbefestigung abgebaut. Die Gesamtkosten lägen bei einer Million DM. Mit dem Abbau werde eine weitere Verbesserung der Beziehungen zu Österreich und zum Westen überhaupt ermöglicht.

Politbüromitglied Imre Pozsgay hatte bereits im Oktober die Sperranlagen als historisch, politisch und technisch überholt bezeichnet.

Der Abbau des 'Eisernen Vorhangs' hatte um acht Uhr morgens begonnen, als Grenzsoldaten mit großen Drahtscheren die ersten Löcher schnitten. Der zweifache Zaun wurde zusammengerollt und auf Lkw und Traktoren verladen. Als Entlohnung für ihre Hilfe sollen ihn örtliche Unternehmen und die helfende Bevölkerung erhalten, die anwesenden Journalisten durften Teile als Souvenir mitnehmen.

Bis Ende 1990 sollen auch die meisten Wachtürme entfernt werden. In Budapest wird darauf verwiesen, das System der Grenzanlagen sei überholt, seit im letzten Jahr das liberalste Reiserecht aller osteuropäischen Staaten eingeführt worden war.

Auf Befürchtungen, künftig könnten Sowjetblockstaaten wie die

48

'DDR', die Tschechoslowakei und Rumänien ihren Bewohnern Reisen in das Bruderland untersagen, um eine Flucht über die grüne Grenze zu verhindern, ging man bei den Ungarn gestern nur indirekt ein. Es sei dies allein eine innere Angelegenheit der betreffenden Staaten.

Morgenpost, 3. Mai 1989

Vocabulary
der Grenzbeamte border official
    nieder.reißen, ei, i, i tear down
die Signalanlagen signal installations
der Stacheldrahtverhau barbed-wire entanglement
    ab.bauen dismantle
das Innenministerium ministry of the interior
der Oberst colonel
die Grenzwache border guard
die Grenzbefestigung border fencing
der Abbau dismantling
    ermöglichen make possible
das Politbüromitglied member of the politburo
die Sperranlagen defensive barriers
    überholt outdated
    bezeichnen describe
die Drahtschere wire-cutters
der LKW (Lastkraftwagen) heavy-goods vehicle
die Entlohnung payment
    örtlich local
    anwesend present
der Wachturm watchtower
    entfernen remove
    untersagen forbid
    ein.gehen (auf + acc.) respond to
    eine innere Angelegenheit der betreffenden Staaten an internal matter of the states concerned

7 May 1989. At the local elections in the GDR the Party List of the National Front (i.e. *SED, CDU, LDPD, NDPD* and *Demokratische Bauernpartei*) is declared to have won 98.77 per cent of the vote. The next day church and opposition groups accuse the authorities of ballot rigging. Over 100 demonstrators are arrested in Leipzig.

4 June 1989. After a visit to China by the Soviet premier Gorbachev the Chinese authorities use military force to break up demonstrations for democracy on Tianenmen Square. A wave of arrests and executions follows ... 8 June 1989. The GDR *Volkskammer* describes events in

Peking as an internal affair of the People's Republic aimed at restoring civil order. The SED gives its approval to the 'Chinese Solution' ... 12–15 June 1989. The Soviet premier Michael Gorbachev visits the Federal Republic.

17 July. After the removal of the barbed-wire barriers on the Hungarian border with Austria an increasing number of East Germans, including those on holiday in Hungary, begin to escape through this breach in the Iron Curtain to Austria and from there to West Germany ... 23 July. Despite continued Hungarian border patrols the numbers escaping over the border steadily rise. Some are detained by the Hungarian authorities and returned to the GDR, where they face prosecution for *Republik-flucht* ... 29 July. In the Soviet Union the first opposition party group is formed in the Supreme Soviet since the Revolution.

3 August. Eighty East Germans seeking to emigrate to West Germany occupy the Permanent Mission of the Federal Republic in East Berlin. They refuse to leave until they are granted visas ... 4 August. The West German Embassy in Budapest in Hungary is occupied by 150 East Germans. The GDR accuses the Hungarians of gross interference in its internal affairs by refusing to hand over the would-be emigrants ... 8 August. Overcrowding in the Permanent Mission of the Federal Republic in East Berlin leads to the closing of the building. The West German government appeals to those wishing to emigrate not to attempt to obtain exit visas via the Mission in East Berlin ... 13 August. By the middle of August 181 East Germans have sought refuge in the West German Embassy in Budapest. The Embassy has to be closed because of over-crowding ... 15 August: 168 East Germans return to the GDR from the West German Embassy in Prague after they have been promised freedom from prosecution and assured that their applications for emigration papers will be dealt with speedily. Most of the occupiers in the Embassy, however, choose to hold out ... 19 August. The Austrian *Paneuropa-Union* and Hungarian opposition groups organize a 'pan-European' picnic near Sopron on the Hungarian–Austrian border. Over 600 East Germans use the occasion to break through a gate, crossing over into Austria, the most dramatic incident so far in the mass escape to the West.

2. 600 East Germans escape into Austria

'Helfen Sie mit, den Eisernen Vorhang niederzureißen!' lautete die Aufforderung der ungarischen Opposition – des Ungarischen

Demokratischen Forums[1] und des Bundes der Freien Demokraten −,[2] die am Samstag unweit der Grenzstadt Sopron (Oden-
burg) gemeinsam mit der Paneuropa-Union[3] Otto von Habsburgs
im ehemaligen Sperrgebiet hart an der Grenze ein internationales
Treffen organisiert hatte. In Flugblättern hieß es auf ungarisch,
englisch, russisch, polnisch, tschechisch, deutsch und rumänisch:
'Europäische Freunde! Die Geschichte hat bewiesen, daß der
einzige Weg zum Frieden über die Abschaffung der Stacheldraht-
zäune und der psychischen Schranken führen kann. ... Im Geiste
der Zukunft möchten wir jedes Jahr − beginnend am 19. August
1989 − an der Stelle des früheren Eisernen Vorhangs an der
ungarisch−österreichischen Grenze ein Treffen von Menschen aus
verschiedenen europäischen Ländern organisieren. Dazu erwarten
wir alle jene, die demonstrieren möchten, daß der Wunsch des
einfachen Menschen das freie, friedliche Europa ist!'
Diese Aufforderung war auch zahlreichen DDR-Touristen zu
Ohren gekommen, für die der 'Odenburger Zipfel' − jenes
ungarische Gebiet südlich des Neusiedler Sees, das tief nach
Österreich hineinreicht − magische Anziehungskraft gewonnen
hat, seit die Nachricht von der Demontage des Eisernen Vorhangs
durch die Ungarn bis in den letzten Winkel des Landes gelangte.
'Früher gab es hier kaum Touristen aus der DDR', sagt ein Ungar.
'Sie trauten sich nicht hierher − und außerdem gab es bereits
im Binnenland Kontrollpunkte der Polizei, die keinen Ostblock-
bewohner durchließen. Seit neuestem aber sind wir geradezu
überschwemmt mit ostdeutschen Campingtouristen. Und die
meisten von ihnen zeigen ein ganz ungewöhnliches Interesse, das
Grenzgebiet zu erwandern und in den grenznahen Wäldern Pilze
zu sammeln. ...'
Jetzt hatte sich wie ein Lauffeuer herumgesprochen, daß die
ungarische Grenzpolizei anläßlich des Oppositionsfestivals den
seit Ende des Zweiten Weltkriegs gesperrten Übergang an der
alten Straße zwischen St. Margarethen im Burgenland und dem
ungarischen Sopron öffnen wird. Ursprünglich war geplant, daß
sich die österreichischen Gäste, unter ihnen einige Politiker, durch
diese Bresche zum Festplatz begeben sollten.
Aber dann kommt alles ganz anders. Mehr als 600 Männer, Frauen
und Kinder aus der DDR, die auf der ungarischen Seite mit den
übrigen Festteilnehmern auf der schmalen Straße zu Fuß bis zur

Grenzlinie gezogen sind, warten nicht ab, bis ungarische Grenzer das Stacheldrahttor auf der Straße öffnen. Sie drücken es ein und hasten im Laufschritt den völlig verdutzten Österreichern, die zahlreich in Festtracht und Dirndl dort stehen, entgegen. Einige werden buchstäblich über den Haufen gerannt. Da laufen Frauen mit kleinen Kindern auf dem Arm, Männer tragen Reisetaschen – offenbar das einzige Gepäck, das sie mitnehmen konnten. Ein junges Paar fällt sich um den Hals, als es auf österreichischem Boden angelangt ist. Das Mädchen bricht in Tränen aus. 'Endlich geschafft! Jetzt sind wir frei!' hört man einen Mann rufen.

Das halbe Dutzend ungarischer Grenzpolizisten, das ursprünglich abkommandiert war, um die Pässe der österreichischen Festgäste zu kontrollieren, macht keinerlei Anstalten, einzugreifen oder die Menge an der Flucht zu hindern. Nach Lage der Dinge hätte nur eines die Menschen zurückhalten können: Wenn die Polizei mit automatischen Waffen das Feuer eröffnet hätte. Das aber würde im heutigen Ungarn auch der schärfste Grenzpolizist nicht mehr wagen – und außerdem waren die ungarischen Grenzer nur mit Pistolen bewaffnet.

Viele aus der DDR, die diesen günstigen Augenblick verpaßten, versuchen später, buchstäblich durchs Gebüsch doch noch nach Österreich zu kommen. Eine viele tausend Menschen zählende Menge sieht plötzlich einem Mann zu, der querfeldein in Richtung Grenze rennt. 'Wenn er bis zum Waldrand kommt, hat er's geschafft', sagt ein Ungar.

Die Welt, 21. August 1989.

Vocabulary

    nieder.reißen, ei, i, i tear down
  die Aufforderung demand, invitation
  das Sperrgebiet prohibited area
    hart an der Grenze close by the border
  das Flugblatt leaflet
  die Abschaffung abolition
  der Stacheldrahtzaun barbed-wire fence
  die psychischen Schranken psychological barriers
    zu Ohren kommen come to the notice of
    hinein.reichen stretch into
  die Anziehungskraft attractive force
  die Demontage dismantling
    bis in den letzten Winkel des Landes gelangen reach the furthest corner of the country

seit neuestem recently
geradezu überschwemmt absolutely flooded
erwandern go rambling across
grenznah close to the border
sich wie ein Lauffeuer herum.sprechen, i, a, o a rumour spreads like wildfire
anläßlich on the occasion of
der **Übergang** crossing point
die **Bresche** breach
der **Festplatz** here: picnic ground
    sich begeben, i, a, e to make one's way
der **Grenzer** border guard
das **Stacheldrahttor** gate in the barbed-wire fencing
    buchstäblich literally
    über den Haufen rennen knock down
    ab.kommandieren detail
    keine Anstalten machen make no move
    ein.greifen, ei, i, i intervene
    nach Lage der Dinge as matters stand/stood
    schärfst strictest
    querfeldein across country

Notes

1 **das Ungarische Demokratische Forum:** A Hungarian intellectual reformist group founded in 1987.
2 **der Bund der Freien Demokraten:** A Hungarian opposition party founded in 1988, evolving out of the Network of Free Initiatives.
3 **Paneuropa-Union:** A conservative organisation serving to promote pan-European co-operation in Central Europe, run by a descendant of the Austrian Habsburg dynasty.

22 August. The West German Embassy in Prague has to be closed down, as no more refugees can be accommodated ... After strong protests from the GDR Hungary strengthens its border patrols to prevent further mass escapes ... 28 August. Unhindered by the Hungarian government 108 East Germans, accompanied by the Red Cross, are allowed to leave the West German Embassy in Budapest to travel to West Germany via Austria ... During August 3,000 East Germans have escaped across the 'green border' between Hungary and Austria to the West.

1 September. Erich Honecker, the East German leader, leaves hospital after a gall-bladder operation... 4 September. After the church service for peace hundreds demonstrate outside the Nikolaikirche in Leipzig demanding 'Reisefreiheit statt Massenflucht'. The demonstration is broken up by security forces.

Figure 1 Police face demonstrators outside the Nikolaikirche in Leipzig, September 1989

3. The East German press attacks the Leipzig demonstrations

Über die Demonstration von mehreren hundert Leuten am Montagabend in der Leipziger Innenstadt wurden wir gestern von einem Leser per Telefon gefragt. Die Antwort ist einfach: Weil diejenigen, die sich da im Anschluß an einen Gottesdienst (!) zusammenrotteten, uns, die Junge Welt, nicht informiert hatten, daß sie in Leipzig eine staatsfeindliche Aktion gegen die DDR anzetteln wollen. Wie anders als staatsfeindlich soll man es denn nennen, wenn dort Rufe laut werden wie 'Mauer weg' oder 'Weg mit den Kommunisten'. Das sind Worte gegen die Gesetze der DDR, gegen die Verfassung, das ist Verleumdung von Millionen Menschen, die unseren Staat mit aufbauten und aufbauen, die fleißig arbeiten, die im Gegensatz zu Ausreißern gern in unserer

Republik leben und diese, ungestört von Egoisten und politischen Rowdys immer attraktiver und freundlicher machen wollen. Erfahren haben wir von dieser Provokation aus dem BRD-Fernsehen, das auf seiner täglichen Suche nach antisozialistischen Elementen wieder mal rechtzeitig von seinen eigenen Statisten eingeladen worden war. Auf den Bildern war freilich auch das Entscheidende zu sehen: Störenfriede haben bei uns keine Chance! Unsere Genossen der VP und anderer Schutz- und Sicherheitsorgane haben entschlossen gehandelt und verhindert, daß der Aufruf zur Verletzung der Gesetze der DDR öffentlich verbreitet wird – was die Westmedien ja schon zur Genüge tun. Und verhindert wurde auch, daß sich Brutalitäten und Unverschämtheiten gegen unsere Genossen ausweiteten. Darüber kann die Junge Welt nur so berichten: Danke, Genossen, für eure Wachsamkeit.

Junge Welt (Organ des Zentralrats der FDJ), 6. September 1989.

Vocabulary
> **im Anschluß an** following
> der **Gottesdienst** church service
> **sich zusammen.rotten** form a mob
> **staatsfeindlich** hostile to the State
> **an.zetteln** foment
> die **Verleumdung** slander
> der **Ausreißer** absconder
> der **Statist** bystander, 'extra'
> die **Schutz- und Sicherheitsorgane** protective and security authorities
> **entschlossen handeln** act resolutely
> der **Aufruf zur Verletzung der Gesetze** the call to break the law
> **zur Genüge** only too well
> die **Unverschämtheit** impertinence
> der **Genosse** comrade
> **sich aus.weiten** spread

7 September. A demonstration is attempted in East Berlin by groups protesting at the rigging of the local election results in the GDR on 7 May. The demonstration, with western media present, is broken up; eighty demonstrators are arrested … 8 September. 177 East Germans who have now spent six weeks in the Permanent Mission of the Federal Republic in East Berlin leave the building. Although receiving no guarantees that they will be allowed to leave the GDR, they are promised legal assistance in submitting their official application for an exit visa.

4. *Stasi* report on East Germans leaving the GDR

Als wesentliche Gründe/Anlässe für Bestrebungen zur ständigen Ausreise bzw. das ungesetzliche Verlassen der DDR – die auch in Übereinstimmung mit einer Vielzahl Eingaben an zentrale und örtliche Organe/Einrichtungen stehen – werden angeführt:

– Unzufriedenheit über die Versorgungslage;

– Verärgerung über unzureichende Dienstleistungen;

– Unverständnis für Mängel in der medizinischen Betreuung und Versorgung;

– eingeschränkte Reisemöglichkeiten innerhalb der DDR und nach dem Ausland;

– unbefriedigende Arbeitsbedingungen und Diskontinuität im Produktionsablauf;

– Unzulänglichkeiten/Inkonsequenz bei der Anwendung/Durchsetzung des Leistungsprinzips sowie Unzufriedenheit über die Entwicklung der Löhne und Gehälter;

– Verärgerung über bürokratisches Verhalten von Leitern und Mitarbeitern staatlicher Organe, Betriebe und Einrichtungen sowie über Herzlosigkeit im Umgang mit den Bürgern;

– Unverständnis über die Medienpolitik der DDR.

Stasi-Bericht, 9. September 1989.

Vocabulary
der Anlaß cause, occasion
die Bestrebung effort, attempt
die Ausreise emigration
  in Übereinstimmung mit in accordance with
die Eingabe petition
die Einrichtung institution
  an.führen mention
die Versorgungslage provision of goods and services
  unzureichende Dienstleistungen inadequate services
die Mängel shortcomings
die Betreuung care
  eingeschränkt limited
die Arbeitsbedingungen working conditions
die Diskontinuität im Produktionsablauf interruptions in production
die Unzulänglichkeit inadequacy
die Inkonsequenz lack of consistency
die Anwendung application
die Durchsetzung implementation

das **Leistungsprinzip** performance-related standards
die **Herzlosigkeit** callousness

10 September. The organisation of dissidents and civil rights activists in the GDR, Neues Forum, isues its first public call for political and social reform in East Germany. The founding members, including the artist Bärbel Bohley and the scientist Jens Reich, appeal for a dialogue between government and the people and the recognition of Neues Forum.

5. The first public statement issued by Neues Forum

In Staat und Wirtschaft funktioniert der Interessenausgleich zwischen den Gruppen und Schichten nur mangelhaft. Auch die Kommunikation über die Situation und die Interessenlage ist gehemmt. Im privaten Kreis sagt jeder leichthin, wie seine Diagnose lautet, und nennt die ihm wichtigsten Maßnahmen. Aber die Wünsche und Bestrebungen sind sehr verschieden und werden nicht rational gegeneinander gewichtet und auf Durchführbarkeit untersucht. Auf der einen Seite wünschen wir uns eine Erweiterung des Warenangebots und bessere Versorgung, andererseits sehen wir deren soziale und ökologische Kosten und plädieren für die Abkehr von ungehemmtem Wachstum. Wir wollen Spielraum für wirtschaftliche Initiative, aber keine Entartung in eine Ellenbogen-gesellschaft. Wir wollen das Bewährte erhalten und doch Platz für Erneuerung schaffen, um sparsamer und weniger naturfeindlich zu leben. Wir wollen geordnete Verhältnisse, aber keine Bevormundung. Wir wollen freie, selbstbewußte Menschen, die doch gemeinschaftsbewußt handeln. Wir wollen vor Gewalt geschützt sein und dabei nicht einen Staat von Bütteln und Spitzeln ertragen. Faulpelze und Maulhelden sollen aus ihren Druckposten vertrieben werden, aber wir wollen dabei keine Nachteile für sozial Schwache und Wehrlose. Wir wollen ein wirksames Gesundheitswesen für jeden, aber niemand soll auf Kosten anderer krankfeiern. Wir wollen an Export und Welthandel teilhaben, aber weder zum Schuldner und Diener der führenden Industriestaaten noch zum Ausbeuter und Gläubiger der wirtschaftlich schwachen Länder werden. ...
Es kommt in der jetzigen gesellschaftlichen Entwicklung drauf an,
– daß eine größere Anzahl von Menschen am gesellschaftlichen Reformprozeß mitwirkt,

– daß die vielfältigen Einzel- und Gruppenaktivitäten zu einem Gesamthandeln finden.

Wir bilden deshalb gemeinsam eine politische Plattform für die ganze DDR, die es Menschen aus allen Berufen, Lebenskreisen, Parteien und Gruppen möglich macht, sich an der Diskussion und Bearbeitung lebenswichtiger Gesellschaftsprobleme in diesem Lande zu beteiligen. Für eine solche übergreifende Initiative wählen wir den Namen.

Neues Forum

Gründungsaufruf des Neuen Forum, 10. September 1989.

Vocabulary
der Interessenausgleich balance of interests
    mangelhaft unsatisfactorily
    gehemmt inhibited
    leichthin without thinking
    gegeneinander gewichtet weighed against each other
    auf Durchführbarkeit überprüfen examine for practicability
die Abkehr von ungehemmtem Wachstum the rejection of unrestricted growth
der Spielraum scope
die Entartung in eine Ellenbogengesellschaft degeneration into a dog-eat-dog
    society
das Bewährte what is tried and tested
    geordnete Verhältnisse an orderly society
die Bevormundung tutelage
    gemeinschaftsbewußt with a sense of community
der Büttel lackey
der Spitzel informer
der Faulpelz idler
der Maulheld loud-mouth
der Druckposten cushy job
    vertreiben, ie, ie throw out
die Wehrlosen those who are defenceless
    krank.feiern skive off work
der Ausbeuter exploiter
der Gläubiger creditor
das Gesamthandeln joint activity
die Bearbeitung here: tackling
    übergreifend comprehensive
der Gründungsaufruf founding statement

During the following weeks calls for the legal recognition of Neues Forum become one of the central demands of public appeals and demonstrations.

6. Neues Forum makes demands

Das Neue Forum muß zugelassen werden!
Das Neue Forum braucht eine eigene Zeitung und Zugang zu den Medien!
Was braucht unsere Gesellschaft? Was benötigt unser Land?
— Wir brauchen Pressefreiheit, Meinungsfreiheit und eine tiefgreifende Medienreform.
— Wir brauchen Versammlungs- und Demonstrationsfreiheit.
— Wir brauchen eine gründliche Reform des Wahlrechts.
— Unabdingbar ist eine umfassende Rechtsreform, besonders der politischen Strafjustiz und des Strafvollzuges.
— Wir brauchen volle Freizügigkeit für jeden, auch für die Jugend. Unser Verhältnis zu Reisen, Auswanderung und Heimkehr muß vom Kopf auf die Füße gestellt und aus dem Umfeld von Verrat und Verbrechen geholt werden.[1]
— Wir brauchen die Offenlegung und den Abbau aller Vergünstigungen und Privilegien. Es darf weder Territorien noch Bevölkerungsschichten mit Sonderversorgung geben.
— Der Wehrdienst muß entrümpelt und reformiert werden. Die Wehrpflicht muß erheblich verkürzt werden (max. 12 Monate). Wir brauchen einen sozialen Ersatzdienst.
— Wir brauchen eine parlamentarische Kontrolle der Polizei – und Sicherheitsorgane. Sie müssen drastisch auf das Maß der tatsächlichen Bedrohung durch Kriminalität reduziert werden.
— Staat und Gesellschaft müssen entflochten und entfilzt werden. Es gibt zuviel Administration und Bürokratie. Die Gemeinden und Kreise müssen selbständiger werden.
— Wir brauchen den Aufbruch von Erziehung und Volksbildung aus der Erstarrung in Disziplin und Langeweile.
— Ein Drittel unserer Gesellschaft sind alte Menschen, Kranke und Behinderte. Ihnen müssen ein menschenwürdiges Leben und soziale Gleichberechtigung garantiert sein.
Die Bevölkerung muß rückhaltlos über den wahren Zustand von Wirtschaft, Umwelt und sozialen Verhältnissen aufgeklärt werden. Wir wollen keine Krisenverschleierung durch Konsumspritzen, die nur die Staatsverschuldung weiter erhöhen. Schluß mit der Geheimniskrämerei um lebenswichtige Informationen und Daten! Der Wirtschaftskrise muß durch Abbau unproduktiver Staatsausgaben,

nicht durch sozialen Abbau begegnet werden! Wir brauchen eine grundsätzliche Neuorientierung der Wirtschaftspolitik. Der Umweltschutz muß neben der sozialen Gerechtigkeit zum Grundwert entwickelt werden.

Neues Forum.

Vocabulary

zu.lassen, ä, ie, a legalise
der Zugang zu access to
die Pressefreiheit freedom of the press
die Meinungsfreiheit freedom of opinion
eine tiefgreifende Medienreform a radical reform of the media
die Versammlungs- und Demonstrationsfreiheit freedom of assembly and freedom to demonstrate
das Wahlrecht electoral law
unabdingbar indispensable
eine umfassende Rechtsreform a comprehensive legal reform
die Strafjustiz criminal justice
der Strafvollzug penal system
die Freizügigkeit freedom of domicile, freedom to travel
die Auswanderung emigration
die Offenlegung disclosure .
der Abbau aller Vergünstigungen the removal of all privileges
das Territorium area
die Bevölkerungsschichten sections of the population
die Sonderversorgung special provision
der Wehrdienst military service, draft
entrümpeln 'clear out', reform
die Wehrpflicht military conscription
max. maximum
der Ersatzdienst community (non-military) service
die Polizei- und Sicherheitsorgane police and security authorities
entflechten, i, e, o break up
entfilzen free of graft and corruption
die Gemeinden und Kreise localities and districts
selbständiger more autonomous
der Aufbruch here: release
die Volksbildung popular education
die Erstarrung ossification
der Behinderte disabled person
menschenwürdig worthy of human beings
die Gleichberechtigung equal rights
rückhaltlos with complete frankness
die Umwelt environment
die sozialen Verhältnisse the social situation
auf.klären inform
die Krisenverschleierung the cover-up of crises

60

die **Konsumspritze** short boost to consumer spending
die **Staatsverschuldung** state deficit
    Schluß mit no more
die **Geheimniskrämerei** secrecy
    lebenswichtig vital
die **Daten** data
der **Abbau** cuts
eine **grundsätzliche Neuorientierund der Wirtschaftspolitik** a fundamental
    reorientation of economic policy
der **Umweltschutz** environmental protection
der **Grundwert** basic value

Notes

1 **Unser Verhältnis ... geholt werden:** 'Our attitude to travel, emigration and
homecoming must be put on a normal footing again (must be put back on its
feet again) and no longer stigmatised as treason and crime.'

11 September. In Leipzig more than seventy members of opposition
groups are arrested as they leave the weekly church service for peace in
the Nikolaikirche ... In Hungary the border to Austria is opened. The
Hungarian government unilaterally suspends the treaty with the GDR
from 1969 by ceasing to detain East Germans wishing to leave ... During
the following three days 15,000 East Germans cross via Austria to
reception camps in the Federal Republic ... The government of the GDR
bitterly attacks the Hungarian government, whom it accuses of sacrificing
its loyalty to a fellow-member of the Warsaw Pact in return for West
German credit and promises of economic support ... 12 September.
A further opposition group, Demokratie Jetzt, is founded, consisting of
civil rights activists close to the Church. They demand 'eine demokratische
Umgestaltung in der DDR' ... 250 of the 450 East Germans who have taken
refuge in the West German Embassy in Prague return to East Germany
after promises of legal assistance in their application for exit visas ...
13 September. A new wave of East German refugees in the West German
Embassy in Prague increases the numbers to 400 ... After the regular peace
service in the Nikolaikirche in Leipzig 100 people are arrested as they
attempt to demonstrate ... 19 September. Neues Forum applies for official
recognition as a legal organisation. The application is rejected by the GDR
authorities on the grounds that Neues Forum is a subversive group ... After
the Permanent Mission in East Berlin and the Embassies in Budapest and
Prague, the West German Embassy in Warsaw has to be closed due to
overcrowding and gradually deteriorating hygienic conditions. Hundreds
continue to dodge guards to clamber into the Embassy compound. Many
have to camp out now in the Embassy grounds. Thousands continue to
escape across the Hungarian–Austrian border and into West Germany
where they receive help and attention from the media.

7. *Neues Deutschland* attacks West German media involvement

Nach dem Medien- und Politikerrummel in der BRD um den
'Tag X' sehen sich die in einer illegalen Nacht-und-Nebel-Aktion
abgeworbenen DDR-Bürger ihrem Schicksal überlassen. Die
meisten der vielen hundert Reporter und Kameraleute, die sich im
Raum Niederbayern versammelt hatten, haben nunmehr jegliches
Interesse an diesen Leuten verloren. ...
Am Dienstag noch überschüttete die BRD-Presse ihre Leser mit
Geschichten, in denen auf der ganzen Klaviatur von triefender
Rührseligkeit bis militantem Nationalismus gespielt wurde.[1]
Nichts war so manchen Medienvertretern billig und abgeschmackt
genug.
Nur selten mischte sich in die von Haß gegen die DDR geprägte
Berichterstattung der BRD-Medien auch Nachdenkliches. So
stellte der ZDF-Reporter Hirsch nach Gesprächen mit zahlreichen
der 'Flüchtlinge' fest: 'Nach der abenteuerlichen Reise wird
manchem erst bewußt, auf was er sich da eingelassen hat.'
Und die 'Süddeutsche Zeitung' zitierte unter der vielsagenden
Überschrift 'Luftballons für die Landsleute von drüben' einen
Grenzbeamten mit den Worten: 'Aber wer kümmert sich in einigen
Wochen um sie, wenn die ganze Aufregung wieder vergessen und
der Alltag eingekehrt ist?' Und auch die 'Stuttgarter Nachrichten'
warfen die Frage auf: 'Mit einigem Argwohn muß gefragt werden:
Was kommt nach dem Medienrummel?' Wieviel Aufmerksamkeit
bleibt noch übrig, wenn die Kameras wieder eingepackt sind und
die Reporter abziehen?
Schon bei ihrer Ankunft in den bayerischen Aufnahmelagern
mußten die Abgeworbenen feststellen, daß ihnen weder in bezug
auf Wohnungen noch auf Arbeitsplätze feste Zusagen gemacht
werden konnten: Auch die zuvor versprochene freie Ortswahl in
der BRD war erheblich eingeschränkt. Für die meisten gebe es
auch keine Chance, so wurde ihnen bedeutet, in ihren erlernten
Berufen zu arbeiten. In den Lagern gab es zwar Schalter des
Arbeitsamtes, doch die seien, so erfuhren die ehemaligen
DDR-Bürger, in erster Linie dazu da, sie als Arbeitslose zu
registrieren.

Neues Deutschland, 13. September 1989.

Vocabulary

der Medien- und Politikerrummel spectacle put on by the media and politicians
die Nacht-und Nebel-Aktion the cloak-and-dagger operation
    ab.werben, i, a, o lure away
    abgeschmackt tasteless
    Nachdenkliches thoughtful reflections
    sich ein.lassen, ä, ie, a (auf + acc.) get involved in
    vielsagend telling
    ab.ziehen, ie, o, o leave
das Aufnahmelager reception camp
die Abgeworbenen those lured away
    ein.schränken restrict

Notes

1 **Am Dienstag noch ... gespielt wurde:** 'On Tuesday the West German press was still inundating its readers with reports covering the whole gamut, from cloying sentimentality to militant nationalism.'

8. *Neues Deutschland* accuses West Germany of a co-ordinated campaign

Unter Anwendung aller Methoden der Versprechungen, der Verlockungen, des psychologischen Drucks und unverhüllter Abwerbung werden Bürger der DDR dazu gebracht, über dritte Länder ihre Heimat zu verlassen. Verbunden ist der Menschenhandel mit einer zügellosen Verleumdungskampagne gegen die DDR. All dies geschieht unter Mißachtung der Staatsbürgerschaft der DDR, unter der Anmaßung einer sogenannten 'Obhutspflicht für alle Deutschen'. Die Aktionen der BRD sind generalstabsmäßig vorbereitet, sie werden skrupellos durchgeführt; so wie es dem Charakter der kapitalistischen Gesellschaft entspricht.

... Alles Gerede in der Bundesrepublik von 'Menschlichkeit' und 'Menschenrechten' erweist sich wieder einmal als Lug und Trug. Der von Kräften der Bundesrepublik organisierte und stabsmäßig geplante Menschenhandel dient allein der revanchistischen, großdeutschen Politik einer Wiederherstellung des 'Großdeutschen Reiches in den Grenzen von 1937', der Revision der Ergebnisse des Zweiten Weltkrieges und der Nachkriegsentwicklung. Es ist der Versuch, das 40jährige sozialistische Aufbauwerk der Bürger der DDR zu diskreditieren. Dieser Versuch wird scheitern, aber verantwortliche politische Kräfte der BRD haben sich vor aller

Welt als diejenigen entlarvt, die in massiver Weise den Prozeß der Entspannung und Zusammenarbeit in Europa gefährden.

Neues Deutschland, 19. September 1989.

Vocabulary
    unter Anwendung making use of
  die Verlockung temptation
  die unverhüllte Abwerbung undisguised enticement
    dazu bringen incite someone to
  der Menschenhandel traffic in human beings
  die zügellose Verleumdungskampagne unbridled defamatory campaign
    generalstabsmäßig vorbereiten plan with military precision
    skrupellos durch.führen carry out unscrupulously
  die Menschlichkeit humanity
  die Menschenrechte human rights
    sich erweisen, ei, ie, ie turn out to be
    Lug und Trug lies and deception
  die Nachkriegsentwicklung post-war development
  das Aufbauwerk work of construction
    diskreditieren discredit
    scheitern fail
    entlarven unmask
    in massiver Weise massively
  die Entspannung detente

20 September. Manfred Gerlach, Chairman of the Liberal 'Block Party' in the GDR, issues a call for a more tolerant attitude by the authorities towards critics, dissidents and civil rights groups; this is one among the tentative chorus of appeals by artists, churchmen, and politicians, including members of the SED ... 24 September. The number of refugees climbing into the Embassy grounds in Prague has reached 900, in Warsaw, about 400 ... The GDR authorities begin direct negotiations with Bonn on ways to solve the crisis, as final preparations are made to celebrate the fortieth anniversary of the GDR ... 25 September. After a lengthy illness and convalescence Erich Honecker returns to his official duties ... In Leipzig about 8,000 demonstrate for freedom of speech, freedom of assembly and against the continued banning of Neues Forum ... Calls for liberalisation are made by, among other people, the Deputy Minister of Culture and the former head of East Germany's secret service, Markus Wolf ... A meeting of nation-wide opposition groups is held in Leipzig. Neues Forum is chosen as the umbrella organisation for the many regional and single-issue reform groups and action groups which have sprung up throughout the GDR ... 26 September 200 of the 1,200 East Germans who have occupied the West German Embassy in Prague return to

East Germany after being given promises that they will be allowed to leave the GDR legally within six months. Most, however, hold out in the Prague Embassy and Embassy grounds in deteriorating conditions ... 27 September. A further demonstration is broken up in Leipzig after the peace service in the Nikolai-Kirche. Many arrests are made.

Among the many public calls for toleration of criticism by the government and for a process of public dialogue is the appeal by the renowned East Berlin theatre founded by Bert Brecht, the Berliner Ensemble.

9. The 'Berliner Ensemble' appeals for dialogue

Das künstlerische Ensemble des Berliner Ensembles hält es für notwendig zu erklären, daß es sich mit allen Möglichkeiten und Mitteln an der Volksaussprache, die sehr dringend notwendig ist zur Klärung der aktuellen krisenhaften Lage, beteiligen wird. Auch angesichts der einzigartigen historischen Chance, die der Abrüstungsdialog zwischen der UdSSR und den USA eröffnet hat und angesichts der globalen Verschärfung ökonomischer und ökologischer Konflikte, die vor den Grenzen unseres Landes nicht haltmachen, brauchen wir eine umfassende und sachliche Analyse, die den Fragen nach der künftigen Entwicklung der DDR, ihrer unverzichtbaren Funktion im politischen Weltprozeß auf dialektische Weise gerecht wird. Die Zeit drängt. Nötig ist die öffentliche Diskussion. Ohne die öffentliche Information über alle Fragen und Probleme werden wir die Menschen dieses Landes nicht nur nicht aktivieren zur Weiterführung des Sozialismus in der DDR, sondern wir werden sie verlieren und nicht nur über die Grenze.

Erklärung der Künstler des 'Berliner Ensembles', 29. September 1989.

Vocabulary
das künstlerische Ensemble the performing company
die Volksaussprache popular debate
    aktuell current
der Abrüstungsdialog dialogue on disarmament
die Verschärfung aggravation
die umfassende und sachliche Analyse a comprehensive and objective analysis
    unverzichtbar indispensable
die den Fragen ... gerecht wird which does justice to the questions
die Weiterführung continuation

30 September. After intensive negotiations between East and West German officials the GDR gives in, allowing the refugees in the West German Embassies to leave for West Germany. In a dramatic statement the West German Foreign Minister, Hans-Dietrich Genscher, announces the breakthrough to the 3,000 refugees in the Prague Embassy grounds. The historic announcement leads to scenes of jubilation. Fulfilling the conditions laid down by the GDR, 5,500 emigrants leave Prague in East German trains of the Reichsbahn, re-routed to pass through the territory of the GDR again so that they are nominally 'expelled'. Eight hundred refugees are also allowed to leave the Embassy in Warsaw for West Germany ... By the end of September a total of altogether 25,000 East Germans have also left Hungary before being accommodated temporarily in reception camps in Bavaria.

Figure 2 East German emigration routes

10. The East Germans in the Prague Embassy are allowed to leave

Dichtgedrängt standen Hunderte von Menschen auf Gleis 8 des Hauptbahnhofs in Hof. Als um 6.14 Uhr bei Nieselregen der erste Zug mit Botschaftsflüchtlingen einfuhr, brandete ihnen Applaus entgegen. Noch größerer Jubel in den Waggons der Deutschen Reichsbahn. Eine Gruppe junger Hofer stimmte zur Gitarren-begleitung einen alten Beatles-Hit an – da konnten die Neuankömmlinge die Tränen nicht mehr zurückhalten. 'Willkommen im freien Teil Deutschlands' begrüßte Entwicklungshilfeminister Jürgen Warnke die meist jungen Familien mit Kindern, die von Verwandten und Freunden in die Arme geschlossen wurden. Der Beginn des neuen Lebens. Ein Tag voller Glück.

Freudentränen, Unglauben, wildfremde Menschen fielen sich in die Arme: 'Ich hatte einen Schock. Ich hatte schon nicht mehr an die Ausreise geglaubt', schildert eine Mutter ... ihre Eindrücke aus der Bonner Botschaft in Prag.

Bundesaußenminister Hans-Dietrich Genscher war am Samstag kurz vor 19 Uhr auf den Balkon des Palais Lobkowicz[1] getreten. Als Genscher die Stimme erhob und 'liebe Landsleute' sagte, brach ohrenbetäubender Jubel los. 'Uns war klar, wir haben es geschafft', meint ein 28jähriger, der wie Genscher in Halle geboren ist.

Die Menschen im schlammigen Botschaftsgarten rissen die Arme hoch, schrien Erleichterung und Freude heraus. 'Die Frauen fielen um wie Fliegen', erinnerte sich ein Dresdner später an den 'größten Moment' seines Lebens. Genschers besondere Bemühungen um die 4000 Flüchtlinge in Prag honorierten die DDR-Bürger mit Hochrufen und Dauerapplaus.

'Wahnsinn, echt totaler Wahnsinn', lautete die Reaktion auf das unerwartete schnelle Ende des Lagerlebens. Daß es noch vor den Feiern zum 40. DDR-Geburtstag am 7. Oktober klappen würde, hatte die blonde Vierzigerin aus Magdeburg immer gehofft. Doch daß ihre noch im Lager geäußerten drei großen Wünsche – 'Ein Schaumbad, ein eigenes Bett und einen Kübel Kaffee im Westen' – so schnell in Erfüllung gehen könnten, hatte sie nicht geglaubt.

Genscher war vor lauter Lärm kaum mehr zu verstehen. 'Es gab nur noch Trubel', berichet der Vater zweier Kinder am Sonntagmorgen in Hof. Nach Genschers Kurzauftritt hatten die

DDR-Flüchtlinge sofort Papiere geholt und gepackt. In Bussen wurden sie zum Bahnhof gefahren.

Acht Stunden dauerte die Zug-Reise. Zunächst ging es – mit einem mulmigen Gefühl in der Magengrube – zurück auf DDR-Gebiet. Dann endlich tauchte hinter Gutenfürst, wenige Kilometer nördlich von Hof, der Stacheldraht-Grenzzaun links und rechts der zweigleisigen Bahnstrecke auf. Zwischen den Absperrungen das Tor zum Westen. Dann weißblaue bayerische Grenzpfähle: 'Es ist geschafft.'

Neue Ruhr-Zeitung, 2. Oktober 1989.

Vocabulary
  bei Nieselregen in drizzle
  die Botschaftsflüchtlinge embassy refugees
    entgegen.branden thunder towards
    an.stimmen begin to sing
  der Neuankömmling new arrival
  der Entwicklungshilfeminister Minister for Development Aid
    wildfremd totally strange
  der Bundesaußenminister Federal Foreign Minister
    ohrenbetäubend deafening
    schlammig muddy
  die Erleichterung relief
  die Bemühung effort
  das Lagerleben camp life
    klappen succeed
  das Schaumbad foam bath
  der Kübel bucket
    vor lauter Lärm because of the sheer noise
  der Trubel excitement
  der Kurzauftritt brief appearance
    mit einem mulmigen Gefühl in der Magengrube with a queasy feeling in the
      pit of the stomach
  der Grenzpfahl post marking the border

Notes
1 **Palais Lobkowicz:** The West German Embassy in Prague

2 October. The GDR press publishes letters from 'ordinary citizens' and 'members of the works' militia', threatening demonstrators with forceful counter-measures if disturbances continue ... A nation-wide liberal–conservative opposition group Demokratischer Aufbruch is founded ... Neues Deutschland publishes a scathing commentary on those who have chosen to abandon their homeland. The article, edited and partly reformulated by Erich Honecker himself, contains wording which causes great offence and serious doubts as to his political judgement even among members of the SED and the Politburo.

11. 'Neues Deutschland' accuse the emigrants of betrayal

Wie der Sprecher des Ministeriums für Auswärtige Angelegenheiten mitteilte, sind die ehemaligen Bürger der DDR, die sich
rechtswidrig in den Botschaften der BRD in Prag und Warschau
aufhielten, über die Deutsche Demokratische Republik in Zügen
der Deutschen Reichsbahn in die BRD abgeschoben worden.
Die DDR sah sich dazu aus humanitären Gründen veranlaßt
angesichts der in den BRD-Vertretungen entstandenen unhaltbaren
Situation, die beim eventuellen Ausbruch von Seuchen auch
Menschen der betreffenden Länder bedroht hätte. Daran hätte
auch die Tatsache nichts geändert, daß die entstandene Situation
nicht durch uns verschuldet war, sondern durch die BRD auf
Grund der Verletzung der völkerrechtlichen Normen für Botschaften. Diese können in Europa kein Asyl gewähren. ...
Zügellos wird von Politikern und Medien der BRD eine stabsmäßig
vorbereitete 'Heim-Ins-Reich'[1]-Psychose geführt, um Menschen
in die Irre zu führen und auf einen Weg in ein ungewisses Schicksal
zu treiben. Das vorgegaukelte Bild vom Leben im Westen soll
vergessen machen, was diese Menschen von der sozialistischen
Gesellschaft bekommen haben und was sie nun aufgeben. Sie
schaden sich selbst und verraten ihre Heimat.
Nun werden einige Bürger der DDR an uns mit Recht die Frage
stellen, warum wir diese Leute über die DDR in die BRD ausreisen
lassen, obwohl sie grob die Gesetze der DDR verletzten. Die
Regierung der DDR ließ sich davon leiten, daß jene Menschen
bei Rückkehr in die DDR, selbst wenn das möglich gewesen
wäre, keinen Platz mehr im normalen gesellschaftlichen Prozeß
gefunden hätten. Sie haben sich selbst von ihren Arbeitsstellen
und von den Menschen getrennt, mit denen sie bisher zusammen
lebten und arbeiteten. Bar jeder Verantwortung handelten Eltern
auch gegenüber ihren Kindern, die im sozialistischen deutschen
Staat wohlbehütet aufwuchsen und denen alle Kindereinrichtungen, alle Bildungs- und Entwicklungsmöglichkeiten offenstanden.
Jene Leute hätten auch Schwierigkeiten bekommen, neue
Wohnungen zu erhalten, da diese natürlich für andere Bürger
vorgesehen sind. Vorzugsbehandlung konnten sie in der DDR nicht
erwarten. Hinzu kommt, daß sich nach bisherigen Feststellungen
unter diesen Leuten auch Asoziale befinden, die kein Verhältnis

zur Arbeit und auch nicht zu normalen Wohnbedingungen haben.

Sie alle haben durch ihr Verhalten die moralischen Werte mit Füßen getreten und sich selbst aus unserer Gesellschaft ausgegrenzt. Man sollte ihnen deshalb keine Träne nachweinen.[2] Wie es ihnen drüben ergeht, zeigen jetzt schon einige Berichte aus der BRD. Einige wurden bereits aus Arbeitsstellen entlassen, weil sie während der Arbeit Besorgungen machen wollten. In einem Autowerk hat man eine Frau ausgelacht, weil sie für ihre Kinder Kindergartenplätze beantragte. Arbeiter haben ihr zugerufen, sie verwechsele die BRD mit der DDR. Wäre sie dort geblieben, brauchte sie sich jetzt keine Sorgen um Kindergartenplätze zu machen.

Neues Deutschland, 2. Oktober 1989.

Vocabulary
der Sprecher spokesperson
das Ministerium für Auswärtige Angelegenheiten Ministry of Foreign Affairs
    mit.teilen inform
    sich rechtswidrig auf.halten illegally occupy
    ab.schieben, ie, o, o deport
    sich dazu veranlaßt sehen feel obliged to
    angesichts in view of
    unhaltbar intolerable
    beim eventuellen Ausbruch von Seuchen in the event of the possible outbreak
      of epidemics
die entstandende Situation the situation which has arisen
    verschulden, durch ... verschuldet cause, to be to blame for
    auf Grund der Verletzung von völkerrechtlichen Normen because of the
      violation of international legal norms
    in die Irre führen mislead
    vor.gaukeln create the illusion
    verraten betray
    grob verletzen grossly violate
    sich davon leiten lassen to be guided by
    bar jeder Verantwortung devoid of all responsibility
    wohlbehütet well-protected
die Angelegenheit affair
die Kindereinrichtungen child-care facilities
    vor.sehen für (+ acc.) reserve for
die Vorzugsbehandlung preferential tratment
    mit Füßen treten, i, a, e trample on
    entlassen, ä, ie, a dismiss
    Besorgungen machen go shopping
    aus.lachen laugh at

beantragen apply for
verwechseln confuse

Notes
1 **Heim ins Reich:** The slogan of National Socialist expansionism; the 'bringing home' of ethnic German communities spread over Eastern Europe.
2 **Sie alle haben ... nachweinen:** The intransigent bitterness of this passage, inserted by Erich Honecker, impelled many, even within the SED and Politburo, to withdraw their support from the GDR leader (cf. Text 21).

2 October. After the peace service in the Nikolaikirche in Leipzig the largest crowd so far, 20,000 people, demonstrates for reforms. The demonstration is broken up by force by the police, supported by units of the works' militia. During October, as the crisis comes to a head, an increasing number of statements are issued by cultural organisations calling for dialogue and reform, such as the following declaration by the Staatsschauspiel Dresden:

12. The demands of the 'Staatsschauspiel Dresden'

Wir nutzen unsere Tribüne, um zu fordern:
1. Wir haben ein Recht auf Information.
2. Wir haben ein Recht auf Dialog.
3. Wir haben ein Recht auf selbständiges Denken und Kreativität.
4. Wir haben ein Recht auf Pluralismus im Denken.
5. Wir haben ein Recht auf Widerspruch.
6. Wir haben ein Recht auf Reisefreiheit.
7. Wir haben ein Recht, unsere staatlichen Leitungen zu überprüfen.
8. Wir haben ein Recht, neu zu denken.
9. Wir haben ein Recht, uns einzumischen.
Wir nutzen unsere Tribüne, um unsere Pflichten zu benennen:
1. Wir haben die Pflicht, zu verlangen, daß Lüge und Schönfärberei aus unseren Medien verschwinden.
2. Wir haben die Pflicht, den Dialog zwischen Volk und Partei- und Staatsführung zu erzwingen.
3. Wir haben die Pflicht, von unserem Staatsapparat und von uns zu verlangen, den Dialog gewaltlos zu führen.
4. Wir haben die Pflicht, das Wort Sozialismus so zu definieren, daß dieser Begriff wieder ein annehmbares Lebensideal für unser Volk wird.

5. Wir haben die Pflicht, von unserer Staats- und Parteiführung zu verlangen, das Vertrauen zur Bevölkerung wiederherzustellen.

'Wir treten aus unseren Rollen heraus'
Erklärung des Staatsschauspiels Dresden, Anfang Oktober 1989.

Vocabulary
  der Widerspruch dissent
    überprüfen keep a check on
    sich ein.mischen interfere, get involved
  die Schönfärberei whitewashing
    erzwingen, i, a, u compel
  das Vertrauen wieder.her.stellen restore their trust in

It remains uncertain whether the GDR authorities will resort to force and risk bloodshed. Nervousness increases throughout East Germany.

13. The rising tension in the GDR

Über alle diese Ereignisse unterhalte ich mich mit dem Taxifahrer. Nach einer Gesprächspause sage ich: 'Wie wird es weitergehen? Etwas muß in den nächsten Tagen geschehen. Die Forderungen der neuen politischen Gruppierungen "Neues Forum", "Demokratische Erneuerung" und anderer Reformkräfte auch innerhalb der Parteien werden angesichts des Flüchtlingsstroms lauter und dringlicher. Immer mehr Leute legen ihre Angst ab und fordern die politische Führung auf, einen offenen Dialog mit der Bevölkerung zu führen. 'Wie es weitergeht?!' antwortet der Taxifahrer. 'Das kann ich Ihnen sagen. Das Land blutet aus. Da helfen auch keine Reformen mehr, die mit dieser Altherrenriege sowieso nicht zu machen sind.' Er schaut verschmitzt zu mir herüber. 'Sie wissen ja, welches Tier vier Beine und sechzig Zähne hat?'
Ich bin einen Moment verblüfft und antworte dann:' Vielleicht ein Krokodil.'
'Ja, aber wissen Sie auch, welches Wesen sechzig Beine hat und vier Zähne?' fährt er fort. Als ich verneine, sagt er, als wäre es das Selbstverständlichste von der Welt:[1] 'Na, das Politbüro natürlich!' Nach kurzem, hartem Lachen schüttelt er energisch den Kopf. 'Ich habe mit diesem Staat abgeschlossen.[2] Seit einem Jahr läuft mein Ausreiseantrag. Bestimmt komme ich bis

Jahresende noch raus. Ich bin doch nicht doof. Lieber lasse ich mich vom Kapitalismus für 15,– DM die Stunde ausbeuten, als daß ich mich vom Sozialismus für 5,– Mark die Stunde angeblich nicht ausbeuten lasse.'[3]

Als ich am Bahnhof aus dem Taxi steige, denke ich: Nicht alle haben mit diesem Staat und mit dem Leben hier so abgeschlossen wie dieser. Zum Glück bleiben viele Engagierte da, die sich die Hoffnung auf Veränderung nicht durch billige Vertröstungen und Phrasen der Regierenden nehmen lassen werden. Aber wie wird die politische Führung reagieren? Wird sie sich am chinesischen Weg der gewaltsamen Unterdrückung orientieren? Nachdem in den Zeitungen der letzten Tage mehr über China zu lesen ist als über den großen Bruder Sowjetunion, und die Aktuelle Kamera des Fernsehens in ihrer Berichterstattung keinen Zweifel daran läßt, daß die derzeitige chinesische Führung zu den besten Freunden des Politbüros der SED gehört, wäre es nicht abwegig, wenn die Partei- und Staatsführung, dem Beispiel Chinas folgend, die Plätze vor der Gethsemanekirche in Berlin, der Nikolaikirche in Leipzig und der Kreuzkirche in Dresden in blutgetränkte Plätze des 'Himmlischen Friedens' verwandelte.

Oder wird man sich in der politischen Führung doch den reformerischen Gedanken öffnen, Fehler beim Namen nennen und im Dialog mit allen Kräften des Volkes, auch den bisher als staatsfeindlich proklamierten Oppositionellen, Lösungen suchen? Voller banger Gefühle steige ich in den Zug.

Christian Weber, *Alltag einer friedlichen Revolution* (Stuttgart, 1990), 6–7.

Vocabulary
die **Gruppierung** group
die **Reformkräfte** reformist groups
  angesichts in view of
der **Flüchtlingsstrom** flood of refugees
  dringlicher more urgent
  ihre Angst ab.legen lay aside their fear
  auf.fordern call on
  aus.bluten bleed to death
die **Altherrenriege** old codgers' team
  verschmitzt slyly
  verblüfft amazed
das **Wesen** creature

der **Ausreiseantrag** application for an emigration visa
    sich aus.beuten lassen allow oneself to be exploited
    angeblich supposedly
die **Engagierten** those politically involved
    billige Vertröstungen threadbare prevarications
die **Berichterstattung** media coverage
    derzeitig at the moment
    es wäre nicht abwegig it would not be wholly unexpected
die **Partei- und Staatsführung** party and state leadership
    blutgetränkt soaked in blood
    verwandeln transform
    sich öffnen (+ dat.) be receptive to
    etwas beim Namen nennen call a spade a spade
    bang anxious

Notes

1 **als wäre es ... Welt:** 'as if it was the most obvious thing in the world'
2 **Ich habe ... abgeschlossen:** 'I want nothing more to do with this state.'
3 **Lieber lasse ich ... lasse:** 'I would rather allow myself to be exploited by capitalism for DM 15 an hour than supposedly not be exploited by socialism for DM 5 an hour.'

III. Protests and Honecker's resignation

3 October. Great anger is caused by the decision to suspend visa-free travel to Czechoslovakia, to prevent East Germans from escaping across the Czech border to Hungary and Austria ... In a new wave of emigrants seeking to reach the Federal Republic by occupying its Embassies the number of East Germans in the West German Prague embassy has again reached 7,000 despite preventive measures by the Czech police, trying to smother protest in their own country ... Once again, thousands of East Germans are allowed to leave Prague and Warsaw by train for the Federal Republic to resolve the crisis in time for the fortieth anniversary celebrations ... 4 October. Many thousands of East Germans assemble at the station in Dresden. As the trains with the refugees pass through there are serious disturbances; the police use water cannon and batons to drive back the crowds. Many try to jump on the trains, as they pass through without stopping ... In Leipzig a large demonstration for democratic reform and for Neues Forum is broken up by the police ... 5 October. As the eve of the GDR's fortieth anniversary approaches there are further demonstrations in Dresden and Magdeburg, which are broken up by security forces ... 6 October. The Soviet Party Chairman and President of the USSR, Mikhail Gorbachev, arrives in East Berlin to take part in the celebration of the founding of the GDR in 1949. There are widespread demonstrations for reform and calls of 'Gorbi, Gorbi' ... In a public address Honecker stresses the unshakeable character of socialism in the GDR and its importance in the continuing confrontation between East and West. He makes reference to the growing crisis arising from the exodus from the GDR and the demonstrations.

14. Erich Honecker on the fortieth anniversary of the GDR

Gerade zu einer Zeit, da einflußreiche Kräfte der BRD die Chance wittern, die Ergebnisse des zweiten Weltkrieges und der Nach-kriegsentwicklung durch einen Coup zu beseitigen, bleibt ihnen nur erneut die Erfahrung, daß an diesen Realitäten nichts zu

75

Figure 3 Erich Honecker (with Egon Krenz in the background)

ändern ist, daß sich die DDR an der Westgrenze der sozialistischen Länder in Europa als Wellenbrecher gegen Neonazismus und Chauvinismus bewährt. An der festen Verankerung der DDR im Warschauer Pakt ist nicht zu rütteln.

Wenn der Gegner derzeit in einem noch nie gekannten Ausmaß seine Verleumdungen gegen die DDR richtet, dann ist das kein Zufall. In 40 Jahren DDR summiert sich zugleich die vierzigjährige Niederlage des deutschen Imperialismus und Militarismus. Der Sozialismus auf deutschem Boden ist ihm so unerträglich, weil die vordem ausgebeuteten Massen hier den Beweis erbringen, daß sie fähig sind, ihre Geschicke ohne Kapitalisten selbst zu bestimmen. ...

Unsere Position ergibt sich nicht aus irgendwelchen veralteten Lehrsätzen, sondern aus der schöpferischen Anwendung des Marxismus-Leninismus, aus den Interessen der Arbeiterklasse und aller Werktätigen. Mit einem Wort, unsere Position ist die einer Politik nach dem obersten Grundsatz, alles zu tun für das Wohl des Volkes und seine friedliche Zukunft. Dementsprechend bleiben wir beim Erreichten nicht stehen, erhalten wir Bewährtes, trennen uns von dem, was überholt ist und hemmt, schreiten wir auf dem Kurs der Einheit von Wirtschafts- und Sozialpolitik[1] voran. In diesem Geist werden wir auch die sozialistische Demokratie in ihren vielfältigen Formen weiterentwickeln. Unser Anliegen ist, daß die Bürger sich immer aktiver und konkreter an den Staatsgeschäften beteiligen.

Erich Honecker zum 40. Jahrestag der DDR, 6. Oktober 1989.

Vocabulary
    einflußreich influential
  die Chance wittern sense a chance
  der Wellenbrecher breakwater
    sich bewähren prove its worth
  die Verankerung anchorage
    in einem noch nie gekannten Ausmaß to an unprecendented extent
  die Verleumdung slander
    sich summieren culminate in
    unerträglich intolerable
    sich ergeben, i, a, e (aus + dat.) result from
  der Lehrsatz tenet
  die Anwendung application
  die Werktätigen workers
    nach dem obersten Grundsatz according to the supreme principle
    dementsprechend in accordance with this
    Bewährtes what has been tried and tested
    hemmen constrain
  das Anliegen concern

Notes
1 **die Einheit von Wirtschafts- und Sozialpolitik:** The unity of social and economic policy proclaimed in the GDR from the early 1970s. This was contrasted with the social legislation of capitalist countries, whose function was merely to rectify the hardships resulting from their economic system.

At a torch-lit march-past in East Berlin about 100,000 take part in what is to be the last organised parade to celebrate the GDR … At a gathering of opposition groups in the Erlöser-Kirche in East Berlin a joint declaration demands free and secret ballots in East Germany under UN supervision… Further declarations from across the GDR call for discussions as a first step towards reform. A typical example is the statement issued by the Gerhart-Hauptmann-Theater in Zittau.

15. Further calls for dialogue from across the GDR

Warum empfinden zigtausend Menschen, Bürger unseres Staates eine immer mehr um sich greifende Perspektivlosigkeit, so daß sie sich gezwungen sehen, unseren Staat zu verlassen?

Warum fragt man nicht nach den Ursachen solcher Haltungen und Beweggründe in öffentlichen, offenen und gemeinsamen Gesprächen, sondern treibt diese Menschen in die Emigration und kriminalisiert sie noch durch unsere Medien?

Warum werden wir aus dem Prozeß von Problemdebatten und Problemlösungen ausgeklammert?

Warum entläßt man uns aus der Geschichte,[1] und warum wird uns der Weg verbaut zu einem eigenen Geschichtsbewußtsein?

Warum werden uns Beschränkungen auferlegt, die uns daran hindern, die Welt kennenzulernen?

Warum werden Anfragen um den richten Weg unseres Staates als staatsfeindlich abgetan, verboten, geahndet?

Warum wurden wesentliche Informationsquellen, Publikationen verboten, und warum werden wir gezwungen, uns einseitig zu informieren?

Wie können wir unter diesen gegebenen Bedingungen weiterarbeiten?

Wir fordern eine öffentliche Diskussion über diese nicht nur uns allein bewegenden Probleme mit allen gesellschaftlichen Schichten unseres Landes!

Den Beginn einer solchen Diskussion sehen wir in einer wertfreien Veröffentlichung aller Ideen, Vorschläge und Überlegungen.

Wir glauben, daß die Probleme unseres Landes nur gemeinsam lösbar sind.

Erklärung der Mitarbeiter des Gerhart-Hauptmann-Theaters Zittau, 6. Oktober 1989.

Vocabulary

eine um sich greifende Perspektivlosigkeit a spreading sense of hopelessness
aus.klammern (aus + dat.) exclude from
Beschränkungen auferlegen (+ dat.) impose constraints
ab.tun, u, a, a dismiss, wave aside
wertfrei impartial

Notes

1 **Warum entläßt ... Geschichte:** 'Why are we left out of history?

7 October. To celebrate the fortieth anniversary of the GDR there are military and naval displays in East Berlin and Rostock ... The number of East Germans crossing the borders to West Germany continues to rise dramatically ... In Schwante (Potsdam) an East German Social Democratic Party is founded to signal the breakaway of East German Social Democrats from union with East German Communists in the SED. The acting party leader is Ibrahim Böhme ... In a news conference Mikhail Gorbachev expresses criticism of the East German Politburo's failure to carry out reforms − 'Wer zu spät kommt, den bestraft das Leben.' ... There are many demonstrations all over the GDR to coincide with the fortieth anniversary celebrations. Most are broken up by the police. Many demonstrators use the presence of the international media and Mikhail Gorbachev to call for democratisation and perestroika in the GDR.

16. The protests on 7 October in East Berlin

Gegen 17 Uhr finden sich, wie an jedem 7. der letzten Monate, einige hundert Jugendliche auf dem Berliner Alexanderplatz ein, um 'auf die Wahlen zu pfeifen'. Zunächst wird diskutiert, dann werden die ersten Sprechchöre laut. Im Gegensatz zu früheren Kundgebungen, bei denen zu hören war 'Wir wollen raus', heißt es diesmal: 'Wir bleiben hier!'. Schnell ist die Gruppe von Neugierigen umringt, westliche Kamerateams, von Sicherheitskräften stark behindert, kommen zu ihren Bildern. Gegen 17.20 Uhr macht sich die Gruppe auf den Weg in Richtung Palast der Republik, wo zu dieser Zeit die Partei- und Staatsführung mit ihren Gästen, darunter Michail Gorbatschow, Todor Shiwkow, Milos Jakes, Wjciech Jaruzelski und Nicolae Ceausescu,[1] Geburtstag feiert. Polizeiketten vor der Spreebrücke verhindern ein weiteres Vorrücken. Die inzwischen auf zwei- bis dreitausend Personen angewachsene Menge skandiert immer wieder 'Gorbi, Gorbi', 'Wir sind das Volk' und 'Gorbi, hilf uns'. Michail Gorbatschow hatte tags zuvor, auf den Reformunwillen der DDR-Führung angesprochen, diplomatisch aber unmißverständlich erklärt: 'Wer zu spät kommt, den bestraft das Leben.'

Um 18 Uhr setzt sich ein geordneter Demonstrationszug mit mehreren tausend Menschen in Richtung des nördlichen Stadtbezirks Prenzlauer Berg in Bewegung. Hier findet seit einer Woche in der Gethsemanekirche eine Mahnwache für politische Gefangene statt. Auf Höhe der staatlichen Nachrichtenagentur ADN rufen die Demonstranten 'Lügner, Lügner' und 'Pressefreiheit – Meinungsfreiheit'. Die ersten Mannschaftswagen fahren heran. Polizisten sperren die Seitenstraßen ab. Es kommt zu Handgreiflichkeiten, zu Verhaftungen und zum Einsatz von Gummiknüppeln. 'Keine Gewalt' ruft die Menge und strebt weiter vorwärts. Ein Fernsehreporter postiert sich vor dem heranrückenden Zug und kommentiert: 'Dies ist die erste größere Protestdemonstration in Ost-Berlin seit dem Arbeiteraufstand am 17. Juni 1953.'

Neben Polizisten werden jetzt auch zivile Sicherheitskräfte gegen die Demonstranten eingesetzt, die untergehakt Keile in den Marschzug treiben, um den Block zu zersplittern sowie Abgedrängte auf Mannschaftswagen zu verladen und 'zuzuführen', wie es später im offiziellen Bericht heißt. Anderthalbtausend Menschen erreichen schließlich die Gethsemanekirche an der Schönhauser Allee. Vor dem Portal brennen Hunderte von Kerzen für die zu unrecht Inhaftierten in Leipzig, Potsdam und Berlin. Drinnen hat eine Fastenaktion für sie begonnen. An den Wänden hängen Berichte über die gewaltsamen Auseinandersetzungen an den Vortagen in Dresden. Vor der Tür wieder Sprechchöre: 'Neues Forum, Neues Formum'.

Unter diesem Namen hatte sich vier Wochen zuvor eine Bürgerinitiative gebildet, die dem bis dahin unartikulierten und unorganisierten Protest Stimme und Gestalt verlieh. Tausende Unterschriften standen inzwischen unter dem 'Aufruf 89' zur Initiierung 'eines demokratischen Dialogs über die Aufgaben des Rechtsstaates, der Wirtschaft und der Kultur'. Wörtlich hieß es in der Erklärung vom 12. September: 'Es kommt in der jetzigen gesellschaftlichen Entwicklung darauf an, daß eine größere Anzahl von Menschen am gesellschaftlichen Reformprozeß mitwirkt,

80

daß die vielfältigen Einzel- und Gruppenaktivitäten zu einem Gesamthandeln finden. Wir bilden deshalb gemeinsam eine politische Plattform für die ganze DDR, die es Menschen aus allen Berufen, Lebenskreisen, Parteien und Gruppen möglich macht, sich an der Diskussion und Bearbeitung lebenswichtiger Gesellschaftsprobleme in diesem Land zu beteiligen.' Die Straße ist ein erster Ort dafür.

Während die Demonstranten weiter ihre Forderungen nach Demokratisierung der Gesellschaft rufen, rüsten Spezialeinheiten der Polizei und der Staatssicherheit zur gewaltsamen Zerschlagung dieser, wie sie finden, konterrevolutionären Ansammlung. Gegen 21 Uhr wird die Gegend um den Bahnhof Schönhauser Allee hermetisch abgeriegelt. Vergitterte Lastwagen und Wasserwerfer fahren auf, Fahrzeuge, die bis dahin in der DDR unbekannt waren. Gegen Mitternacht kommt der Befehl zum Losschlagen, genau wie in Leipzig, Dresden, Plauen, Jena, Magdeburg, Ilmenau, Arnstadt, Karl-Marx-Stadt und Potsdam, wo an diesem Feiertag politische Demonstrationen ebenfalls gewaltsam aufgelöst werden. Was sich dabei ereignet, verändert das Leben grundlegend. Zeugen geben später Details zu Protokoll: 'Als ich gegen Mitternacht zum Bahnhof Schönhauser Allee kam, traf ich auf eine größere Menschengruppe, die diskutierend zwischen Polizeikordons stand. Die gesamte Straße war abgeriegelt. Auf Befehl rückte die Sperrkette vor, um uns abzudrängen, obwohl wir bisher allen Aufforderungen, wie etwa zur Räumung der Fahrbahn, nachgekommen waren. Plötzlich und völlig unmotiviert sprangen dahinter Spezialeinheiten mit Gummiknüppeln hervor, die wahllos auf alle einschlugen. Mir galt offensichtlich ein besonderer Einsatz, da ich bis zu diesem Zeitpunkt versucht hatte, mit einem befehlskräftigen Offizier zu diskutieren. Wenigstens drei Polizisten stürzten gleichzeitg auf mich los. Sie schlugen auch noch auf mich ein, als ich bereits am Boden lag. Mehrere Schläge waren auf meinen Kopf gerichtet, die anderen trafen meine Rippen und meine rechte Hand, mit der ich versuchte, mich an einem Fußgängergeländer festzuhalten. Auf einen Freund, der schrie, sie mögen damit endlich aufhören, gingen sie ebenfalls mit gezücktem Gummi-knüppel los. Als ich der Zuführung zu entkommen suchte und von einem Bereitschaftswagen sprang, wurde ich von einem anderen Polizei-Lkw angefahren, der nach kurzem

Stop weiterbrauste. Insgesamt habe ich drei Wochen mit einem schweren Schädelhirntrauma, zwei Platzwunden am Hinterkopf und perforiertem Trommelfell in den Krankenhäusern zugebracht.'
(Klaus Laabs)

Am gleichen Abend findet in dem kleinen Ort Schwante am nördlichen Rand von Berlin die Gründung einer Sozialdemokratischen Partei (SDP)[2] für die DDR statt. In den Statutengrundsätzen heißt es:

'Die SDP bemüht sich um die Entmonopolisierung, Demokratisierung und Teilung der Macht in Staat und Gesellschaft mit dem Ziel des Aufbaus einer ökologisch orientierten sozialen Demokratie.' Gleichzeitig verabschiedete Grundpositionen zur Erarbeitung des Parteiprogramms enthalten unter anderem die Forderungen nach strikter Gewaltenteilung, Trennung von Staat und Partei, ökologisch orientierter sozialer Marktwirtschaft mit demokratischer Kontrolle ökonomischer Macht, nach dem Recht auf freie Gewerkschaften nebst Streikrecht, Reisefreiheit und Auswanderungsrecht sowie Anerkennung der Zweistaatlichkeit Deutschlands,[3] bei gleichzeitiger Option für mögliche Veränderungen im Rahmen einer europäischen Friedensordnung.

Die anwesenden Personen wählen einen Vorstand und bereiten alles für die schnelle Aufnahme weiterer Mitglieder vor. Staatliche Stellen werden nicht um Genehmigung gefragt, ihnen wird die Parteigründung mitgeteilt.

Christoph Links and Hannes Bahrmann, *Wir sind das Volk* (Berlin and Weimar, Wuppertal, 1990), 7–11.

Vocabulary
> **pfeifen auf (+ acc., coll.)** whistle at, not give a damn for
> **die Polizeikette** police cordon
> **skandieren** chant
> **der Reformunwillen** unwillingness to reform
> **unmißverständlich** unmistakably
> **die Mahnwache** vigil
> **auf Höhe (+ gen.)** level with
> **der Mannschaftswagen** personnel carrier
> **ab.sperren** cordon off
> **die Handgreiflichkeit** scuffle
> **der Einsatz von Gummiknüppeln** the use of rubber truncheons
> **heranrückend** approaching
> **der Zug** here: procession

ein.setzen (gegen + acc.) deploy against
zu.führen arrest
die zu unrecht Inhaftierten those wrongfully arrested
die Fastenaktion hunger vigil
die Auseinandersetzung confrontation
die Bürgerinitiative citizens' action group
das Gesamthandeln joint actions
der Lebenskreis walk of life
die Bearbeitung here: deliberation
rüsten prepare for
die Spezialeinheit special unit
die Zerschlagung dispersal
die Ansammlung crowd
hermetisch ab.riegeln hermetically cordon off
der Befehl zum Losschlagen the order to attack
die Sperrkette cordon
einer Aufforderung nach.kommen obey an order
wahllos ein.schlagen, ä, u, a (auf + acc.) beat indiscriminately
befehlskräftig authorised to give orders
das Fußgängergelände pedestrian railing
die mit gezucktem Gummiknüppel with truncheon drawn
die Zuführung arrest
der Bereitschaftswagen riot police van
weiter.brausen roar by
das Schädelhirntrauma concussion
die Platzwunde am Hinterkopf wound at the back of the head
das perforierte Trommelfell perforated ear-drum
die Entmonopolisierung demonopolisation
der Aufbau construction
die Grundposition basic position
die Gewaltenteilung separation of powers
nebst together with
im Rahmen einer europäischen Friedensordnung in the framework of a
European peace order
die Aufnahme acceptance
staatliche Stellen state authorities
die Genehmigung permission
eine Partei gründen found a party

Notes

1 **Gorbachev, Zhivkov, Jakes, Jaruzelski, and Ceaucescu,** the party leaders of
the Soviet Union, Bulgaria, Czechoslovakia, Poland and Romania.
2 **SDP (Sozialdemokratische Partei Deutschlands):** Initially the East German
social democrats underlined their separate identity from the West German
SPD.
3 **die Anerkennung der Zweistaatlichkeit:** The recognition of the sovereignty of
the Federal Republic and of the GDR, still not formally acknowledged by
Bonn.

8 October. In further demonstrations in East Berlin and other cities many arrests are made. Demonstrators are subjected to brutal treatment before being released again. As the confrontations increase in intensity, there are fears of a total clampdown, leading to a further exodus of those who have given up hope of reform. At this juncture no-one is certain if there will not be a repetition of the crushing of the demonstrations for democracy in China, a step demonstratively approved of by the GDR leadership by the presence of Egon Krenz in Peking.

17. An eyewitness report on the treatment of protesters

In einem Kasernengelände, von Stacheldraht umgeben, endet die Fahrt. 'Die Frauen nach links, Männer rechts!' schnarrt eine befehlende Stimme. Ein junges Mädchen, die aus Angst oder Verwirrung ihrem Freund in die falsche Richtung folgt, erhält einen Schlag mit dem Gummiknüppel ins Genick und wird unter Beschimpfungen 'Wasch dir die Ohren, du Schlampe', zu den Frauen gezerrt, die unter Püffen und Tritten zu einer Reihe formiert worden sind. Während eine Uniformierte von Ines und den anderen Frauen die Ausweise einsammelt, werden die Männer gegenüber auf Garagentore verteilt und müssen sich mit dem Gesicht zur Tür mit weit gespreizten Armen und Beinen schräg in sogenannter Fliegerstellung an das kalte Blech lehnen. Da nach Ansicht der Polizisten keiner die Beine weit genug spreizt, brüllen die Uniformierten und treten mit Stiefeln nach ihnen, bis die gewünschte Stellung erreicht ist.

Das Mädchen neben Ines, das geschlagen wurde, weint. Ines kramt nach einem Taschentuch, reicht es ihr und sagt einige tröstende Worte. Da erhält auch sie einen Schlag mit dem Knüppel von hinten auf den Kopf, unter dem sie zusammenbricht.

Im Neonlicht einer Garage kommt sie wieder zu Bewußtsein. Außer einem Tisch in der Mitte ist der Raum leer. Ein dumpfer Schmerz zieht sich über ihre linke Kopfhälfte bis in den Nacken. Sie betastet die Schwellung. Zum Glück ist die Haut nicht aufgeplatzt, so daß kein Blut austritt. 'Aufstehen, ausziehen', brüllt eine Stimme. Hinter ihr steht eine Polizistin in Zivil, den Revolver im Gürtel ihres Rockes. Mit einem Gummiknüppel schlägt sie gleichmäßig einen Takt an die Betonwand der Garage. Alle

Kleidungsstücke, die Ines auszieht, wirft die Beamtin auf den Tisch und durchsucht sie. Durch den Sturz ist der Mantel dreckverschmiert. Die Polizistin gibt ein Zeichen. Auch den Slip runter. Als Ines nur noch im Hemd dasteht, muß sie dieses hochhalten und mit gespreizten Knien in die Hocke gehen. Sie spürt, wie die Kälte aus dem Betonfußboden in ihre nackten Füße kriecht, und zittert vor Scham und Angst. Wärend die Polizistin sie umkreist, klatscht sie mit dem Knüppel auf ihre flache Handfläche. Dann bedeutet sie Ines, daß sie sich wieder anziehen könne, und verstaut die Handtasche, die Halskette, die Fahrscheine aus der Manteltasche sowie das Buch, das Ines ihrer Freundin schenken wollte, in einer Plastetüte.

Ines wird in einen riesigen Lagerraum geführt und zwischen den etwa dreißig Frauen eingereiht, die hier in einem Meter Abstand mit dem Gesicht zur Wand stehen. Darüber, daß sie schweigen, wachen Polizisten mit Gummiknüppeln und Hunden. Zur Toilette begleitet sie eine uniformierte Beamtin, die sie die ganze Zeit über nicht aus den Augen läßt. Mitternacht ist längst vorbei, als Ines allen Mut zusammennimmt und den Polizisten, der hinter ihr vorbeidefiliert, fragt, ob sie nicht ihrer neunjährigen Tochter, die allein zu Hause wartet, eine Nachricht zukommen lassen könne. Doch der Uniformierte hebt sofort den Arm, und Ines kann froh sein, daß er seinen Knüppel nicht auf sie niedersausen läßt, sondern nur 'Schnauze' brüllt.

Im Morgengrauen werden sie gruppenweise in Gefängnis-Lkws verladen. So dicht gedrängt sitzen sie in den Zellen, daß Ines das Mädchen, dem sie ihr Taschentuch gegeben hat, auf den Schoß nimmt, weil sie nicht mehr sitzen kann. Durch das Rütteln und Gegeneinandergeworfenwerden hat sich der Grind am Schienbein gelöst. Ines spürt, wie das Blut langsam am Bein hinabrinnt. Sie ist müde und möchte sich am liebsten zusammenkrümmen, so schmerzt ihr Magen.

'Bestimmt bringen sie uns ins gelbe Elend[1] nach Bautzen', murmelt eine heisere Stimme. In dieses berüchtigte Gefängnis! denkt Ines entsetzt. Wie oft hat sie es von der Autobahn aus liegen gesehen, wenn sie zur Schwiegermutter nach Horka fuhren. Die schlimmsten Gerüchte laufen um über die Bedingungen, die in diesem Gebäude aus gelbem Backstein herrschen.

Der Lkw bremst und rollt aus. Noch während er fährt, wird die

Tür aufgerissen. Unter dem Gebrüll von Gefängniswärtern, die eine Gasse gebildet haben, steigen die Frauen aus. 'Hände auf den Rücken! Im Laufschritt!' Die Wärter schlagen mit Fäusten und Knüppeln nach ihnen. Abgehetzt erreichen die Frauen einen Saal, in dem sie sich auf schmale Holzbänke setzen dürfen. Wieder müssen sie stundenlang warten. Dann, 18 Stunden nach ihrer Verhaftung, erhält Ines das erste Mal etwas zu essen und zu trinken. Der Tee ist lauwarm wie die Suppe. Automatisch kaut sie das dunkle Brot. Ihre Hände zittern vor Erschöpfung und Übermüdung, so daß ihr fast der Löffel aus der Hand fällt.

Nach dem Geschirreinsammeln und erneuter Leibesvisitation, zum Glück ohne Ausziehen, werden die Frauen einzeln geholt. Das Verhör findet im Keller statt. Der Offizier hinter dem Tisch in dem leeren, gekalkten Raum wirkt genauso abgespannt und müde wie die Frauen. Er erklärt Ines, daß dies kein Verhör sei, sondern eine Befragung zwecks Klärung eines Sachverhalts. Gegen die Beschuldigung, daß sie an einer gesetzeswidrigen Zusammenrottung teilgenommen habe, protestiert sie nicht. Aber sie weigert sich, das Protokoll zu unterschreiben, das er ihr über den Tisch schiebt. Seine Blicke werden gefährlich scharf, und er preßt die Lippen zusammen. 'Unterschreiben', zischt er. Doch in Ines regt sich nach der Kette von Beleidigungen und Erniedrigungen der letzten Stunden ein triumphierendes Gefühl, als sie leise, aber bestimmt, beharrt: 'Niemals.' Der Offizier überlegt einen Moment und läßt sie mit den Worten: 'Das werden Sie noch bereuen' in den Saal zurückbringen, in dem die anderen Frauen warten.

Endlich, am Spätnachmittag, werden kleine Gruppen aus dem Saal gerufen. Ines gehört der letzten Gruppe an. In einem Kellerraum teilt ihnen ein Uniformierter mit, daß entschieden worden sei, keine Strafverfolgung einzuleiten. Mit den Worten: 'Wie Sie nach Dresden zurückkommen, ist Ihre Sache. Geld haben Sie ja', teilt er die abgenommenen Sachen aus. Es ist gegen 19 Uhr, als Ines mit den anderen Frauen ihrer Gruppe auf dem Bahnsteig in Bautzen steht. Und wie sie beim Verabschieden der neunjährigen Carola versprochen hat, ist es genau 21 Uhr, als sie zu Hause ihre Wohnungstür öffnet. Allerdings schließt sie mit vierundzwanziger Verspätung das verängstigte, ratlose Kind in die

Arme, welches sie kaum zu erkennen scheint, weil Ines um Jahre gealtert aussieht.

Christian Weber, *Alltag einer friedlichen Revolution* (Stuttgart, 1990), 11−15.

Vocabulary

das Kasernengelände the grounds of a barracks
der Stacheldraht barbed-wire
    schnarren bark, rasp
    mit dem Gummiknüppel ins Genick with a truncheon in the nape of her neck
    unter Beschimpfung accompanied by abuse
die Schlampe slut
    unter Püffen und Tritten with thumps and kicks
    spreizen spread apart
    in sogenannter Fliegerstellung in the aeroplane position, as it is known
    kramen nach (+ dat.) rummage for
    tröstend comforting
    zu Bewußtsein kommen regain consciousness
der Nacken nape of the neck
die Schwellung swelling
    auf.platzen open up (wound)
    in Zivil in civilian clothing
    dreckverschmiert covered with dirt
der Slip panties
    umkreisen circle around
    verstauen pack away
die Plastetüte plastic bag
    vorbei.defilieren parade past
    nieder.sausen come crushing down
    Schnauze! shut it!
    dicht gedrängt tightly crowded
    sich zusammmen.krümmen double up
die Bedingungen, die herrschen the prevailing conditions
der Gefängniswärter prison warder
eine Gasse bilden form a double line
    im Laufschritt at the double
    ab.hetzen drive to exhaustion
die Übermüdung exhaustion
die Leibesvisitation strip search
das Verhör interrogation
    abgespannt weary
die Beschuldigung accusation
eine gesetzeswidrige Zusammenrottung an illegal assembly
das Protokoll statement
die Beleidigung insult
die Erniedrigung humiliation
    bereuen regret
    keine Strafverfolgung ein.leiten not to prefer charges
    um Jahre gealtert looking years older

Notes
1 **das gelbe Elend:** the yellow nightmare – a reference to the notorious, yellow-brick prison for political offenders in Bautzen.

9 October. The first and most dramatic of the mass demonstrations takes place in Leipzig as more than 70,000 people take to the streets. For the first time the call is heard, 'Wir sind das Volk', challenging the claim of the SED to represent the people. There are insistent calls to avoid violence and provocation. An appeal is issued by the *Kapellmeister* of the Leipzig *Gewandthausorchester*, Kurt Masur, and by regional SED functionaries to avoid clashes with security forces. The police and assembled riot forces do not intervene to break up the demonstration. It becomes clear that there will be no 'Chinese Solution' to crush the democracy movement in East Germany.

18. 9 October. The first mass demonstration in Leipzig

Der demonstrative Aufmarsch der Staatsgewalt folgt eine Stunde später: Mit Blaulicht umkurven lange Lkw-Kolonnen, beladen mit Volkspolizei, den Ring, der die Leipziger Innenstadt einfaßt. Die Wagen halten in Seitenstraßen nahe der Kirche, die Mannschaften bleiben unter den Planen versteckt.

In der Nikolaikirche, wo um 17 Uhr das traditionelle Friedensgebet beginnt, ist bereits eine halbe Stunde zuvor nicht einmal mehr ein Stehplatz frei. Im Fenster über dem Eingang hängt ein großes Schild 'wegen Überfüllung geschlossen'; dazu der Hinweis, daß in drei weiteren Gotteshäusern zur gleichen Zeit Andachten stattfinden.

Vor der Kirche wird die Menge immer dichter. Sie schweigt. Die Ansammlung wächst auf einige hundert Meter durch die Grimmaische Straße bis hin zum Karl-Marx-Platz, an dem das Neue Gewandhaus[1] und die Oper stehen. Um fünf sind es einige tausend, um halb sechs mehr als 10 000, um sechs, als die Nikolaikirche die 3000 Frommen und Neugierigen entläßt, die drinnen Platz gefunden haben, ist der Karl-Marx-Platz schwarz von Menschen, 20 000 mindestens. Zaghaft ertönen erste Rufe: 'Gorbi, Gorbi', 'Demokratie jetzt', 'Wir sind keine Rowdys'.

Die Menge wartet weiter. Plötzlich, ohne erkennbare Regie, setzt sich der Zug von der Nikolaikirche in Bewegung, biegt in die

88

Figure 4 The peaceful demonstration by 70,000 people in Leipzig on 9 October 1989

Grimmaische Straße, rollt, sich lawinenartig vergrößernd, über den Karl-Marx-Platz auf den Georgiring Richtung Bahnhof. 'Schließt euch an, schließt euch an', skandieren die Marschierer.

Als die Spitze der Kolonne den Platz der Republik vor dem Leipziger Hauptbahnhof erreicht, sind dem Ruf rund 70 000 gefolgt. Junge Leute und ältere, Männer mit langen Haaren und solche mit akkuratem Messerschnitt. 'Gorbi, Gorbi', schallt es zu den Häuserfronten hoch und, vom Beton verstärkt, zurück. Auch ältere Ehepaare, den obligaten Einkaufsbeutel am Handgelenk,[2] klatschen dazu rhythmisch in die Hände.

'So etwas', stößt ein Mann mit leicht zitternder Stimme hervor, 'hat Leipzig noch nicht erlebt.' Und er fällt in den Schrei der 10 000 um ihn herum ein: 'Wir sind das Volk, wir sind das Volk.' Die Masse wälzt sich am Hauptbahnhof vorbei. Wenn jetzt Polizei dazwischenginge, um die 'nicht genehmigte Veranstaltung', wie der Auflauf im Ostbürokratendeutsch heißt, auseinanderzutreiben, sie hätte keine Chance – außer mit der Waffe.

Die Vopo ist kaum zu sehen. Die Stasi hat sich verkrümelt. Hinter verschlossenen Bahnhofstüren stehen einige Dutzend martialische Gestalten mit Helmen und Knüppeln, das ist alles. Doch die Demonstranten gucken nicht einmal hin. Der Lindwurm kriecht um die Stadt, die Parolen wiederholen sich: 'Freiheit, Gleichheit, Brüderlichkeit', 'Keine Gewalt', und immer wieder 'Gorbi, Gorbi'.

Die Stimmung ist beängstigend friedlich. Selbst als der Zug an der Bezirksverwaltung der Stasi vorbeizieht, ist kein Ruf 'Stasi raus' zu hören. Statt dessen pflanzt sich durch die Reihen der Appell an die vor dem Eingang aufgebauten Volkspolizisten fort: 'Polizisten, schließt euch an, schließt euch an.'

Verkehrspolizisten schaffen der stillen Demo freie Bahn; und selbst dort, wo Autos oder Straßenbahnen plötzlich zwischen die Menge geraten, bleibt die Stimmung sanft und gelassen. 'Hupen, hupen', schallt es, und zögerlich erst, dann kräftiger, kommt Antwort zurück.

Die Sympathien derer am Rand sind unübersehbar und deutlich zu hören. Vor dem Hotel International steht die Belegschaft Spalier, aus einem Fenster des Neuen Gewandhauses hält eine junge Frau eine Wunderkerze, von den Balkonen der Häuser winken und klatschen viele Bewohner. Die Demonstranten auf der Straße quittieren jede Zustimmung mit dankbarem Beifall.

So plötzlich, wie sich der Zug gebildet hat, löst er sich auf – wenig später in der Goethestraße hinter dem Karl-Marx-Platz verblüffende Szenen: Einige Demonstranten sprechen mit Männern der Betriebskampfgruppen, jener Arbeitermiliz, die noch kurz zuvor gedroht hätte, sie sei bereit, 'diese konterrevolutionären Aktionen endgültig und wirksam zu unterbinden. Wenn es sein muß, mit der Waffe in der Hand!'

90

'Wen wollt ihr schützen?' fragt ein junger Mann einen weiß-
haarigen Kampfgruppenkommandeur. Der antwortet: 'Ich bin
auch nicht gern rausgegangen. Ich habe meinen Leuten gesagt:
Vergeßt nicht, das sind unsere Menschen, die da draußen
demonstrieren.'
'Warum seid ihr dann ausgerückt?'
'Wir mußten verhindern, daß etwas zerstört wird.'
'Da habt ihr recht', sagt der junge Mann.

Als der Zug fast vorbei ist, ertönt plötzlich aus den Lautsprechern
des Leipziger Stadtfunks, die an markanten Punkten der Innenstadt aufgestellt sind, Musik — und das erste sensationelle Echo
der Partei: ein Appell, unterzeichnet vom Chefdirigenten des
Gewandhaus-Orchesters, Kurt Masur, dem Pfarrer Peter Zimmermann, Mitglied im Hauptvorstand der CDU, dem Kabarettisten
Bernd Lutz Lange von den Leipziger 'Akademixern' und
sensationellerweise, drei Sekretären der Bezirksleitung der SED.
Text:

Unsere gemeinsame Sorge und Verantwortung hat uns heute
zusammengeführt. Wir sind von der Entwicklung in unserer Stadt
betroffen und suchen nach einer Lösung. Wir alle brauchen einen
freien Meinungsaustausch über die Weiterführung des Sozialismus
in unserem Land. Deshalb versprechen die genannten Leute allen
Bürgern, die ganze Kraft und Autorität dafür einzusetzen, daß
dieser Dialog nicht nur im Bezirk Leipzig, sondern auch mit
unserer Regierung geführt wird. Wir bitten Sie dringend um
Besonnenheit, damit der friedliche Dialog möglich wird.

Den Aufruf zur Besonnenheit hören die meisten nicht mehr. Sie
sind gegangen, viele mit leuchtenden Gesichtern, in denen der
Stolz steht, sich endlich bekannt zu haben — gegen die Machthaber.
'Heute waren wir 70 000', sagt einer um die 50 selbstbewußt und
angstfrei, 'nächsten Montag werden es 100 000 sein.'

Der Spiegel. Spezial II, 1990.

Vocabulary
> **umkurven** drive around
> **ein.fassen** run around
> **die Mannschaft** unit
> **die Plane** tarpaulin
> **der Stehplatz** room to stand
> **wegen Überfüllung** due to overcrowding

die **Andacht** service
die **Ansammlung** assembly
die **Frommen** churchgoers
die **Neugierigen** curious spectators
    ertönen sound out
    ohne erkennbare Regie without visible leadership
    lawinenartig like an avalanche
    schließt euch an join the demo
    skandieren chant
    sich wälzen throng
    dazwischen.gehen intervene
    sich verkrümeln slip off
der **Lindwurm** here: long procession
    beängstigend alarming
die **Bezirksverwaltung** regional administration
    sich fort.pflanzen spread, propagate
    freie Bahn schaffen clear the path for
    zögerlich hesitantly
    unübersehbar conspicuously
    Spalier stehen line the route
die **Wunderkerze** sparkler
    quittieren here: respond to
    verblüffend amazing
die **Betriebskampfgruppe** works' militia
die **Arbeitermiliz** workers' militia
der **Kampfgruppenkommandeur** militia commander
    aus.rücken turn out
    ertönen sound
das **Mitglied im Hauptvorstand** member of the executive committee
der **Kabarettist** performer of political satire
die **Bezirksleitung** district executive
    betroffen concerned
    ein freier Meinungsaustausch a free exchange of views
    ein.setzen bring to bear
die **Besonnenheit** prudence
    sich bekennen declare one's views

Notes

1 **das Neue Gewandhaus:** the famous concert hall in Leipzig, rebuilt after the war.
2 **den obligaten ... Handgelenk:** 'with the inevitable shopping bag on their arms (wrist)'. The East Germans were reputedly ever-ready to pick up scarce items whenever sudden consignments happened to turn up in shops.

19. Slogans at the 9 October Leipzig demonstration

Wir sind das Volk!***Wir bleiben hier!***Wir sind keine
Rowdys!***Neues Forum zulassen!***Demokratie jetzt oder
nie!***Gorbi, Gorbi!***Stasi raus!***Schließt Euch an!***
Polizisten, schließt Euch an!***Freie Wahlen!

Vocabulary
   sich anschließen join the demonstration

9 October. In Dresden, there is also a demonstration of 12,000 people.
The SED *Bürgermeister*, Wolfgang Berghofer, who comes to enjoy
transitional prominence as a reformist figure, receives a deputation of
demonstrators. In a nine-point programme there are demands, among
other things, for freedom of opinion, freedom to travel and hold
demonstrations, for free elections, the legalisation of Neues Forum and
for an investigation into the brutality of security forces the day before...
10 October. The GDR news media continue to describe protesters as
rowdies, troublemakers and criminal elements ... At a crisis meeting of
the SED Politburo Honecker is called upon to submit a situation report
on recent developments ... 11 October. The Politburo of the Central
Committee of the SED issues a statement calling on all citizens of the
GDR to make a united effort to solve the current problems. This is widely
interpreted as a willingness to enter into a dialogue. This is confirmed
in an interview given by Central Committee Secretary, Kurt Hager,
hitherto one of the most outspoken opponents of reform ... The police
again use force to break up demonstrations in Magdeburg and Halle ...
In the following few days and weeks there are further calls for reform
and the avoidance of violence ... 15 October. At the beginning of the
traditional autumn holidays there is a dramatic increase in the exodus of
East Germans via Hungary and Austria to the reception camps in West
Germany ... For the first time unprecedented critical comments on the
situation are made in Neues Deutschland and in the TV news programme
'Aktuelle Kamera'. This marks a dramatic shift in the policies of the East
German media ... 16 October. After a meeting of the presidium, the GDR
Schriftstellerverband issues a critical statement, in which the need for
revolutionary change in East German society is emphasised and in which
the conformist and uncritical role of the media is condemned ... In Dresden
10,000 assemble outside the *Rathaus* to be informed of the results of
negotiations between a deputation and the *Bürgermeister* ... In Leipzig
100,000 demonstrators call for a democratic renewal of the GDR in the
largest demonstration in East Germany since the uprising of 17 June 1953.

20. Slogans at the 16 October Leipzig demonstration

Pressefreiheit, Reisefreiheit! *** Stasi in die Volkswirtschaft! ***
Die führende Rolle dem Volk! *** Rechtssicherheit statt Staatssicherheit! *** Wahlsystem reformieren! *** Reise-, Presse-,
Meinungsfreiheit! *** Ökologie vor Ökonomie! *** Sozialarbeit
ist nötig − Zivildienst ist ein Menschenrecht!

18 October. At an emergency meeting of the SED Central Committee
Erich Honecker is called upon to resign. The leading figures in Honecker's
removal from office are Egon Krenz, Günter Schabowski and Willy
Stoph. Honecker asks to be relieved of his functions 'for reasons of
health'. Leading SED figures Günter Mittag and Joachim Herrmann
also leave the Politburo and lose their functions as Central Committee
members responsible for economic policy and for agitation and
propaganda. Politburo member Egon Krenz is unanimously elected new
General Secretary of the Central Committee.
The immediate situation leading to Honecker's resignation is described
in the *Frankfurter Rundschau.*

21. Erich Honecker's resignation

Vor allem zwei Sätze des Kommentars[1] hatten die Menschen in
der DDR aufgebracht, in Wut geraten lassen. 'Sie alle haben
durch ihr Verhalten die moralischen Werte mit Füßen getreten
und sich selbst aus unserer Gesellschaft ausgegrenzt. Man sollte
ihnen deshalb auch keine Träne nachweinen.' ...
Schabowski[2] verwies immer wieder auf jene beiden Sätze, die
schließlich den Wandel auslösten. Den bösen Satz, den
Ausgereisten sei keine Träne nachzuweinen, hatte nämlich der
damalige SED-Generalsekretär Honecker höchstpersönlich in
den amtlichen Kommentar der DDR-Nachrichtenagentur ADN
hineingeschrieben. Als Schabowski und Krenz diese Tatsache
erfahren hatten, verlangten sie, unterstützt von anderen, die
Zurücknahme gerade dieses Satzes. Und sie fühlten sich wohl
auch gestärkt durch den Auftritt des KPdSU-Generalsekretärs
Michail Gorbatschow in Ost-Berlin aus Anlaß der Feiern zum 40.
Gründungstag der DDR. Dieser hatte der SED damals ins Stammbuch geschrieben: 'Wer zu spät kommt, den bestraft das Leben.'

Doch Honecker habe von einer Zurücknahme des 'Tränen'-Satzes partout nichts wissen wollen. 'Wenn ihr das heute beschließt, dann sind wir geschiedene Leute', habe jener auf der Politbürositzung[3] am 11. Oktober zu Krenz gesagt, berichtete Schabowski. Bedauernd habe Honecker noch hinzugefügt: 'Und ich hatte doch noch so viel mit dir vor.'[4] Doch der ehemalige Sicherheitschef und das jahrelange Ziehkind Honeckers, Krenz, habe 'tapfer widerstanden'. Nach sechsstündiger Diskussion habe es dann im Politbüro, dem damals einzigen Führungszirkel in der DDR, eine Mehrheit für einen Absatz gegeben ...

Das Zentralkomitee[5] tagte tags darauf um 14 Uhr. Über diese Sitzung liegen bereits Berichte von Teilnehmern vor. Nachdem der Mehrheitsbeschluß vor diesem Gremium verlesen worden war, waren alle auf Honeckers Reaktion gespannt. 'Als er zum Podium ging, wußte keiner, was jetzt geschehen würde', sagte einer der Teilnehmer der Sitzung später. Manche fürchteten, der Generalsekretär würde die Verhaftung der Rebellen verkünden und womöglich gar einen Ausnahmezustand ankündigen. Doch der Mann, der schleppenden Schrittes zum Podium ging, hatte wohl nach zwei schweren Operationen im Juli und September nicht mehr die Kraft, sich gegen die Absetzung zu wehren. Am Rednerpult verkündete er seinen Rücktritt und setzte sich für Krenz ein, der alle seine drei Ämter (Generalsekretär, Staatsratsvorsitzender, Vorsitzender des Nationalen Verteidigungsrates)[6] übernehmen sollte. Das Zentralkomitee folgte diesem Vorschlag. Um 14.34 Uhr bereits meldete die DDR-Nachrichtenagentur ADN, Egon Krenz sei zum neuen Generalsekretär gewählt worden. Wenig später sagte der Nachfolger, ihn erwarte 'viel Arbeit; Arbeit, Arbeit und nochmals Arbeit'.

Am 30. November trat das neue Politbüro zusammen mit dem Zentralkomitee angesichts immer neuer Enthüllungen über das ausschweifende Leben mancher Politbüro-Mitglieder geschlossen zurück. Am 8. Dezember meldete ADN, der Generalsstaatsanwalt ermittele gegen Honecker und andere ehemalige Politbüro-Mitglieder wegen Amtsmißbrauches und schwerer Korruption. Am vergangenen Wochenende waren von den aus dem höchsten Gremium Ausgeschiedenen, Günther Kleiber, Werner Krolikowski, Erich Mielke, Günter Mittag, Gerhard Müller, Willi Stoph und Harry Tisch in Untersuchungshaft.[7]

Karl-Heinz Baum, "Eine Träne zuwenig – oder: Wie Erich Honecker stürzte" in: *Frankfurter Rundschau*, 11. November 1989.

Vocabulary
der **Kommentar** commentary
   aufgebracht indignant
   in Wut geraten lassen enrage
   sich aus.grenzen ostracise themselves
   höchstpersönlich in person
die **Nachrichtenagentur** news agency
die **Zurücknahme** withdrawal
der **Auftritt** performance
   aus Anlaß on the occasion of
   jemandem ins Stammbuch schreiben tell them in no uncertain terms
   partout at all
die **Politbürositzung** meeting of the Politburo
das **Ziehkind** here: protégé
der **Absatz** deposition, dismissal
der **Mehrheitsbeschluß** majority decision
das **Podium** rostrum
die **Verhaftung** arrest
   verkünden announce
   schleppenden Schrittes with shuffling steps
   am Rednerpult at the rostrum
der **Rücktritt** resignation
das **Amt** office
der **Generalsekretär** General Secretary
der **Staatsratsvorsitzende** Chairman of the Council of State
der **Nationale Verteidigungsrat** National Defence Council
das **ausschweifende Leben** extravagant life
   geschlossen zurück.treten resign *en bloc*
   ermitteln investigate
der **Amtsmißbrauch** abuse of office
die **Untersuchungshaft** detention awaiting trial

Notes
1 cf. p. 70.
2 **Günter Schabowski:** The head of the Berlin SED, a key figure in the deposing of Erich Honecker. He took a lead in discussions with demonstrators and announced the opening of the Berlin Wall.
3 **Politburo:** The centre of power in the SED, a 'cabinet' elected by the Central Committee, meeting weekly to discuss major decisions.
4 **Und ich ... vor:** 'And I had such plans for you.'
5 **Zentralkomitee:** The wider body within the SED which met between Party Congresses to implement SED policies.
6 **Generalsekretär, Staatsratsvorsitzender, Vorsitzender des Nationalen Verteidigungsrates:** General Secretary of the SED, Chairman of the Council of State and Chairman of the highest military body, the National Defence Council.

7 **Günter Kleiber, Werner Krolkowski,** leading members of the SED Politburo, **Erich Mielke,** head of the MfS (*Stasi*), **Günter Mittag,** Secretary for Economic Affairs in the Central Committee, in charge of East German economic policy, **Gerhard Müller,** leading member of the Politburo, **Willi Stoph,** a leading SED figure, in 1989 Chairman of the Ministerial Council (*Ministerrat*), the highest executive body of the GDR, **Harry Tisch,** head of the *FDGB* (*Freier Deutscher Gewerkschaftsbund*).

18 October. In a speech on television Egon Krenz, the new head of the SED, concedes that the Party has 'made an inaccurate analysis' of the situation in the past months, thus impairing the relationship of trust between the Party and the people. He announces that the SED has opened the door to dialogue and promises a programme of reforms.

22. Egon Krenz's statement on East Germany television

Mehr als hunderttausend — darunter nicht wenig junge Leute — sind aus unserem Land weggegangen. Das ist ein weiteres Symptom für die entstandene komplizierte Lage. Ihren Weggang empfinden wir als großen Aderlaß. Jeder von uns kann die Tränen vieler Mütter und Väter nachempfinden. Wir haben manchen menschlichen, wir haben politischen und ökonomischen Verlust erlitten. Diese Wunde wird noch lange schmerzen. Nicht wenige Äußerungen von Ausgereisten vor der Kamera westlicher Fernsehstationen haben aber auch die Würde und den Stolz ihrer Eltern, Freunde und Kollegen und vieler von uns verletzt. Das entbindet jedoch niemanden von der Pflicht, bei sich und in seiner Umgebung darüber nachzudenken, warum uns so viele Menschen den Rücken gekehrt haben. Nur wenn wir uns rückhaltlos den Ursachen, die in unserer Gesellschaft entstanden sind, zuwenden, werden wir denen, die sich auch jetzt noch mit dem Gedanken der Ausreise tragen, möglicherweise einen Anstoß geben, ihren Entschluß zu überdenken. Wir brauchen sie.

Mit der Erklärung des Politbüros vom 11. Oktober wurde im Sinne unserer Politik von Kontinuität und Erneuerung die Tür breit geöffnet für den ernstgemeinten innenpolitischen Dialog. Die sozialistische Gesellschaft braucht den selbstbewußten und kritischen Bürger, den mündigen Bürger. Unsere Gesellschaft verfügt über genügend demokratische Foren, in denen sich die unterschiedlichsten Interessen der verschiedensten Schichten der Bevölkerung für einen lebenswerteren Sozialismus äußern können. Die breite Entfaltung der sozialistischen Demokratie in der DDR sollte jedoch von niemandem als Freibrief für verantwortungsloses Handeln mißverstanden oder gar für Gewalt- und Zerstörungsakte mißbraucht werden. Auf solche Handlungen kann es nur eine Antwort geben: Sicherung von Ruhe und Ordnung, der friedlichen Arbeit der Bürger, der Schutz der Werte, die wir alle geschaffen und für die wir alle zu bezahlen haben. Wer sich gegen die Grundlagen unserer gesellschaftlichen Ordnung wendet, der muß sich indes fragen lassen, ob er ein anderes gesellschaftliches System als die übergroße Mehrheit unseres Volkes will. Für uns ist klar: Der Sozialismus auf deutschem Boden steht nicht zur Disposition! ...

Das Politbüro hat der Regierung der DDR den Vorschlag unterbreitet, einen Gesetzentwurf über Reisen von DDR-Bürgern ins Ausland vorzubereiten. Wir gehen davon aus, daß dieser Entwurf nach öffentlicher Aussprache in der Volkskammer behandelt und beschlossen werden sollte.

Egon Krenz

Vocabulary

der Aderlaß loss of blood
nach.empfinden empathise
die Ausgereisten those who have emigrated
verletzen hurt the feelings
entbindet niemanden von der Pflicht relieves no one of their duty
rückhaltlos with complete frankness
einen Anstoß geben encourage, stimulate
ihren Entschluß überdenken think over their decision
der mündige Bürger the sovereign citizen
verfügen (über + acc.) to have available
das Forum (en) forum
lebenswert worth living
der Freibrief license
verantwortungsloses Handeln irresponsible actions
die Gewalt- und Zerstörungsakte acts of violence and destruction
sich wenden (gegen + acc.) oppose
die Grundlagen foundations
zur Disposition stehen here: to be in any doubt
der Gesetzesentwurf draft law
davon aus.gehen expect
nach öffentlicher Aussprache after public discussion
beschließen, ie, o, o pass

19 October. In response to the widespread call for freedom to travel the *Ministerrat* announces plans for a reform of the laws on travel abroad; these remain too restrictive and bureaucratic to satisfy people ... East German television launches a series of critical live discussions between politicians, academics, journalists and members of the public ... In Zittau 10,000 people attend a meeting organised by Neues Forum, although it is still not officially recognised ... 20 October. Leading church figures publicly question the SED's constitutional monopoly on power and political leadership ... There are further demonstrations for democratic reforms − 50,000 in Dresden, 5,000 in Karl-Marx-Stadt ... 21 October. Demonstrations continue throughout the GDR − East Berlin, Dresden, Plauen, Potsdam, Karl-Marx-Stadt − but there are no further clashes with the police ... In East Berlin a public discussion is held between demonstrators and leading Politburo member Günter Schabowski ... Independent commissions of inquiry are demanded by angry demonstrators to investigate many cases of police brutality ... 22 October. In the Leipzig Gewandhaus a public discussion with SED politicians takes place, chaired by Kurt Masur. The 'Sunday Discussions', which channel criticism and anger and prevent outbreaks of violence, continue during the following weeks ... 23 October. On the eve of Egon Krenz's election as *Staatsratsvorsitzender* 300,000 demonstrate in Leipzig for free elections and against a new concentration of power in the hands of the SED. There are calls for the opening of the borders, and the dismantling of the Berlin Wall.

23. Slogans at the 23 October Leipzig demonstration

Egon, mach die Grenze auf! *** Das ZK ins Altersheim! *** Junge Leute ins ZK! *** Die Mauer muß weg! *** Freie Wahlen *** Kein Machtmonopol für eine Partei! *** Schluß mit der vormilitärischen Ausbildung von Schülern und Studenten! *** Demokratie − jetzt oder nie! *** Für Demokratie und Marktwirtschaft! *** Freie Wahlen unter UNO-Aufsicht! *** Die Demokratie in ihrem Lauf halten weder Ochs noch Esel auf![1] *** Wir fordern: Mehrparteiensystem! *** Demokratie legalisieren: Vereinigungs- und Demonstrationsrecht! *** Freiheit für alle politischen Gefangenen! *** Freiheit − Selbstbestimmung − Menschenrechte! *** Rowdys raus! ***

Vocabulary
das **Altersheim** old people's home
    vormilitärische Erziehung preparatory military training
    unter UNO-Aufsicht under UN supervision
das **Mehrparteiensystem** multi-party system
das **Vereinigungs- und Demonstrationsrecht** freedom of association and freedom
       to demonstrate
die **Selbstbestimmung** self-determination

Notes
1 **Die Demokratie ... auf:** An ironic rejoinder to Honecker's recent assertion,
'Den Sozialismus in seinem Lauf hält weder Ochs noch Esel auf.'

There are also large demonstrations in East Berlin, Dresden and other
East German cities ... The legal authorities promise a comprehensive
investigation into all accusations of police brutality ... 24 October. Egon
Krenz is elected in the *Volkskammer* as *Staatsratsvorsitzender* and
Vorsitzender des Nationalen Verteidigungsrates. For the first time there
are also votes against and abstentions in the *Volkskammer* ... Krenz
announces that there will be a 'social dialogue' and a fresh approach to
political questions in the *Volkskammer* and *Staatsrat* ... In the evening
there are demonstrations against Krenz in East Berlin ... 25 October.
East German lawyers call for legal reform, a new electoral law, legal
redress against the state and for freedom to travel ... There are more
widespread demonstrations in East Berlin, Greifswald and Halberstadt ...
26 October. At a public meeting in Dresden attended by over 100,000
with the First Secretary of the Dresden SED, the reformer Hans Modrow
and the *Bürgermeister*, Wolfgang Berghofer, promises are made of
'revolutionary changes' ... For the first time representatives of Neues
Forum meet with a leading SED representative, Günter Schabowski ...
The West German Chancellor, Helmut Kohl, telephones Egon Krenz ...
27 October. A serious crisis is developing in the GDR due to acute
shortages and understaffing in key areas, as professional and young
skilled workers leave the country ... The GDR authorities announce an
amnesty for those who choose to return to the GDR. They release those
imprisoned for '*Republikflucht*' ... The temporary restrictions on travel
to Czechoslovakia are lifted ... Further widespread demonstrations are
held in many East German towns and cities ... 28 October. Public discussions are held in many towns, including in front of the *rote Rathaus*
in East Berlin.

24. The first public discussions in the GDR

'Offene Türen – offene Worte' heißt das Motto der ersten Großveranstaltung in Berlin, auf der sich Spitzenpolitiker der Diskussion mit der Bevölkerung stellen. Der vorgesehene Magistratssaal im Roten Rathaus erweist sich als viel zu klein. 20 000 sind gekommen. Die Debatte wird ins Freie verlegt, entwickelt sich zu einer Kundgebung. Sie beginnt mit einer Schweigeminute: 'Man muß an diejenigen denken, die eine individuelle Lösung ihres Problems mit dem Leben bezahlen mußten, in Minenfeldern oder durch Selbstschußanlagen oder die im Wasser der Spree[1] für ihr Begehren, sich einmal die Welt anzuschauen, zu Tode gekommen sind', erklärt ein Redner. All dieser Opfer einer vergangenen, ungenügend an den Realitäten orientierten Politik gelte es zu gedenken.[2] In der folgenden Debatte ergreifen der Berliner SED-Chef Günter Schabowski, Polizeipräsident Friedhelm Rausch, Oberbürgermeister Erhard Krack sowie zahlreiche andere Vertreter von Parteien und Organisationen das Wort, um die auf sie herniederprasselnden Fragen zu antworten. Bereits zu Beginn der Aussprache haben sich hinter den Mikrophonen auf dem Rathausvorplatz Dutzende Bürger aufgereiht, um von der Führung Rechenschaft zu fordern und ihre Meinung öffentlich kundzutun. Schabowski erhält Beifall für die Zusage, daß Demonstrationen künftig zur politischen Kultur Berlins gehören werden, womit einer Hauptforderung der letzten Wochen, das demokratische Grundrecht der Versammlungsfreiheit zu garantieren, nunmehr nachgegeben wird. Er räumt dies aber nur für Berlin ein und macht darauf aufmerksam, daß es in der Führung weiter Streit über den künftigen Weg gebe. Hart kritisiert werden dann im Verlauf der insgesamt sechsstündigen Aussprache die 'Schutz- und Sicherheitsorgane', namentlich das Ministerium für Staatssicherheit, deren Auflösung hier erstmals öffentlich gefordert wird. Der Präsident des Schriftstellerverbandes Hermann Kant[3] erklärt zu den Schlagstockeinsätzen um den 40. Jahrestag: 'Meine Polizei soll nicht mein Volk schlagen', schließlich heiße sie 'Volks-Polizei'. Als sich nach mehrmaliger Aufforderung Polizeipräsident Rausch endlich für die Übergriffe entschuldigt, gellen Pfiffe über den Platz. Stürmischer Beifall hingegen für den Vorschlag, die Politbürosiedlung in Wandlitz[4] bei Berlin in ein Heim für geschädigte Kinder umzuwandeln und die Privilegien für Führungsfunktionäre in Staat und Partei vollständig abzuschaffen. Gegen Ende noch einmal scharfe Angriffe auf das SED-Politbüro. Viele bezweifeln, ob nur zwei, drei Leute an der tiefen gesellschaftlichen Krise schuld seien. Auch die anderen müßten zurücktreten.

Ähnliche Forderungen stellt man auch bei Diskussionsveranstaltungen in Karl-Marx-Stadt und Leipzig. 'Der Patient Leipzig ist krank,[5] Rezepte nutzen nichts mehr, wir brauchen radikale chirurgische Korrekturen', heißt es dort in der siebeneinhalbstündigen Diskussion im Gewandhaus. Dem größten industriellen Ballungszentrum der DDR müsse mehr Aufmerksamkeit zukommen. Alle nach Berlin zwangsdelegierten Bauarbeiter[6] sollten sofort zurückkommen, um den weiteren Verfall der Innenstadt aufzuhalten und überfällige Arbeiten an der Infrastruktur vorzunehmen. Honeckers Politik des schnellen, repräsentationsorientierten Aufbaus der Hauptstadt habe dem ganzen Land schweren Schaden zugefügt.

Im Anschluß an die sonntäglichen Gottesdienste kommt es auch in vielen anderen Städten zu Demonstrationen, so in Ueckermünde am Oderhaff, in Rostock und im thüringischen Bad Salzungen. Unter der Losung 'Wir sind das Volk' richten sich die Forderungen unter anderem auf die Zulassung des 'Neuen Forums', die Schaffung eines zivilen Wehrersatzdienstes und die Durchsetzung von Pressefreiheit.

Am Abend kündigt der Chefredakteur der 'Aktuellen Kamera', Klaus Schickhelm, an, künftig 'schnelle und wahrheitsgetreue Informationen' in dieser Hauptnachrichtensendung des DDR-Fernsehens zu vermitteln, was mit Berichten von den zahlreichen Kundgebungen dann auch tatsächlich geschieht. Die Fernsehjournalisten wollten ihren Zuschauern künftig offen in die Augen sehen können, meint der Chefredakteur im Namen aller Mitarbeiter.

Christoph Links and Hannes Bahrmann, *Wir sind das Volk* (Berlin, Weimar and Wuppertal, 1990), 60–3.

Vocabulary
 die **Großveranstaltung** large meeting
 der **Spitzenpolitiker** leading politician

sich der **Diskussion stellen** face discussion
der **Magistraatssaal** city council chamber
  ins **Freie verlegen** transfer outside
die **Kundgebung** rally
die **Schweigeminute** a minute's silence
die **Selbstschußanlage** automatic machine-gun emplacement
das **Begehren** desire
das **Wort ergreifen, ei, i, i** start to speak
  hernieder.prasseln hail down
  Rechenschaft fordern demand accountability
  kund.tun make known
die **Versammlungsfreiheit** freedom of assembly
  einer Hauptforderung nach.geben give in to a major demand
  im Verlauf in the course of
die **Aussprache** discussion
die **Auflösung** dissolution
der **Schlagstockeinsatz** the use of batons
  nach mehrmaliger Aufforderung after being asked several times
  gellen ring out
die **Politbürosiedlung** Politburo residential area
  geschädigte Kinder children with illnesses
  um.wandeln convert
der **Führungsfunktionär** leading fuctionary
  ab.schaffen abolish
  zurück.treten, i, a, e resign
  radikale chirurgische Korrekturen radical corrective surgery
das **Ballungszentrum** conurbation
  zwangsdeligieren forcibly transfer
der **Verfall** dilapidation
  überfällig overdue
  vor.nehmen carry out
  im Anschluß following
die **Losung** slogan
der **Wehrersatzdienst** alternative non-military service
die **Durchsetzung** implementation
der **Chefredakteur** editor-in-chief
  vermitteln here: broadcast

Notes

1 **Spree:** The river along parts of the border between East and West Berlin.
2 **All dieser ... zu gedenken:** (He said) 'they must now remember all these victims of a past policy insufficiently oriented to realities.' The SED terminology still employed here is a sign of euphemistic caution, or of bitter sarcasm.
3 The controversial East German writer **Hermann Kant** was later ostracised by fellow-writers for alleged collaboration with the SED in pressuring critical writers to leave the GDR.
4 **die Politburosiedlung in Wandlitz:** The enclosed wooded estate, where leading SED figures had villas and enjoyed a life-style of relative luxury.
5 **Der Patient Leipzig ist krank:** A reference to the run-down nature of Leipzig's infrastructure and housing stock and the exceptionally high levels of pollution.

6 **Alle ... zwangsdelegierten Bauarbeiter:** The building brigades taken from construction work in Leipzig to concentrate on construction projects in the 'show-case' of East Berlin.

30 October. Egon Krenz continues to underline the irreconcilable differences between socialism and capitalism ... East German television makes a public commitment to more objective news coverage ... The agitational programme 'der schwarze Kanal' with Karl-Eduard von Schnitzler is dropped ... Further demonstrations take place across the GDR, including 200,000 in Leipzig.

25. Slogans at the 30 October Leipzig demonstration

Stasi aus der Demo raus! *** Deutsche Demagogische Republik – nie wieder! *** Entmilitarisierung von Schule und Studium! *** Konkrete Friedenserziehung statt Wehrkundeunterricht! *** Margot Honecker[1] muß gehen! Weg für Bildungsreform, Trennung Schule – SED-Organisation! *** Neues Forum ist des Volkes Wille – Egon, schlucke diese Pille! *** Demokratischer Sozialismus ohne Machtmonopol der SED! *** Demokratie statt Machtmonopol der SED! *** Alu-Chips[2] sind nichts wert auf der Welt, wir brauchen ab sofort Valutageld! *** Privilegierte aller Länder, vereinigt Euch! *** Dem Volke zum Wohle, die Stasi in die Kohle! *** Enteignung des SED-Medienmonopols! *** Frauen: die Hälfte der Welt – den Frauen die Hälfte der Politik! *** In Espenhain die Filter rein, die Luft soll wieder sauber sein! *** Ihr im ZK habt Wasser gepredigt und Wein gesoffen – nun zahlt auch die Zeche![3] *** Neues Forum! Es geht nur ohne Gewalt!

Vocabulary
 die Entmilitarisierung demilitarisation
 der Wehrkundeunterricht military education
 das Valutageld hard foreign currency
     in die Kohle down the pits
 die Enteignung confiscation

Notes
1 **Margot Honecker:** The wife of Erich Honecker, Minister of Education in the GDR and a leading figure in the SED.
2 **Alu-Chips:** Aluminium chips. The derogatory East German description of their own, non-convertible coinage and currency, regarded as worthless compared with the Western D-Mark.

Figure 5 Demonstrators in Leipzig on 30 October 1989 quote Mikhail Gorbachev

3 **Ihr im ZK ... Zeche:** 'You in the Central Committee have preached to others
the virtues of drinking water, while boozing wine – now you can foot the bill.' –
A play on a proverbial and an idiomatic expression in German.

1 November. Egon Krenz meets with Mikhail Gorbachev in Moscow.
Krenz expresses his support for the principles underlying Gorbachev's

policy of Perestroika. He categorically rejects the idea of German reunification ... Further demonstrations take place in Neubrandenburg, Frankfurt/Oder and Dresden ... For the first time statistics on air pollution in the area around Leipzig-Halle-Bitterfeld, previously kept secret, are published ... Several leading SED politicians are forced to resign, including Margot Honecker and Harry Tisch and a number of regional SED functionaries ... 3 November. On television Egon Krenz announces an SED action programme for political and social reform in the GDR. These include the establishment of a constitutional court, an administrative court, the introduction of community service as an alternative to national military service and reforms in economic and educational policy ... Further leading members of the SED Politburo are forced to resign, hastening the process of political disintegration in the GDR. These include Hermann Axen, Kurt Hager und Erich Mielke ... East Germans continue to cross into West Germany in increasing numbers. By the first week of November 40,000 have left the GDR in the mass exodus ... 4 November. A massive demonstration takes place in East Berlin attended by more than one million people. The historic five-hour march and demonstration, called by cultural organisations, are broadcast on East German television. There are calls for free elections, freedom of the press, freedom of expression and assembly.

26. The mass demonstration in East Berlin on 4 November

Massendemonstrationen hat es in der DDR zuhauf gegeben: am 1. Mai jeden Jahres, Mitte Januar zum Gedenken an die Ermordung der kommunistischen Ahnherren Rosa Luxemburg und Karl Liebknecht,[1] oder alle paar Jahre die Fackelzüge und Umzüge des Staatsjugendverbandes. Das Fernsehen schwelgte dann immer in Zahlen. Doch die Menschen waren alle hinbefohlen. Im Betrieb hatte man ihnen den 'Stellplatz' zugewiesen. Funktionäre überreichten ihnen Spruchbänder mit vorgeschriebenen Texten. Über Lautsprecher hallten simulierte Sprechchöre, die Fröhlichkeit vorspiegeln sollten, doch lustlos bewegten sich die Menschen zur Tribüne hin, wo die Mächtigen des Staates Huldigungen entgegennahmen; dort angekommen, klatschten die unten denen oben artig zu, setzten pflichtgemäß ein Lächeln auf, um dann, kaum hatten sie die Pflicht getan, im Laufschritt der U- oder S-Bahn zuzueilen. Transparente wurden achtlos weggeworfen, von der Müllabfuhr abtransportiert. 'Eine machtvolle Kampfdemonstration', schrieben tags darauf die Zeitungen.

An diesem Samstag war alles anders. Vor 14 Tagen hatten Ost-Berliner Künstler und Schriftsteller zu einer Demonstration für Pressefreiheit und freie Meinungsäußerung aufgerufen. Staatliche Stellen versuchten noch, den Termin mit fadenscheinigen Begründungen hinauszuschieben. Doch als klar ist, daß an diesem Tag auf jeden Fall Tausende demonstrieren werden, gibt es die staatliche Genehmigung.

Tagelang waren Menschen in Ost-Berlin damit beschäftigt, Transparente zu entwerfen, zu bemalen, zu befestigen, alles wieder wegzuwerfen, weil es nicht so recht gelungen schien, von vorn anzufangen, um alles noch schöner, noch treffender, noch witziger zu gestalten. Das war nicht nur in Ost-Berlin so. Am Morgen kamen viele mit dem Auto oder mit der Bahn angereist, um mit eigenen Werken dabei zu sein. Aus Sachsen, Thüringen, Mecklenburg, Brandenburg oder Pommern.

Der Demonstrationszug setzt sich 40 Minuten vor der Zeit in Bewegung. Der Platz vor dem Gebäude des Allgemeinen Nachrichtendienstes (ADN) kann die von allen Seiten zuströmenden Menschen nicht mehr fassen. Nach eineinhalb Stunden hat die Spitze des Zuges die knapp vier Kilometer lange Wegstrecke zurückgelegt: am Palasthotel vorbei zum Palast der Republik, wo die Volkskammer ihren Sitz hat, über den Marx-Engels-Platz zum Amtssitz des neuen Staatsratsvorsitzenden Egon Krenz, über die Breite Straße zum Alexanderplatz. Dort warten bereits Zehntausende. Es dauert noch eine halbe Stunde, bis die letzten Demonstranten überhaupt erst losziehen können.

So viele fröhliche, lachende, ungezwungene und zugleich selbstbewußte Menschen hat die DDR, deren verdecktes Markenzeichen bisher die schlechte Laune der Menschen ist, noch nie gesehen. Schweigend ziehen sie die Straßen entlang, manche Kerzen in der Hand, auch das im deutlichen Kontrast zu sonst üblichen Aufmärschen. Sie brauchen keine simulierten Sprechchöre, ihre große Zahl, ihre selbstgefertigten Spruchbänder sind auch so politische Demonstration genug. An der Volkskammer und am Staatsratsgebäude gibt es vereinzelte, spärliche Sprechchöre: 'Alle Macht dem Volke, nicht der SED.' Die Demonstranten klatschen und jubeln Menschen zu, die auf den Balkons stehen und mit eigenen Plakaten winken. Sie vergessen nicht die Solidarität mit noch immer Bedrängten in der Welt, mit dem CSSR-Dramatiker Vaclav Havel[2] oder den Farbigen in Südafrika. Sie fordern die Rehabilitierung eines Rudolf Bahro,[3] eines Robert Havemann,[4] und der Opfer des Stalinismus in der DDR. Sie lachen herzlich, als vor dem Gebäude des Staatsrats Schauspieler die bisher übliche Huldigungszeremonie simulieren, winkend mit abgeschlaffter, zitternder Hand, nickend mit wackelndem Kopf, den anderen Arm mühsam aufgestützt.

Wieviel es sind, die da demonstrieren, wer vermag es zu sagen? 'Mindestens 500 000', rechnen später die Veranstalter, andere kommen auf 800 000, auf eine Million. Es können noch 100 000 mehr gewesen sein.

'Gegen den Führungsanspruch der SED' und 'freie Wahlen' oder 'neue Wahlen für neuen Weg', das sind die auf den Transparenten immer wieder gestellten Forderungen — oft auch beide zusammen — Forderungen, die genau auf den Punkt bringen, was die Menschen in der DDR angesichts der politischen Krise, von der die SED intern selbst spricht, jetzt für unbedingt nötig halten. Das aber sind auch genau die Punkte, von denen die SED gegenwärtig noch nichts wissen will, wenn man über anderes durchaus reden kann. Das Bild von der Eingangstür der DDR-Volkskammer mit dem Plakat 'freie Wahlen' wird die SED auch künftig daran erinnern.

Viele der Spruchbänder strotzen nur so von Phantasie, Humor und politischen Anspielungen.[5] Sie sind es wert, in einem Museum für deutsche Geschichte der Nachwelt erhalten zu werden.

Karl-Heinz Baum, "An diesem Samstag war alles anders", in *Frankfurter Rundschau*, 6. November 1989.

Vocabulary

    zuhauf in great numbers
  die Ahnherren forebears
 der Fackelzug torch-lit parade
 der Umzug procession
 der Staatsjugendverband state youth association
    schwelgen in (+ **dat.**) revel in
    hin.befehlen, ie, a, o order to turn up
 der Stellplatz allotted position

das **Spruchband** banner
    mit vorgeschriebenen Texten with ready-formulated slogans
    hallen echo
    simulierte Sprechchöre simulated slogan-chanting
    vor.spiegeln create the illusion of
    lustlos half-hearted
die **Huldigung** tribute, adulation
    entgegen.nehmen receive
    artig well-behaved
    pflichtgemäß dutifully
    im Laufschritt at the double
das **Transparent** banner
die **Müllabfuhr** refuse disposal
die **Kampfdemonstration** militant demonstration
    auf.rufen, u, ie, u appeal
die **staatliche Genehmigung** state permission
    entwerfen draft
    befestigen stick
    noch treffender more aptly
    fassen accommodate, hold
der **Amtssitz** official residence
    ungezwungen spontaneous
das **verdeckte Markenzeichen** concealed trade-mark
    selbstgefertigte Spruchbänder home-made banners
    auch so by themselves
    vereinzelt sporadic
    spärlich scattered
die **noch immer Bedrängten** those still being oppressed
die **Rehabilitierung** rehabilitation
die **Huldigungszeremonie** ceremonial adulation
    simulieren simulate
    abgeschlafft limp
    vermögen, vermag, vermochte, vermocht be able to
    auf den Punkt bringen put in a nutshell
    unbedingt nötig absolutely necessary
die **Anspielung** allusion
der **Nachwelt erhalten** preserved for posterity

Notes

1 **Rosa Luxemburg, Karl Liebknecht:** Leading revolutionary German socialists opposed to the reformism and 'revisionism' of the Social Democrats. They broke with the SPD in 1914 for supporting Imperial Germany's war effort in the Reichstag. Both were murdered by the right-wing *Freikorps* in 1919.
2 **Vaclav Havel:** The Czech dramatist and leading dissident. A founder member of Charta 77. He succeeded the communist Husak after the Czech Revolution as President of Czechoslovakia.
3 **Rudolf Bahro:** A former SED technocrat, who became a leading critic of Stalinism and 'real existing socialism'. The author of *Die Alternative in Osteuropa* (1977), Bahro was imprisoned and later released to live in the West.

4 **Robert Havemann:** A scientist and communist, who became East Germany's best-known dissident. An outspoken critic of SED orthodoxy and a proponent of a reform socialism, Havemann spent many years under house-arrest.

5 **strotzen nur so ... Anspielungen:** 'are positively bursting with imaginative invention, humour and political allusion.'

Among the speakers on the Alexanderplatz are Markus Wolf, the former head of East Germany's secret service and the writers Christa Wolf,[1] Stefan Heym[2] and Christoph Hein.[3]

Notes

1 **Christa Wolf:** The GDR's internationally best-known writer. A critical member of the SED. The author of *Der geteilte Himmel, Nachdenken über Christa T., Kindheitsmuster,* etc.

2 **Stefan Heym:** The author of *Collin, 5 Tage im Juni, Schwarzenberg,* etc. A critical socialist, who spent the war years in the USA. While publishing in the West, Heym refused to live outside the GDR. A leading inspirer of reform socialism in the GDR.

3 **Christoph Hein:** A GDR writer of the younger generation, widely read outside the GDR. The author of plays, essays and the stories, including *Drachenblut, Horns Ende* and *Der Tangospieler.*

27. The speech by Christa Wolf on 4 November

'Liebe Mitbürgerinnen und Mitbürger, revolutionäre Bewegung befreit auch die Sprache. Was bisher so schwer auszusprechen war, geht uns auf ein Mal frei von den Lippen. Wir staunen, was wir offenbar schon lange gedacht haben und was wir uns jetzt laut zurufen. 'Demokratie – jetzt oder nie!', und wir meinen Volksherrschaft. Wir erinnern uns der steckengebliebenen oder blutig niedergeschlagenen Ansätze in unserer Geschichte und wollen die Chance, die in dieser Krise steckt, daß sie alle unsere produktiven Kräfte weckt, nicht wieder verschlafen. ...
Revolutionen gehen von unten aus, unten und oben wechseln ihre Plätze in dem Wertesystem, und dieser Wechsel stellt die sozialistische Gesellschaft vom Kopf auf die Füße. Große soziale Bewegungen kommen in Gang. Soviel wie in diesen Wochen, ist in unserem Land noch nie geredet worden, miteinander geredet worden, noch nie mit dieser Leidenschaft, mit so viel Zorn und Trauer, aber auch mit so viel Hoffnung. Wir wollen jeden Tag nutzen. Wir schlafen nicht oder wenig. Wir befreunden uns mit

Menschen, die wir vorher nicht kannten, und wir zerstreiten uns schmerzhaft mit anderen, die wir zu kennen glaubten. Das nennt sich nun 'Dialog'. Wir haben ihn gefordert. Nun können wir das Wort fast nicht mehr hören.[1] Und haben doch noch nicht wirklich gelernt, was es ausdrücken will. Mißtrauisch starren wir auf manche, plötzlich ausgestreckte Hand, in manches vorher so starre Gesicht. Mißtrauen ist gut,[2] Kontrolle noch besser. Wir drehen alte Losungen um, die uns gedrückt und verletzt haben und geben sie postwendend wieder zurück. Wir fürchten, benutzt zu werden, verwendet. Und wir fürchten ein ehrlich gemeintes Angebot auszuschlagen. In diesem Zwiespalt befindet sich nun unser ganzes Land. Wir wissen, wir müssen die Kunst üben, den Zwiespalt nicht in Konfrontation ausarten zu lassen.[3] Diese Wochen, diese Möglichkeiten werden uns nur einmal gegeben − durch uns selbst. ...

Zu Huldigungsvorbeizügen und verordneten Manifestationen werden wir keine Zeit mehr haben. Dies ist eine Demo, genehmigt, gewaltlos. Wenn sie so bleibt bis zum Schluß, wissen wir wieder mehr über das, was wir können und darauf bestehen wir dann. 'Ein Vorschlag für den 1. Mai: Die Führung zieht am Volk vorbei.' (Alles nicht von mir, alles nicht von mir. Das ist literarisches Volksvermögen.) Unglaubliche Wandlung, das Staatsvolk der DDR geht auf die Straße, um sich als Volk zu erkennen. Und dies ist für mich der wichtigste Satz dieser letzten Wochen: der tausendfache Ruf: 'Wir sind das Volk!' Eine schlichte Feststellung und die wollen wir nicht vergessen.'

Christa Wolf

Vocabulary
 die **Volksherrschaft** power of the people
 der **Ansatz** attempt
      verschlafen, ä, ie, a sleep through, not wake up in time for
      in Gang kommen, o, a, o be under way
      sich zerstreiten ei, i, i fall out with
      mißtrauisch mistrustful
      starren (auf + acc.) stare at
      starr rigid
      um.drehen turn round
      drücken oppress
      postwendend 'by return', immediately
      aus.schlagen, ä, u, a reject

der **Zwiespalt** conflict, dilemma
der **Huldigungsvorbeizug** adulatory march-past
    verordnete Manifestationen pre-arranged popular demonstrations
    literarisches Volksvermögen the literary property of the people
eine **schlichte Feststellung** a simple statement of fact

Notes
1 **Nun ... hören:** 'Now we are sick and tired of the word.'
2 **Mißtrauen ist gut ... noch besser:** A play on Lenin's dictum, 'Vertrauen [trust] ist gut, Kontrolle ist besser.'
3 **Wir wissen ... zu lassen:** We know we have to practise the art of preventing this dilemma from degenerating into confrontation.

28. The speech by Stefan Heym on 4 November

Liebe Freunde, Mitbürger, es ist, als habe einer die Fenster aufgestoßen nach all den Jahren der Stagnation, der geistigen, wirtschaftlichen, politischen, den Jahren von Dumpfheit und Mief und bürokratischer Willkür, von amtlicher Blindheit und Taubheit. Welche Wandlung! Vor noch nicht vier Wochen: Die schön gezimmerte Tribüne, hier um die Ecke, mit dem Vorbeimarsch, dem bestellten, vor den Erhabenen. Und heute Ihr, die Ihr Euch aus eigenem freien Willen versammelt habt, für Freiheit und Demokratie und für einen Sozialismus, der des Namens wert ist.

In der Zeit, die hoffentlich jetzt zu Ende ist, wie oft kamen da die Menschen zu mir, mit ihren Klagen. Dem war Unrecht geschehen, und der war unterdrückt und geschurigelt worden, und allesamt waren sie frustriert. Und ich sagte, so tut doch etwas. Und sie sagten resigniert, wir können doch nichts tun. Und das ging so in dieser Republik, bis es nicht mehr ging, bis es soviel Unbilligkeit angehäuft hatte im Staate und soviel Unmut im Leben der Menschen, daß ein Teil von ihnen weglief. Die anderen aber, die Mehrzahl, erklärten, und zwar auf der Straße, öffentlich: Schluß, ändern, wir sind das Volk!

Einer schrieb mir – und der Mann hat recht: Wir haben in diesen letzten Wochen unsere Sprachlosigkeit überwunden und sind jetzt dabei, den aufrechten Gang zu erlernen, und das, Freunde, in Deutschland, wo bisher sämtliche Revolutionen danebengegangen sind und wo die Leute immer gekuscht haben, unter dem Kaiser, unter den Nazis und später auch.

Aber sprechen, frei sprechen, gehen, aufrechtgehen, das ist nicht genug. Laßt uns auch lernen zu regieren. Die Macht gehört nicht in die Macht eines Einzelnen oder ein paar weniger oder eines Apparats oder einer Partei. Alle, alle müssen teilhaben an dieser Macht. Und wer immer sie ausübt und wo immer, muß unterworfen sein der Kontrolle der Bürger. Denn Macht korrumpiert, und absolute Macht, das können wir heute noch sehen, korrumpiert absolut. Der Sozialismus – nicht der Stalinsche, der Richtige –, den wir endlich erbauen wollen, zu unserem Nutzen und zum Nutzen ganz Deutschlands, dieser Sozialismus ist nicht denkbar ohne Demokratie. Demokratie aber, ein griechisches Wort, heißt Herrschaft des Volkes. Freunde, Mitbürger üben wir sie aus, diese Herrschaft.

Stefan Heym

Vocabulary
auf.stoßen, ö, ie, o push open
die **Dumpfheit** torpor
der **Mief** fug, claustrophobic atmosphere
die **Willkür** arbitrariness
die **Erhabenen** those in high places
unterdrücken suppress
shurigeln bully
allesamt all of them
die **Unbilligkeit** injustice
der **Unmut** annoyance
die **Sprachlosigkeit** muteness, speechlessness
den aufrechten Gang erlernen learn to walk upright, on two legs, unbowed
daneben gehen fail, flop
kuschen cringe
unterwerfen subject
erbauen construct

29. The speech by Christoph Hein on 4 November

Liebe mündig gewordene Mitbürger, es gibt nun für uns alle viel zu tun, und wir haben wenig Zeit für diese Arbeit. Die Strukturen dieser Gesellschaft müssen verändert werden, wenn sie demokratisch und sozialistisch werden soll, und dazu gibt es keine Alternative. Es ist auch von den schmutzigen Händen, von den schmutzigen Westen zu sprechen, Verfilzung, Korruption,

Amtsmißbrauch, Diebstahl von Volkseigentum. Das muß aufgeklärt werden, und diese Aufklärung muß auch bei den Spitzen des Staates erfolgen, sie muß dort beginnen. Hüten wir uns davor, die Euphorie dieser Tage mit den noch zu leistenden Veränderungen zu verwechseln. Die Begeisterung und die Demonstrationen sind hilfreich und erforderlich, aber sie ersetzen nicht die Arbeit. Lassen wir uns nicht von unserer eigenen Begeisterung täuschen! Wir haben es noch nicht geschafft: Die Kuh ist noch nicht vom Eis.[1] Und es gibt noch genügend Kräfte, die keine Veränderungen wünschen, die eine neue Gesellschaft fürchten und auch zu fürchten haben. Ich möchte uns alle an einen alten Mann und wahrscheinlich jetzt sehr einsamen Mann erinnern. Ich spreche von Erich Honecker. Dieser Mann hatte einen Traum. Und er war bereit, für diesen Traum ins Zuchthaus[2] zu gehen. Dann bekam er die Chance, seinen Traum zu verwirklichen. Es war keine gute Chance, denn der besiegte Faschismus und der übermächtige Stalinismus waren dabei die Geburtshelfer. Es entstand eine Gesellschaft, die wenig mit Sozialismus zu tun hatte. Von Bürokratie, Demagogie, Bespitzelung, Machtmißbrauch, Entmündigung und auch Verbrechen war und ist diese Gesellschaft gezeichnet. Es entstand eine Struktur, der sich viele gute, kluge und ehrliche Menschen unterordnen mußten, wenn sie nicht das Land verlassen wollten. Und keiner konnte mehr erkennen, wie gegen diese Struktur vorzugehen sei, wie sie aufzubrechen ist. Und ich glaube, auch für diesen alten Mann ist unsere Gesellschaft keinesfalls die Erfüllung seiner Träume. Selbst er, an der Spitze dieses Staates stehend und für ihn und seine Erfolge, aber auch für seine Fehler, Versäumnisse und Verbrechen besonders verantwortlich, selbst er war den verkrusteten Strukturen gegenüber fast ohnmächtig. Ich erinnere an diesen alten Mann nur deshalb, um uns zu warnen, daß nicht auch wir jetzt Strukturen schaffen, denen wir eines Tages hilflos ausgeliefert sind. Schaffen wir eine demokratische Gesellschaft, die einklagbar ist! Einen Sozialismus, der dieses Wort nicht zur Karikatur macht. ...

Ohne diese Demonstrationen wäre die Regierung nicht verändert worden, könnte die Arbeit, die gerade erst beginnt, nicht erfolgen. Und da ist an erster Stelle Leipzig zu nennen. Der Oberbürgermeister unserer Stadt sollte im Namen der Bürger Berlins, da wir alle gerade mal hier zusammenstehen, dem Staatsrat der

Volkskammer vorschlagen, die Stadt Leipzig zur Heldenstadt der DDR zu ernennen. Wir haben uns an den langen Titel 'Berlin – Hauptstadt der DDR' gewöhnt, ich denke, es wird leichter sein, uns an ein Straßenschild 'Leipzig – Heldenstadt der DDR' zu gewöhnen. Der Titel wird unseren Dank bekunden, er wird uns helfen, die Reformen unumkehrbar zu machen, er wird uns an unsere Versäumnisse und Fehler in der Vergangenheit erinnern, und er wird die Regierung an die Vernunft der Straße mahnen, die stets wach blieb und sich wieder zu Wort meldet.

Christoph Hein

Vocabulary

mündig sovereign, politically mature
die schmutzigen Westen those with a dubious record
die Verfilzung graft
das Volkseigentum property of the people
auf.klären investigate
die Aufklärung investigation
sich davor hüten be on one's guard against
die Begeisterung enthusiasm
ersetzen replace
das Zuchthaus prison
übermächtig over-powerful
der Geburtshelfer 'midwife'
die Bespitzelten those subject to surveillance
der Machtmißbrauch abuse of power
die Entmündigung deprival of their democratic rights, sovereignty
zeichnen here: leave its mark
sich unter.ordnen subordinate oneself
vorgehen (gegen + acc.) tackle, attack
auf.brechen, i, a, o break down
die Versäumnisse shortcomings
verkrustet ossified
ohnmächtig impotent
ausgeliefert at the mercy of
bekunden publicly declare
unumkehrbar irreversible
sich zu Wort melden begin to speak out

Notes

1 **Die Kuh ... Eis:** 'We haven't got the cow off the ice yet. The tricky part is not over yet.'
2 Erich Honecker spent eight years in prison under the Nazis for underground resistance work.

6 November. At a further demonstration in Leipzig support is expressed
for the revolution taking place in Czechoslovakia. Calls are made to
disband the *Stasi*. There is widespread criticism of the planned 'reform'
of laws on travel abroad.

30. Slogans at the 6 November Leipzig demonstration

Bonzen raus!***Wir kommen wieder!***Montags sind wir
wieder da!***Basisdemokratie kontra Politbürokratie!***Es lebe
der Prager Frühling!***Visapflicht, das paßt uns nicht!***Teilt
die Macht!***Egon, spiel nicht Blindekuh, laß das Neue Forum
zu!***Rücktritt der Regierung und provisorische Regierung bis
zu Neuwahlen!***Egon, mach die Stasi dicht, eher glaubt das
Volk Dir nicht!***Vorschlag für den 1. Mai: Die Regierung
zieht am Volk vorbei!***Zeigt eure moralische Überlegenheit,
protestiert schweigend und gewaltfrei an der Stasi vorbei − Neues
Forum!***Räumt die Stasi-Festung aus und macht schönen
Wohnraum draus!***Stasi-Gelder für saubere Umwelt und
gesunde Wälder!***Eine Schlange häutet sich, bleibt aber eine
Schlange!***Zementsäcke statt Betonköpfe!***Das Reisegesetz
beweist: Es herrscht der alte Geist!***Freiheit für politische
Gefangene!***Egon, hau Du ab, dann bleiben täglich Tausende
im Lande!***Schluß mit dem Machtmonopol der SED − Staats-
sicherheit, Entmündigung, Diktatur!***Egon, jetzt wollen wir
Taten sehn, oder sollen wir in den Westen gehn?***SED, gib Deine
Führung ab, sonst werden hier die Leute knapp!***Auferstanden
aus Ruinen,[1] die uns die SED hinterlassen hat!***Ausreisen ohne
Visum!***"Krumme Ecke",[2] Schreckenshaus − wann wird ein
Museum draus?

Vocabulary
 die Bonzen bigwigs
 die Basisdemokratie grass-roots democracy
   ... paßt uns nicht we've had it up to here with ...
 die Blindekuh blind-man's-buff
   zu.lassen legalise
   dicht machen close down
 die Überlegenheit superiority
   aus.räumen clear out
   sich häuten shed their skin

der Betonkopf hard-liner
　　hau ab! get lost!
die Entmündigung deprival of ther democratic rights, sovereignty
das Schreckenshaus house of terror

Notes
1 **Auferstanden … Ruinen:** An ironic illusion to the lines of the GDR's national anthem referring to the ruins of the Second World War.
2 **Krumme Ecke:** the derogatory name for the *Stasi* headquarters in Leipzig.

IV. The Wall crumbles

7 November. The Constitutional and Legal Committee of the *Volks-kammer* rejects the planned laws on travel abroad as 'inadequate'. The government of the GDR under *Ministerpräsident* Stoph resigns, having forfeit all claim to political support by the parliament, a major stage in the disintegration of the established political structures of the GDR ... 8 November. At a meeting of the SED Central Committee the Politburo resigns *en bloc*. Egon Krenz is confirmed as the new General Secretary of the SED. Among the newly formed Politburo is the reformer Hans Modrow from Dresden. The Central Committee recommends to the *Volkskammer* that Modrow be elected new *Ministerpräsident* ... There are renewed demonstrations for free elections and an end to travel restrictions ... In the West German *Bundestag* Chancellor Helmut Kohl makes economic assistance to the GDR conditional upon the end of the SED's monopoly on power, the acceptance of independent political parties and free elections ... 9 November. At a historic moment in Germany's history, Günter Schabowski announces that all GDR citizens can travel to the West at short notice and unconditionally. Those wishing to go to the West can obtain visas immediately. Despite unclarity as to the precise meaning of the decree it is generally interpreted as an order to open the border and the Berlin Wall and to end all restrictions on travel. There are scenes of wild jubilation as thousands of East Germans cross the border to West Berlin.

31. The first East Germans cross the border to West Berlin

Der Werkzeugmacher Ralf Dickel, 34, aus dem Ost-Berliner Bezirk Prenzlauer Berg ist einer der ersten, die an jenem Donnerstagabend durch die Mauer kommen. Zuerst sehen wir nur seinen Kopf, den er neugierig um die Beton-Mauer reckt – wie jemand, der einen scheuen Blick in ein verbotenes Zimmer riskiert. Dann geht er zögernd ein paar Schritte weiter und schaut sich verstohlen um,

118

als ob er fürchtet, doch noch an seinem grünen Parka zurückgehalten zu werden. Schließlich ist er da.

Am Grenzübergang Bornholmer Straße klatschen jetzt ein paar
hundert West-Berliner Beifall, rufen, pfeifen und lassen Sektkorken knallen. Es ist genau 20.45 Uhr, Ralf Dickel reißt die
Arme hoch und schreit: 'Wahnsinn!'

Ein Wort, das wie kein anderes die neue Situation in Berlin und
bald auch überall an der deutschen Grenze beschreibt: Fassungslosigkeit, Überraschung, Ungläubigkeit, Glück.

Als die Regierung der DDR die Grenzübergänge öffnet und Tag
für Tag und Nacht für Nacht neue Breschen in den Beton der
Berliner Mauer schlägt, taumelt die Stadt wie im Fieber. Am
Kurfürstendamm liegen sich wildfremde Menschen weinend in den
Armen, klatschen unzählige Hände auf die Dächer und Kühler-
hauben der Trabants und Wartburgs,[1] die mühsam durch die
Spaliere der Schaulustigen kriechen. ...

Auch dort, zwischen Brandenburger Tor und Potsdamer Platz,
Massenszenen, wie sie der russische Revolutionsfilmer Eisenstein
nicht eindringlicher hätte drehen können: Menschen stehen dicht
an dicht, mit erhobenen Armen, die Finger zum Victoryzeichen
gespreizt. Sie sitzen in den Bäumen, tanzen auf der hier zwei Meter
breiten Mauerkrone und singen 'We shall overcome'.

Hunderte machen sich mit Hämmern und Meißeln am Betonwall
zu schaffen, biedere Familienväter aus Castrop-Rauxel und Günz-
burg, aufgeregte Hausfrauen aus Uelzen und Wanne-Eickel, die
sich bei der brisanten Werkelei von ihrem halbwüchsigen Anhang
ablichten lassen. Immer wieder wird skandiert: 'Die Mauer muß
weg.'

Überflüssig ist sie jetzt ohnehin geworden. Von Donnerstag nacht
bis Sonntag abend strömen weit über zwei Millionen DDR-Bürger
in den Westteil der Stadt — um den Ansturm zu bewältigen, schlägt
der SED-Staat zehn neue Übergänge in die Mauer. ...

Stern extra, Nr. 3/1989.

Vocabulary
der **Werkzeugmacher** tool-maker
　　recken stretch
　　verstohlen furtively
　　lassen Sektkorken knallen let the champagne corks pop
　　Wahnsinn! incredible! crazy!

die **Fassungslosigkeit** bewilderment
    taumeln reel
die **Kühlerhaube** car bonnet
das **Spalier** double-line, guard of honour
die **Schaulustigen** onlookers
    eindringlich dramatic
die **Werkelei** handiwork
    sich ablichten lassen have their photos taken
    skandieren chant

Notes
1 **Trabant, Wartburg:** East German makes of car.

32. Scenes of jubilation in West Berlin

Die Mauer provoziert. Sie steht da, als hätte sie an diesem Abend keine Nachrichten gehört. Als wüßte sie noch gar nicht, wie sinnlos sie geworden ist. Vor dem Brandenburger Tor ist sie so breit wie die Betten, aus denen viele Berliner soeben gestiegen sind, um in dieser Nacht dabeizusein. Die Nacht, 'auf die wir 28 Jahre gewartet haben' (Momper).[1] Die Fernsehteams haben die Mauer taghell ausgeleuchtet, ein Wasserwerfer spritzt noch schüchtern von Ost nach West, mehrere hundert, vielleicht tausend umlagern die historische Stätte. Strahlende Gesichter, Siegesgeheul, Kinder unterm Weihnachtsbaum.
Irgendwann ist der Erste raufgeklettert, magisch angezogen von dem symbolträchtigsten und meistgehaßten Bauwerk dieser Stadt. Dann werden Hände gereicht, 'Leitern' gebaut, wird gezerrt und geschoben. Die Berliner stürmen die Mauer. Kaum einer kommt oben an, ohne zu jauchzen und die Arme hochzureißen. 'Die Mauer muß weg! Die Mauer muß weg!' heißt die Parole des Abends. Nur: der Chor ist schon von der Realität überholt. Das Gebrüll der Leute erscheint fast wie ein nachträglicher Vollzug, wie die hundertstimmige Bestätigung dessen, was viele noch immer nicht fassen können. Die Mauer ist weg. Das meistgebrauchte Wort: 'Wahnsinn! Ick globb's nich!'[2]
Die unten staunen, die oben jubeln, und nicht nur die Kids. Auch einige ältere Herrschaften probieren den Klimmzug oder baumeln zentnerschwer an kräftig ziehenden Armen. Oben stehen Lackschühchen neben Springerstiefeln, Sektpullen kreisen, die ersten

Besoffskis grölen, Blicke kreisen von hüben nach drüben. Volksfest. Die Geste des Abends ist die Umarmung.

Die Wasserwerfer jenseits der Mauer haben den Hahn wieder zugedreht. Polizei und aufmarschierte Nationale Volksarmee haben längst begriffen: Der Versuch, die Berliner von der Mauer zu spritzen, paßt nicht in diese Zeit, nicht in diese Nacht, nicht zu dieser deutsch-deutschen Mauer-Fiesta.

Einige Ost-Berliner sind 'legal' rübergekommen und dann auf der Westseite hochgeklettert. Am frühen Morgen findet endlich die direkte Verbrüderung statt: Von beiden Seiten wird das Bauwerk genommen. Ost und West sind obenauf, fallen sich in die Arme. Vereinzelt klettern West-Berliner auf der Ostseite wieder runter und laufen durchs Brandenburger Tor. Die DDR-Grenzer sind verlegen, hilflos, zucken die Achseln, gewähren freien Eintritt. 'Ich war die ganze Nacht drüben und hab' mich erst heute morgen von einem Trabi zur Grenze bringen lassen', berichtet eine taz-Kollegin mit leuchtenden Augen am Morgen. ...

Der Star dieser Nacht, ein rauschebärtiger Hüne, hat von all dem nichts bemerkt, arbeitet weiter wie besessen und entzückt die Massen. Er hat Fäustel und Meißel mitgebracht und schon mal begonnen, die Mauer abzutragen. Die obere Kante ist auf der Westseite bereits sichtbar angeknabbert. Kein Zementstück, das ohne Beifall und Triumphchöre in die Menge splittert. Ein ganz Schlauer holt sich ein Bröckchen und steckt es als 'erste Devotionalie' breit grinsend ein. Die letzten Wetten werden abgeschlossen, wann der materielle Fall der Mauer dem politischen folgen wird.

Manfred Kriener, "Das Volksfest auf der Mauer", in *die Tageszeitung*, 11. November 1989.

Vocabulary
- **aus.leuchten** illuminate
- **symbolträchtigst** most symbolic
- **meistgehaßt** most hated
- **jauchzen** cheer
- **von der Realität überholt** overtaken by reality
- **das Gebrüll** roaring
- **ein nachträglicher Vollzug** carried out belatedly
- **die Bestätigung** confirmation
- **die Herrschaften** ladies and gentlemen

probieren den Klimmzug have a go at pulling themselves up
baumelt zentnerschwer dangles hundredweight-heavy
die Lackschühchen little patent-leather shoes
die Springerstiefel bovver-boots
    Sektpullen kreisen champagne bottles are passed round
die Besoffskis (coll.) drunks
    grölen bawl
die Verbrüderung fraternisation
    vereinzelt sporadic
die Achseln zucken shrug their shoulders
    gewähren grant
eine taz-Kollegin a colleague from the *Tageszeitung*
der rauschebärige Hüne a full-bearded giant
    entzückt delighted
der Fäustel hammer
der Meißel chisel
    ab.tragen carry off
    an.knabbern nibble away
der ganz Schlaue a bright spark
das Bröckchen small piece
die Devotionalie devotional object, holy relic
    Wetten ab.schließen lay bets

Notes
1 **Walter Momper:** The SPD Mayor of West Berlin at the time of the collapse of the GDR.
2 **Ich globb's nich:** Berlin dialect – 'Ich glaube es nicht!'

33. East Germans in West Berlin

Die Mauer vorm Brandenburger Tor gleicht einer nächtlichen Disco-Tanzfläche mit Tausenden von Gästen, der Kurfürstendamm ist eine einzige Fußgängerzone, die Verkaufspassagen des Europacenters geben ein improvisiertes Nachtlager für Hunderte her. An den Grenzübergängen kommt man nicht mehr nach beim Begrüßen der Besucher von drüben. Das Konfetti ist schon lange ausgegangen, und in der Innenstadt gibt es 'wie im Osten' keine Bananen mehr.
Radio DDR meldet die 'zweihundertprozentige Auslastung der Züge nach Helmstedt' und die Abfahrt eines Sonderzuges aus Leipzig Richtung Berlin. Der Verkehrsfunk-West konstatiert resigniert 'stehenden Fußgängerverkehr auf dem Tauentzien'.[1]
In der Einkaufszone Wilmersdorfer Straße gibt es kein Brot mehr

zu kaufen, bei Karstadt am Hermannplatz geht beinahe viertel-stündlich eine kleine Nicole, Daniela oder Sylvia verloren 'und soll bitte sofort von ihrer Mutti' abgeholt werden. Fuß- und Fahrradwege der Stadt sind übersät von Sektflaschen und Colabüchsen, die nun Coca heißen.

Wer auch immer will, bearbeitet die Mauer mit Hammer und Meißel, als ob sie vor allem 'dem Westen' gehöre. Ein Souvenir muß her,[2] den Freunden und Eltern in Westdeutschland längst versprochen. Auch von Osten her wird die Mauer in Eigenarbeit abgerissen. Fünf Meter neben dem offiziellen Abrißkommando der Grenzpolizei haben sich am Prenzlauer Berg DDR-Bürger mit kleinen Hämmern am 'antifaschistischen Schutzwall'[3] zu schaffen gemacht. Unter dem Beifall der Umstehenden feiern sie hier ihr Fest, konkurrieren mit dem offiziellen Bautrupp, wer wohl schneller sei. ...

In der Innenstadt ist der Autoverkehr zusammengebrochen, die U-Bahn hoffnungslos heißgelaufen. Wegen Überfüllung und Unfallgefahr müssen einige Linien eingestellt werden, und an ein Taxi ist kaum zu denken, auch wenn sich an den Rufsäulen wie selbstverständlich Chauffeure mit DDR-Kennzeichen eingereiht haben. Das einzig zuverlässige Verkehrsmittel ist das Fahrrad, nur daß die Luft zum Ersticken ist.

Überall dort, wo eine Menschenmenge gesichtet wird, befindet sich ganz sicher eine Sparkasse. Die ersten haben sich hier nachts um zehn angestellt, um morgens um neun ihre hundert D-Mark Begrüßungsgeld[4] in Empfang zu nehmen. Mehrere hundert Meter lang sind die Schlangen, ringeln sich gleich mehrfach um Plätze und Straßenkreuzungen. Diese 'Schlangenarbeit' gewohnt, harren die DDR-BürgerInnen geduldig aus – kein Murren, kein Vor-drängeln. Pflichtbewußt wird jedes im Paß eingetrage Kind dem Schalterbediensteten vorgezeigt, damit auch alles seine Richtigkeit hat beim Bezug des Geldes. Mittendrin in der Schlange die fast schon unvermeidliche Westberliner Rentnerin, die sich ausge-rechnet an diesem Tag ihres Kontostands vergewissern muß.

Ob der hundert D-Mark Begrüßungsgeld – an diesem Wochenende millionenfach ausgezahlt – schlägt die Stunde des Einzelhandels. Der kleinste Second-hand-Laden wittert seine Chance. Als gelte es, Verhungernde vor dem Tode zu retten, öffnen etliche Kaufhäuser auch am Sonntag ihre Tore für die Besucher aus der DDR und ihre Kassen für das frischgedruckte Geld. Es gibt kein Geschäft, das nicht dichte Menschentrauben anzieht. Video- und HiFi-Läden stehen auf der Hitliste ganz oben an, aber gekauft werden vor allem Lebensmittel.

'Ne echte Coca zu trinken' gehört zum Westbesuch dazu, wenn man nur wüßte, wie diese verdammte Büchse aufgeht. Einige Supermarktregale sehen aus wie nach einer lang andauernden Versorgungskrise, Süßigkeiten sind Mangelware, und beinah schon flehentlich fragt eine Frau: 'Wo gips denn hier de Fruchtzwersche?'[5]

Vor den Gemüseständen bekommen Kinder Nachhilfeunterricht in exotischen Südfrüchten, am Ende bleiben nur noch Kohlköpfe in den Regalen liegen. Kebab-Buden und Pizzerien feiern Hochkonjunktur, bei den Zeitungskiosken steigt der Umsatz von Pornoheften. Viele jedoch überlegen sehr gut, wofür sie den kostbaren Hunderter ausgeben. Die meisten sind erschlagen von dem verwirrenden Angebot um sie herum und wenn abends die Trabiwelle wieder in Richtung Ost-Berlin rollt, sieht man nicht nur viele erschöpfte, sondern auch viele nachdenkliche Gesichter.

Ganz findige West-Berliner eröffnen den Handel auch in die entgegengesetzte Richtung: Am Potsdamer Platz wirbt ein Mini-Cooper mit der aufgesprühten Offerte: 'Suche Antiquitäten aus der DDR: Tel ...' Auch der Tausch 'West-Auto gegen Ost-Datscha' ist im Gespräch.

Berlin an diesem Wochenende − eine Stadt, in der jede Stunde Schlaf ein verpaßtes Erlebnis ist. Irgendwann jedoch muß wieder ein Stück Normalität einziehen, muß die Stadt wieder Luft holen können, damit die jetzt noch euphorische Feiertagsstimmung nicht in ein explosives Gemisch umschlägt. Schon jetzt grummelt der Unmut an vielen Ecken, und die ersten trauen sich, ihn öffentlich zu machen: 'Momper, denk an unsere Kinder. Sie ersticken!' trotzt ein Balkontransparent gegen den Trabi-Gestank[6] an. Fahrverbot für PKWs, Einreisesperre für die Zweitakter, heißen die Forderungen nicht nur an Kneipentischen.

Besonders bei den Jüngeren, die nicht mehr nachvollziehen können, was diese Tage historisch bedeuten, wächst auch der Neid auf 'die Ossis': 'Ich muß 2 Mark 70 zahlen im Bus, und die zeigen einfach ihren blauen Paß hoch!' 'Überall kommen sie umsonst hin, zum Fußball, ins Theater, is' doch ungerecht.'

Ärger auch über das Begrüßungsgeld: 'Wer soll denn das bezahlen, is doch alles unser Geld!' Nicht mehr lange, so die Befürchtung im Bekanntenkreis, dann schlägt die Stimmung um. Den DDR-Besuchern, die durch die Stadt schwärmen, ist dieses Problem durchaus bewußt. Zurückhaltend und höflich bemühen sie sich, nichts falsch zu machen, niemandem zur Last zu fallen. 'Ist doch auch nicht schön für euch', meint entschuldigend eine Frau in der U-Bahn. 'Nein, das kann auch nicht so weitergehen.'
Am liebsten würden sie nicht auffallen, diese Menschenmassen, aber wie macht man eine Million Menschen unsichtbar? Wie eine Normalisierung dieser im wahrsten Sinne atemberaubenden Situation aussehen wird, entzieht sich im Moment jeder Phantasie. Nur auf einen gemeinsamen Nenner können sich schon jetzt alle verständigen: Wenn dieser Berliner Endlosfilm einmal ein Ende findet, wird nichts mehr sein wie zuvor.

Vera Gaserow, "Berlin – eine wahrlich atemberaubende Stadt", in *die Tageszeitung*, 13. November 1989.

Vocabulary
> **gleichen** resemble
> die **Fußgängerzone** pedestrian precinct
> die **Verkaufspassage** shopping mall
> ein **improvisiertes Nachtlager** a makeshift place to bed down
>> **aus.gehen** run out
>> **melden** announce
> die **zweihundertprozentige Auslastung** capacity stretched to double; 200 per cent full
> die **Einkaufszone** shopping area
>> **übersäen** *here:* litter
>> **bearbeiten** go to work on
>> **in Eigenarbeit** do-it-yourself
>> **zusammen.brechen, i, a, o** break down
>> **heiß.laufen, äu, ie, au** overheat
>> **überfällig** overdue
> die **Unfallgefahr** accident risk
>> **ein.stellen** suspend
> die **Rufsäule** emergency telephone
>> **zuverlässig** reliable
>> **zum Ersticken** asphyxiating
> die **Sparkasse** savings bank
> das **Begrüßungsgeld** greetings money
> die **'Schlangenarbeit' gewohnt** used to queuing
>> **aus.harren** hold out
> das **Murren** complaints

vor.drängeln jump queues
pflichtbewußt dutiful
ausgerechnet an diesem Tag today of all days
der **Kontostand** bank balance
schlägt die Stunde *here:* do a roaring trade
der **Einzelhandel** retailers
seine Chance wittern sense an opportunity
etliche a good number of
die **Menschentrauben** clusters of people
die **Versorgungskrise** critical shortages
die **Mangelware** scarce commodity
flehentlich plaintively
der **Nachhilfeunterricht** coaching *here:* an object lesson
der **Kohlkopf** nerd
die **Kebab-Bude** kebab stall
Hochkonjunktur feiern enjoy a boom
der **Umsatz steigt** turnover increases
das **Pornoheft** porn magazine
erschlagen bowl over
nachdenklich thoughtful
in entgegengesetzte Richtung in the opposite direction
werben, i, a, o advertise
die **Antiquität** antique
die **Ost-Datscha** *dacha* in East Germany
ein verpaßtes Erlebnis a lost opportunity to experience
die **Feiertagsstimmung** holiday mood
um.schlagen, ä, u, a (in + acc.) change into
grummeln rumble
der **Unmut** annoyance
ersticken choke
an.trotzen defy
der **Trabi-Gestank** the Trabi stench
der **Kneipentisch** bar-room table
die **Stimmung schlägt um** the mood turns ugly
sich bemühen take pains
atemberaubend breathtaking
sich jeder Phantasie entziehen beggar imagination
ein gemeinsamer Nenner a common denominator
sich verständigen reach agreement
der **Endlosfilm** never-ending film

Notes

1 **Radio DDR ... Tauentzien:** 'Radio GDR announces 'the trains to Helmstedt are 200% full' and that a special train is leaving from Leipzig to Berlin. The radio traffic report from the West announces resignedly a standstill of pedestrians crossing the Tauentzien check-point.'
2 **Ein Souvenir muß her:** 'They've got to get a souvenir.'
3 **antifaschistischer Schutzwall:** anti-fascist bulwark – the standard SED description of the Berlin Wall.

4 **Begrüßungsgeld:** The DM 100 greetings money paid to every East German visiting West Germany.
5 **Wo gips denn hier de Fruchtzwersche?:** East German dialect – Wo gibt es denn hier die Fruchtzwerge? 'Where have they got the mini fruit-blancmanges?'
6 **Irgendwann jedoch ... umschlägt:** 'But at some point things have got to get back to normal a little; the city has to be able to get its breath back again, so that what is still a euphoric holiday mood does not suddenly become transformed into an explosive mixture. Annoyance is already rumbling on many corners and people are beginning to find the courage to come out with it. 'Momper, don't forget our children. They are choking to death': on a balcony a placard challenges the stench from the Trabis (Trabant cars).'

34. The end of an era

Die neue Freiheit wuchs den Deutschen gänzlich überraschend binnen einer Woche zu, nachdem SED-Chef Egon Krenz – seit drei Wochen Nachfolger Erich Honeckers – eben noch ein umständliches Reisegenehmigungsrecht angekündigt hatte. 28 Jahre plus knapp 3 Monate war Berlin mit Mauern und Sperranlagen geteilt, 40 Jahre lang die Nation getrennt.

Selbst die kühnsten politischen Propheten hätten die Mauer allenfalls durchlässig gesehen am Ende eines visionären Zeitraums, in dem die seit Jahrzehnten in Kaltem Krieg und Blockdenken erstarrten Hälften West- und Osteuropa in ein 'gemeinsames Haus' einziehen sollten, wie es der sowjetische Reformator Michail Gorbatschow entwarf.

Schon in der fünften Woche nach einer pompös zelebrierten 40-Jahr-Feier, bei der bestellte Jubler vor den Tribünen 'der Erhabenen' (so der DDR-Schriftsteller Stefan Heym) defilieren mußten, war die Erstarrung im deutschen Zweitstaat dahin.

Erstmals in der jüngeren deutschen Geschichte, dies der unglaublichste Aspekt in einem historischen Monatszeitraum, siegte das Volk gegen die Herrschenden, zwang ihnen seinen Willen auf – ohne Gewalt. Die Nacht rückte, mancher ahnte es schon, die Wiedervereinigung in greifbare Nähe.

Eine Nation, deren Größenwahn Europa an den Abgrund gebracht hatte und die nach der Niederlage von den Siegern gezielt und vermeintlich dauerhaft zerteilt worden war, hatte sich über das Zeitalter fast zweier Generationen hinweg ein offenbar dauerhaftes Zusammengehörigkeitsgefühl erhalten. ...

Am späten Nachmittag des 9. Novembers hatte Günter Schabowski, gerade erst ernannter Informationssekretär des SED-Zentralkomitees und Mitglied des einst allmächtigen Politbüros, auf einer im Fernsehen live übertragenen Pressekonferenz mitgeteilt, ab sofort könnten die DDR-Bürger problemlos in den Westen reisen, ohne Verwandte, ohne Anlaß, nach Lust und Laune. Die Behörden seien angewiesen, Paß und Visum schnell und unbürokratisch auszustellen.

Es dauerte drei Stunden, bis die aus Erfahrung stets mißtrauischen DDR-Bürger die Nachricht wirklich glaubten. Gegen 22 Uhr bildeten sich an den Berliner Grenzübergängen dichte Menschentrauben. Die Leute streckten ihre Personalausweise durch die Eisengitter und forderten die Wachposten auf, sie durchzulassen – ab in den Westen.

Dann geriet die Lage, wie so manches in den voraufgegangenen Wochen, der SED außer Kontrolle. Plötzlich war die Grenze offen – für alle. Die Grenzer, tags zuvor noch abweisende Hüter des realen Sozialismus, bekamen von den Nachtschwärmern Blumen. Und sie schauten dem Treiben freundlich zu.

Erst in den frühen Morgenstunden griffen am Brandenburger Tor DDR-Grenzer mit Wasserschläuchen und Lautsprechern ein, drängten Mauerspringer in den Westen zurück, bildeten einen dreifachen Kordon, um das Symbol der deutschen Einheit abzuriegeln und, für ein Weilchen noch, die Mauer davor zu konservieren, die am 13. August 1961 gebaut worden war.

Der Spiegel, Spezial II, 1990.

Vocabulary

    zu.wachsen (+ dat.) fall to
der Nachfolger successor
das umständliche Reisegenehmigungsrecht a complicated law on permission to
    travel abroad
    an.kündigen announce
die Sperranlage barrier
    kühnst boldest
    allenfalls at best
    durchlässig permeable
das Blockdenken bloc mentality
    erstarren ossify
    entwerfen, i, a, o draft
    bestellte Jubler those ordered in to cheer

defilieren parade
der **Zweitstaat** second state
unglaublichst most unbelievable
auf.zwingen, i, a, u impose
die **Wiedervereinigung** reunification
in greifbare Nähe rücken come within immediate grasp
der **Größenwahn** megalomania
an den Abgrund bringen bring to the brink of disaster
gezielt deliberately
vermeintlich supposedly
dauerhaft for good
das **Zusammengehörigkeitsgefühl** sense of belonging together
live übertragen broadcast live
ohne Anlaß *here:* without a stated cause for travel
nach Lust und Laune whenever they feel like it
an.weisen, ei, ie, ie instruct
das **Visum** visa
aus.stellen issue
mißtrauisch suspicious
der **Personalausweis** identity papers
das **Eisengitter** grille
auf.fordern order
der **Wachposten** border guard
außer Kontrolle geraten get out of control
der **Grenzer** border guard (military)
der **Wasserschlauch** water hose
der **Mauerspringer** wall jumper
konservieren conserve

35. *Neues Deutschland* reports the trips by East Germans across the border

Am Freitagmittag an der Grenzübergangsstelle Marienborn.[1]
Ohne Verzug rollt ein PKW nach dem anderen aus Richtung
Magdeburg in die BRD. Die Genossen von den Grenztruppen und
des Zolls können über die genaue Anzahl der Männer, Frauen und
Kinder, die die Grenze passieren, keine Angaben machen, denn
stündlich wächst der Verkehr an, es gibt viel zu tun. Auf der anderen Seite, wenige Kilometer entfernt von der BRD-Stadt Helmstedt,
werden die DDR-Bürger nicht nur mit lautem Rufen und Winken
von hier versammelten Menschen, sondern auch von Reportern
westlicher Medien empfangen. Welche Auskünfte diese Journalisten
bekommen, wissen wir nicht. Aber auf unsere Fragen hörten wir
immer wieder: 'Eine prima Sache! Heute abend sind wir zurück!'

Besonders eilig haben es Andrea und Andreas Schwier, die mit ihren beiden Kindern (sechs und ein Jahr alt) unterwegs sind. 'Ich will pünktlich zur Nachtschicht antreten', erklärte uns der 27jährige junge Mann, der im Magdeburger Fernmeldeamt arbeitet. 'Warum wir fahren? Wir wohnen im Grenzort Oebisfelde und wollen uns ganz einfach einmal unsere Heimat von der anderen Seite betrachten.' Sich mal umsehen will auch Hans-Joachim Herzberg aus Hohlstedt im Harz, der mit seiner Frau fährt. 'Wenn es so bleibt, daß jeder mal in die BRD fahren darf, reißt auch der Strom der Aussiedler ab', bekundete er seine feste Überzeugung. Ähnlicher Meinung auch der 71jährige Fritz Knackmuß aus Oebisfelde, der mit seiner Frau regelmäßig Freunde in Wolfsburg besucht. 'Die jungen Leute sollen sich ruhig ansehen, was drüben los ist. Wer will schon Weihnachten in einem Notquartier verbringen?'

Wir schließen uns dem Strom der PKW in Richtung Westen weiter an. In Helmstedt[2] sind auf Parkplätzen und an Straßenrändern 'Trabant' und 'Wartburg' kein Einzelfall. Passanten schlendern durch die Kleinstadt, betrachten die gepflegten Fachwerkhäuser sowie die bunten Schaufenster. 'Wir fahren jetzt wieder nach Haus!' berichteten uns Elektromeister Ortwin Görke und Schlosser Matthias Zwetko. 'Uns hat vor allem das Brunnental gegenüber unseren Heimatorten Behnsdorf und Morsleben interessiert. Demnächst nehmen wir unsere Frauen und Kinder mit, wenn die neue Regelung mit dem kommenden Reisegesetz weiter bestehen bleibt. Wir wurden hier freundlich begrüßt. Sogar kostenloses Essen wurde angeboten. Aber wir fahren lieber hungrig nach Haus, schließlich hat man doch so etwas wie Stolz. Und als Bettler geben wir uns nicht aus.[3] Die Regierungen unseres Landes und der BRD sollten hier eine vernüftige Regelung finden, damit wir unser Geld, das wir uns durch gute Arbeit verdient haben, zu einem annehmbaren Satz umtauschen können.'

Neues Deutschland, 11./12. November 1989.

Vocabulary
    ohne Verzug without delay
    keine Angaben machen without application formalities
  die Auskunft information
    zur Nachtschicht an.treten arrive for the night shift

der **Grenzort** border town
    sich mal um.sehen just have a look round
    ab.reißen, ei, i, i come to an end
das **Notquartier** temporary accommodation
    sich an.schließen, ie, o, o join
der **Einzelfall** isolated case
    schlendern stroll
der **Elektromeister** fully qualified electrician
der **Schlosser** fitter
    zu einem annehmbaren Satz um.tauschen convert at a reasonable rate of exchange

Notes
1 **Marienborn:** the autobahn crossing-point in and out of West Berlin.
2 **Helmstedt:** The autobahn transit point in North Germany.
3 **Wir fahren ... aus:** 'We would rather return home hungry; after all, you do have your pride, don't you? And we're not making ourselves out to be beggars.'

10 November. Hundreds of thousands of East Germans continue to cross the border into West Berlin ... The East German authorities begin to break new crossing-points through the Berlin Wall to cope with the flood of visitors to the West, the majority of whom return after collecting their 'greetings money' and a short shopping spree. Thousands, however, also continue to leave East Germany for good ... Neues Forum is finally recognised as a legal organisation ... Leading figures in the GDR, including the writer Christa Wolf, issue a call to their fellow-citizens not to abandon East Germany for the West.

36. An appeal to East Germans to stay in their country

'Liebe Mitbürgerinnen, liebe Mitbürger,
wir sind alle tief beunruhigt. Wir sehen die Tausende, die täglich unser Land verlassen. Wir wissen, daß eine verfehlte Politik bis in die letzten Tage hinein ihr Mißtrauen in die Erneuerung dieses Gemeinwesens bestärkt hat. Wir sind uns der Ohnmacht der Worte gegenüber Massenbewegungen bewußt, aber wir haben kein anderes Mittel als unsere Worte. Die jetzt noch weggehen, mindern unsere Hoffnung. Wir bitten Sie, bleiben Sie doch in Ihrer Heimat, bleiben Sie bei uns!
Was können wir Ihnen versprechen? Kein leichtes, aber ein nützliches Leben. Keinen schnellen Wohlstand, aber Mitwirkung an großen Veränderungen. Wir wollen einstehen für

Figure 6 Cartoon

Demokratisierung, freie Wahlen, Rechtssicherheit und Freizügigkeit. Unübersehbar ist: Jahrzehntealte Verkrustungen sind in Wochen aufgebrochen worden. Wir stehen erst am Anfang des grundlegenden Wandels in unserem Land.

Helfen Sie uns, eine wahrhaft demokratische Gesellschaft zu gestalten, die auch die Vision eines demokratischen Sozialismus bewahrt. Kein Traum, wenn Sie mit uns verhindern, daß er wieder im Keim erstickt wird. Wir brauchen Sie. Fassen Sie zu sich und zu uns, die wir, hierbleiben wollen, Vertrauen.'

Neues Deutschland, 10. November 1989.

Vocabulary
  die verfehlte Politik a misguided policy
     bestärken strengthen
  die Mitwirkung involvement
     ein.stehen (für + acc.) take responsibility for
  die Rechtssicherheit legal constitutionality
  die Freizügigkeit freedom to travel
     unübersehbar obvious
     jahrzehntealte Verkrustungen the ossified structures of decades
     im Keim ersticken nip in the bud
     Vertrauen fassen zu (+ dat.) place confidence in

10 November. Lothar de Maizière is elected new Chairman of the CDU of the GDR ... 12 November. In a message to US President Bush Mikhail Gorbachev expresses his approval of the opening of the borders between the two German states ... Lines of cars up to 65 kilometres long form as millions of East Germans in *Trabis* (Trabants) drive over the border into West German cities to look round and shop ... Between 9 November and 12 November over 4 million visas are issued to East Germans to travel to the West ... 13 November. The border zone between East and West Germany is 'demilitarised'. The order to shoot at those crossing illegally is suspended ... Hans Modrow is elected new *Ministerpräsident* by the *Volkskammer*. While rejecting the idea of German reunification, he proposes the idea of a Contractual Community between the two German states to further forms of co-operation. The regular Monday demonstrations continue in Leipzig.

37. Slogans at the 13 November Leipzig demonstration

SED – unser Land gehört nicht Dir! *** Für Volksentscheid, freie Wahlen *** Die Macht dem Volk, nicht der Partei, macht endlich die Verfassung frei! Wir fordern: freie Wahlen! *** Die Perestroika in ihrem Lauf halten weder Ochs noch Egon auf![1] *** Die Mauer hat ein Loch, aber weg muß sie doch! *** Durch Reisen lassen wir uns nicht kaufen! *** Meinungsfreiheit in den Schulen! *** Die Ruinenstadt Leipzig fordert sofort alle Bauarbeiter zurück![2] *** Deutschland, einig Vaterland! *** Aus eigener Kraft, das wird's geschafft – soziale Marktwirtschaft[3] muß her! *** Schickt unsere Soldaten heim, wir haben keine Feinde! *** Das Volk braucht keine SED, aber die SED das Volk! *** Volksentscheid über deutsche Frage!

Vocabulary
der Volksentscheid referendum
die Verfassung constitution

Notes
1 **Die Perestroika ... auf!** Egon – Egon Krenz. A further play on Honecker's defiant 'Den Sozialismus in seinem Lauf hält weder Ochs noch Esel auf!'
2 **Die ... zurück:** A reference to the building brigades transferred to East Berlin to modernise the city in time for the fortieth anniversary.
3 **soziale Marktwirtschaft:** The social and economic system of the Federal Republic, claiming to reconcile competitive capitalism with social legislation to protect the individual.

17 November. Modrow is sworn into office and puts forward proposals for comprehensive political, social and economic reforms in the GDR.

38. The disintegration of the SED state. Hans Modrow becomes Ministerpräsident

Nach dem Rücktritt der Regierung der DDR (Ministerrat) wurde am 17. November 1989 der SED-Politiker Hans Modrow neuer Ministerpräsident der DDR. Modrow, der bislang SED-Bezirkssekretär in Dresden gewesen war, galt als Reformer und Anhänger der Politik Gorbatschows. Wie vor ihm Krenz, nannte auch er die Erneuerung der sozialistischen Gesellschaft und den Erhalt der Eigenstaatlichkeit der DDR als Ziele seiner Regierung. In der Amtszeit Modrows versuchte die SED-PDS, einen Teil ihres ehemaligen Vermögens zu sichern. Überall wurden Akten vernichtet, um eine Strafverfolgung unmöglich zu machen. Die Bevölkerung sah die Versuche der SED-PDS, ihre Macht zu restaurieren, mit Skepsis. So gingen in den Städten und Gemeinden der DDR die Demonstrationen weiter. Immer häufiger wurde die staatliche Einheit Deutschlands gefordert. 'Wir sind ein Volk!' riefen die Demonstranten nun. Während die SED-PDS weiter auf Zweistaatlichkeit setzte, griffen Christdemokraten und Liberale in Ost und West die Forderung der Demonstranten schnell auf. ...
Unterdessen ging die Demontage der ehemaligen Staatspartei SED weiter. Durch die Medien, die inzwischen frei berichten konnten, wurden immer neue Fälle von Korruption und Machtmißbrauch bekannt. Die Bevölkerung reagierte mit wütenden Protesten. Am 1. Dezember 1989 änderte die Volkskammer die Verfassung der DDR. Die führende Rolle der SED wurde gestrichen. Zugleich wurden die bislang der SED unterstehenden etwa 400 000 Mann starken 'Kampfgruppen der Arbeiterklasse' aufgelöst. Am 3. Dezember 1989 trat das Politbüro und das ZK der SED zurück. Weitere führende Funktionäre wurden aus der SED ausgeschlossen, andere wie der FDGB[1]-Vorsitzende Harry Tisch und das Politbüromitglied Günter Mittag[2] inhaftiert. Anfang Dezember traten die Blockparteien aus dem 'Demokratischen Block'[3] aus. Wegen der anhaltenden Proteste der Bevölkerung mußte Egon Krenz am 6. Dezember 1989 vom Amt des Vorsitzenden des

Staatsrates der DDR zurücktreten. Sein Nachfolger wurde der LDPD⁴-Vorsitzende Manfred Gerlach. Schon zuvor hatte Krenz sein Amt als Generalsekretär der SED niederlegen müssen. Michael Richter, "1989–1990. Von der friedlichen Revolution zur deutschen Einheit", in Bundeszentrale für politische Bildung (eds.), *Geschichte der DDR* (Munich, 1991), 44.

Vocabulary
der Bezirkssekretär District Party Secretary
  gelten, gilt, galt, gegolten have the reputation
der Erhalt der Staatlichkeit – the maintenance of state sovereignty
das Vermögen wealth, holdings
  restaurieren restore
die Skepsis scepticism
  setzen (auf + acc.) hope for
die Demontage demolition
die Kampfgruppe militia
  auf.lösen disband
  aus.schließen, ie, o, o exclude
  inhaftieren arrest
  treten, i, a, e (aus + dat.) leave
  sein Amt nieder.legen resign from office

Notes
1 **FDGB:** Freier Deutscher Gewerkschaftsbund. The trade union organisation of the GDR.
2 **Günter Mittag:** cf. p. 97, n. 7.
3 **Demokratischer Block:** cf. p. 7.
4 **LPDP:** cf. p. 7.

18 November. There are further demonstrations throughout the GDR against the SED ... In Leipzig 15,000 people attend the first legal meeting of Neues Forum ... The European Community offers economic assistance to East Germany, Hungary and Poland on condition that they hold free elections ... 19 November. Further demonstrations take place in Frankfurt/ Oder, Karl-Marx-Stadt, Gera, Erfurt, Potsdam and East Berlin ... A top-level meeting takes place in East Berlin with West German officials on the setting-up of a joint currency fund and on co-operation in the fields of post, communications, transport and the environment ... In a message to the European Community Hans Modrow opens up the prospect of free elections in the GDR ... 22 November. The SED Politburo offers opposition groups wide-ranging consultations in the form of a Round Table.

39. The role of opposition groups in the GDR

Anders als in der CSSR und Polen, wo sich oppositionelle Gruppen wie 'Charta 77'[1] und 'Solidarität'[2] bereits Ende der 70er Jahre organisieren konnten, hatte eine Opposition in der DDR lange Zeit keine Chance. Sie war verboten und galt offiziell als überflüssig, weil alle 'vernünftigen Kräfte' sowieso nur am 'Aufbau des Sozialismus' mitarbeiten konnten. ... Das 'Neue Forum' erhielt rasch Zulauf und wurde mit rund 200 000 Mitgliedern (Stand: Ende Januar 1990) bald stärkste aller oppositionellen Gruppen. Es versteht sich bis heute nicht als neue Partei, sondern als Bürgerbewegung, will aber am 18. März zur Wahl antreten. Im November und Dezember bildeten sich zahlreiche weitere Parteien und Gruppen, die zumeist aus kirchlichen Friedens- und Menschenrechtsgruppen hervorgingen. Unter ihnen sind der Demokratische Aufbruch, der programmatisch der West-CDU nahesteht, und die SPD von besonderer Bedeutung, da ihnen zuzutrauen ist, daß sie Wähler in großer Zahl anziehen werden. Die Sozialdemokraten hatten sich zunächst unter dem Namen SDP − Sozialdemokratische Partei in der DDR − gesammelt, um nicht von Gegnern als Ableger der West-SPD diffamiert zu werden. Seit ihrem Parteitag am 13./14. Januar 1990 treten sie mit Zustimmung der Bonner SPD-Führung wieder als SPD auf. 'Ich fordere von der SED die sozialdemokratische Hand aus dem Parteiemblem zurück',[3] rief eine Delegierte aus. Diese Forderung war konkret gemeint: Die SPD verlangt die Rückgabe von Druckereien, Gebäuden und Grundstücken, die ihr nach der Zwangsvereinigung 1946 abgenommen worden waren. Alle Gruppen haben große Mühe mit dem Aufbau einer eigenen Organisation. Es fehlt an einfachsten technischen Voraussetzungen: Es gibt kaum Büroräume, die man mieten kann. Es gibt fast keine Telefonanschlüsse, weil das Netz der DDR hoffnungslos veraltet ist. Es gibt kein Zeitungspapier, es sei denn, die SED bewilligt eine Zuteilung. Es gibt keine Druckkapazitäten, es sei denn, die Zeitungen der SED räumen gelegentlich den oppositionellen Gruppen eine Seite ein. Beinahe alle neuen Gruppierungen wurden im November von dem immer lautstärker formulierten Wunsch nach der Einheit Deutschlands bei den Demonstrationen überrascht. Die Opposition hatte anfangs Mühe, zu dieser Frage Stellung zu nehmen. Anders als die Bürgerrechtsbewegungen in Polen und der CSSR hat es die Opposition bisher versäumt, einen Vorschlag für ein Wahlgesetz vorzulegen, die Abschaffung des politischen Strafrechts durchzusetzen, den Einfluß der Kommunisten in der Regierung zu verkleinern und sich Zugang zu Rundfunk und Fernsehen zu verschaffen. Seit dem 7. Dezember 1989 spricht die Opposition jede Woche einmal am 'Runden Tisch' mit der Regierung und den sie tragenden Kräften. Die Stellung dieses Gremiums war schwierig. Die Opposition wollte über alle Entscheidungen der Regierung mitreden. Unter anderem deshalb haben alle am 'Runden Tisch' anwesenden Oppositionsparteien und -gruppierungen dann auch am 28. Januar 1990 zugestimmt, jeweils einen Minister ohne Geschäftsbereich in die Regierung Modrow zu entsenden.

Peter Behnen *et al.*, *Revolution in der DDR* (Hanover, 1990), 18.

Vocabulary

> **gelten, gilt, galt, gegolten** to be described
> **überflüssig** superfluous

der Zulauf support

> **sich bilden** form
> **hervor.gehen (aus + dat.)** result from
> **da ihnen zuzutrauen ist** as they can be expected

der Ableger offshoot

> **diffamieren** defame

die Rückgabe return
die Druckerei printing works
das Grundstück land, property
die Voraussetzung prerequisite

> **mieten** rent

der Telefonanschluß phone connection

> **hoffnungslos veraltet** hopelessly antiquated
> **es sei denn** unless

die Zuteilung allocation

> **bewilligen** grant

die Druckkapazität printing facilities
die Bürgerrechtsbewegung civil rights movement
die Abschaffung des politischen Strafrechts the abolition of political criminal law

> **verkleinern** reduce
> **sich Zugang verschaffen** obtain access

das Gremium committee
der Minister ohne Geschäftsbereich minister without portfolio

Notes

1 **Charta 77:** The Czech civil rights group, which issued their charter in 1977.
2 **Solidarität:** The Polish opposition trade-union movement (led by Lech Walesa), which grew out of the shipyard strike in Danzig in 1980. Solidarity was banned in 1982 but grew to form the basis of the post-communist Polish government.
3 **Ich fordere … zurück:** A reference to the 'enforced' amalgamation of the KPD and SPD in 1946, symbolized by the handshake depicted on SED insignia.

20 November. There are further demonstrations in Leipzig, calling for reform and for punishment for those responsible for the crisis in the GDR. For the first times there are audible demands for a reunification of Germany.

40. Slogans at the 20 November Leipzig demonstration

Gebt die Akten[1] raus! *** Protest ist die erste Bürgerpflicht![2] *** SED − 40 Jahre Betrug! *** SED − immer noch fest im Griff: Medien, Wirtschaft, Organisationen, Sport, Justiz, Verwaltung, Schule, Polizei, Kultur usw.! *** Auch im Schafsfell bleibt der Wolf ein Wolf − weg mit der Vorherrschaft der SED! *** Immer war nur einer schuld: Wilhelm, Adolf, Walter, Erich![3] *** Aufklärung und Bestrafung der stalinistischen Verbrechen in der DDR! *** Wir fordern: Umbau der Stasi-Gebäude zu Pflegeheimen! *** Honecker vors Volkstribunal! *** Vereinigung DDR-BRD − Volksentscheid! *** Deutschland, einig Vaterland! *** Nur die Einheit Deutschlands kann unsere Rettung sein! *** Für e i n deutsches Zimmer im europäischen Haus! *** SDP − ein Weg in die Zukunft! *** Neue Kutscher, alter Karren − Egon, wir sind keine Narren! *** Schluß mit Bevormundung und Bespitzelung in der Schule, im Beruf! Lehrer, lernt: Demonstranten sind k e i n e Rowdys und Idioten! *** Für harte Arbeit hartes Geld![4] *** Gegen Subventionen, jedoch bei sozialer Gerechtigkeit! *** Marktwirtschaft statt Planwirtschaft! *** Tschechen, Slowaken[5] − vergebt unserem Volk, wir hoffen mit Euch! *** Das Geld fürs Militär braucht unsere Umwelt mehr!

Vocabulary
 die Akte dossier
 die Bürgerpflicht citizen's duty
  fest im Griff in tight control

das **Schafsfell** 'sheep's clothing'
die **Vorherrschaft** predominance
der **Umbau** transformation
das **Pflegeheim** nursing-home
das **Volkstribunal** people's tribunal
der **Kutscher** coach-driver
der **Karren** cart

Notes

1 **die Akten:** the millions of dossiers on those under Stasi surveillance.
2 **Protest ... Bürgerpflicht:** An ironic play on the nineteenth-century reactionary dictum, 'Ruhe ist die erste Bürgerpflicht.'
3 **Immer war ... Erich:** A bitter comment on the alleged German tendency to blame their disasters on their leaders, Kaiser Wilhelm, Adolf Hitler, Walther Ulbricht and Erich Honecker, to avoid the question of wider guilt.
4 **hartes Geld:** fully convertible currency.
5 **Tschechen, Slowaken ...:** An apology to the citizens of Czechoslovakia (in the process of carrying out their own revolution) for the role of East Germany in crushing the reform communist movement in the Prague Spring of 1968.

23 November. East Germans are now allowed to travel to any country of their choice without an exit visa ... The GDR authorities have to take measures to stop West Germans from clearing the shops of cheap goods in East Germany, an increasing problem resulting from the open borders and the favourable exchange-rate ... As a result of grass-roots pressure the SED takes steps to expel Erich Honecker and other leading figures from the Party. Egon Krenz argues for a complete separation of SED Party structures and state bodies; he recommends a comprehensive purging of the SED and proposes a removal of Article 1 from the Constitution of the GDR which formulates the SED's monopoly on political power in East Germany ... There are further demonstrations in many parts of East Germany ... 24 November. East German television shows film of the privileged Party functionaries' residential park in Wandlitz and of their hunting-lodges and holiday homes. These reports generate widespread rage and accelerate the SED's loss of moral and political support ... 27 November. The dismantling of the armed border, minefields and military installations separating East and West Germany begins ... Further demonstrations take place against the SED.

41. Slogans at the 27 November Leipzig demonstration

Das Volk braucht die SED wie der Fisch das Fahrrad! *** Herr Kohl, hilf uns und unseren Kindern − jetzt Wiedervereinigung! *** Sozialismus und Demokratie − nie wieder Parteimonarchie! *** Wir fordern: Raus mit der SED aus den Betrieben! *** Bestrafung, Enteignung aller Funktionäre, die ihre Macht auf Kosten des Volkes mißbraucht haben! *** Wir wollen einen Volksentscheid für die deutsche Einigkeit! *** Berlin erscheint in neuem Glanz, in Sachsen zerfallen die Städte ganz! *** Richard v. Weizsäcker[1] − Präsident aller Deutschen! *** Keine Experimente mehr, Wiedervereinigung jetzt! *** Deutsche an einen Tisch! *** Ja zu Reformen, Nein zur Wiedervereinigung! *** Wo sind die Millionen D-Mark?[2] Aufklärung sofort! *** Gegen Reisepanik − behaltet Eure Würde! *** Ich möchte in der Schule meine Meinung sagen!

Vocabulary
der Betrieb factory
die Enteignung confiscation
die Wiedervereinigung reunification

Notes
1 **Richard von Weizsäcker:** The West German Federal President.
2 **die Millionen D-Mark:** The enormous amount of West German currency revealed to have been transferred to secret accounts abroad by, among others, Alexander Schalck-Golodkowski. Cf. pp. 20, 37, 149, n. 1.

28 November. *Bundeskanzler* Helmut Kohl presents a ten-point plan to the *Bundestag*. This goes beyond the 'contractual community' proposed by Modrow and aims at overcoming the division of Germany. Kohl proposes 'confederative structures' between the two German states with the long-term aim of unifying the two countries. The gradual unification of Germany must take place within the framework of European unification and must involve steps towards international disarmament. He promises rapid and comprehensive economic support for the collapsing East German economy, if the GDR leadership works with opposition groups to change the constitution and to draft a new electoral law. The first reaction from abroad is sceptical; it is argued initially that German unification is not on the immediate agenda … 29 November. Responding to the first suggestion of German unification and the abandonment of a separate socialist state in the GDR, leading figures in cultural and political life of the GDR issue an appeal, 'Für unser Land'.

42. An appeal for the survival of the GDR

Unser Land steckt in einer tiefen Krise. Wie wir bisher gelebt haben, können und wollen wir nicht mehr leben. Die Führung einer Partei hatte sich die Herrschaft über das Volk und seine Vertretungen angemaßt, vom Stalinismus geprägte Strukturen hatten alle Lebensbereiche durchdrungen. Gewaltfrei, durch Massendemonstrationen hat das Volk den Prozeß der revolutionären Erneuerung erzwungen, der sich in atemberaubender Geschwindigkeit vollzieht. Uns bleibt nur wenig Zeit, auf die verschiedenen Möglichkeiten Einfluß zu nehmen, die sich als Auswege aus der Krise anbieten.

Entweder können wir auf der Eigenständigkeit der DDR bestehen und versuchen, mit allen unseren Kräften und in Zusammenarbeit mit denjenigen Staaten und Interessengruppen, die dazu bereit sind, in unserem Land eine solidarische Gesellschaft zu entwickeln, in der Frieden und soziale Gerechtigkeit, Freiheit des einzelnen, Freizügigkeit aller und die Bewahrung der Umwelt gewährleistet sind.

Oder wir müssen dulden, daß, veranlaßt durch starke ökonomische Zwänge und durch unzumutbare Bedingungen, an die einflußreiche Kreise aus Wirtschaft und Politik in der Bundesrepublik ihre Hilfe für die DDR knüpfen, ein Ausverkauf unserer materiellen und moralischen Werte beginnt und über kurz oder lang die Deutsche Demokratische Republik durch die Bundesrepublik Deutschland vereinnahmt wird.

Laßt uns den ersten Weg gehen. Noch haben wir die Chance, in gleichberechtigter Nachbarschaft zu allen Staaten Europas eine sozialistische Alternative zur Bundesrepublik zu entwickeln. Noch können wir uns besinnen auf die antifaschistischen und humanistischen Ideale, von denen wir einst ausgegangen sind.

Alle Bürgerinnen und Bürger, die unsere Hoffnung und unsere Sorge teilen, rufen wir auf, sich diesem Appell durch ihre Unterschrift anzuschließen.

Berlin, den 26. November 1989.

Neues Deutschland, 28. November 1989.

Vocabulary

    sich an.maßen arrogate to oneself
    durchdringen, i, a, u penetrate
    sich vollziehen, ie, o, o take place
  die Bewahrung preservation
  der Ausverkauf sell-out
    vereinnahmen swallow up, monopolise
    sich an.schließen, ie, o, o join

Figure 7 GDR soldiers demolish the Wall at the Potsdamer Platz

V. The calls for unification

East Germans continue to travel across the border to shop and look round towns and cities in the Federal Republic ... As the economic situation in the GDR worsens, even larger numbers decide to leave for the West for good ... Resentment begins to be voiced in West Germany, particularly due to the aggravation of the unemployment problem and the tight housing situation.

1 December. The political *Liedermacher* and dissident, Wolf Biermann, deprived of his citizenship in 1976, gives a concert in Leipzig, his first public performance in East Germany for twenty-five years ... An interim report by a *Volkskammer* committee discloses corruption and abuse of office among the SED leadership on a massive scale; these and subsequent revelations provoke outrage and widespread protest throughout the GDR ... The *Volkskammer* removes the SED's claim on the monopoly of political power from the constitution.

43. The new role of the Volkskammer

Angesichts des massiven Verlustes an Autorität und Vertrauen der SED in der Bevölkerung verlagerte sich die Macht von der Partei auf den Staat. Der Volkskammer fiel damit eine ganz neue Rolle zu. War sie bisher ein 'Feierabendparlament', so erhielt sie nun die Chance, durch häufigere Tagungen intensiv in das politische Geschehen einzugreifen. Sie setzte einen Zeitweiligen Ausschuß zur Überprüfung von Fällen des Amtsmißbrauchs, der Korruption, der persönlichen Bereicherung und anderer Handlungen, bei denen der Verdacht der Gesetzesverletzung besteht',[1] ein, der alle ehemaligen politischen Führer der Reihe nach vorlud und vernahm.
Eine Kommission der Volkskammer ist beauftragt, ein Gesetz zur Änderung und Ergänzung der Verfassung auszuarbeiten.
Der Ministerrat wurde in seiner Bedeutung entschieden aufgewertet.

Die Regierung bestand bis Ende Januar 1990 nur noch aus 28 Ministern (vorher 44, danach 36). Die Regierung bereitet u.a. ein Wahlgesetz, ein Mediengesetz, ein Investitionsschutzgesetz, ein Gesetz zur Verwaltungsreform und ein Gesetz zur Entschärfung des politischen Strafrechts vor. Die Regierung hat ferner eine Amnestie für Häftlinge mit einem Strafmaß bis zu drei Jahren verfügt. Die Spitze des Verteidigungsministeriums hat sie umgebildet und die Politische Hauptabteilung aufgelöst, die für den Einfluß der SED in der Armee verantwortlich war. Während die Regierung Modrow mit diesen Maßnahmen Vertrauen in der Bevölkerung erwarb, geriet sie in der Affäre um den Staatssicherheitsdienst ins Zwielicht. Am 7. Dezember erklärte der Ministerpräsident Modrow den Staatssicherheitsdienst für aufgelöst; er solle in ein Amt für Nationale Sicherheit umgewandelt werden. Die Zahl der Mitarbeiter solle reduziert werden. In den nächsten Wochen stellte sich heraus, daß ehemalige Stasi-Mitarbeiter Anfeindungen in der Bevölkerung ausgesetzt waren und erhebliche Mühe hatten, eine neue Beschäftigung zu finden. Anfang Januar wurde bekannt, daß die Regierung den Stasi-Leuten drei Jahre lang ein Überbrückungsgeld zahlen wollte, daß die Stasi in großem Stil alte Akten vernichtete und daß sie noch immer nicht entwaffnet war. Die Empörung in der Bevölkerung war unter dem Eindruck des blutigen Kampfes gegen den Geheimdienst in Rumänien kaum einzudämmen. Die Opposition forderte am 'Runden Tisch' ultimativ Aufklärung über die Vorgänge und erhielt vor laufenden Fernsehkameras von den Regierungsverantwortlichen eine in keiner Weise befriedigende Antwort. Darauf erschien eine Woche später der Ministerpräsident selbst am 'Runden Tisch', zu spät, wie sich zeigte, denn eine aufgebrachte Menschenmenge hatte bereits die Zentrale der Staatssicherheit in Ost-Berlin gestürmt. Modrow erklärte vor der Volkskammer, er gebe den Plan auf, noch vor den Volkskammerwahlen einen Verfassungsschutz und einen Geheimdienst einzurichten.

Peter Behnen *et al.*, *Revolution in der DDR* (Hanover, 1990), 20.

Vocabulary
    sich verlagern shift
    zu.fallen, ä, ie, a (+ dat) fall to
  das Feierabendparlament spare-time parliament

in das politische Geschehen ein.greifen, ei, i, i become involved in political
    events
die Ergänzung amendment
    entschieden auf.werten decisively enhance the importance of
das Investitionsschutzgesetz law on investment guarantees
die Verwaltungsreform administrative reform
die Entschärfung loosening, liberalisation
die Amnestie amnesty
das Strafmaß sentence
    verfügen proclaim
die Politische Hauptabteilung political headquarters
    ins Zwielicht geraten come under suspicion
    um.wandeln convert
    sich heraus.stellen turn out to be
das Überbrückungsgeld interim payment
    in großem Stil on a large scale
    entwaffnen disarm
die Empörung outrage
    ein.dämmen stem
die ultimative Aufklärung final and complete clarification
die Regierungsverantwortlichen those holding government office
die aufgebrachte Menschenmenge outraged crowd
die Zentrale headquarters
der Verfassungsschutz Agency for the Protection of the Constitution
der Geheimdienst secret service
    ein.richten establish

Notes

1 **Sie setzte ... besteht:** 'It appointed an *ad hoc* committee to examine cases of
abuse of office, corruption, misappropriation and other actions involving the
suspected violation of the law.'

2 December. A demonstrating crowd of several thousand SED Party
members, angered by disclosures of corruption, gathers before the Central
Committee headquarters in East Berlin and demands the immediate
resignation of the Politburo and Central Committee. Egon Krenz is
booed by the crowd ... There are widespread demonstrations throughout
East Germany in response to the reported cases of privilege, corruption
and abuses of power by former office-holders ... 3 December. At an
emergency congress SED members force the resignation of Egon Krenz
and the whole of the Politburo and Central Committee of the Party
which has ruled the GDR for forty years. Erich Honecker, Willy Stoph
and Erich Mielke, until recently heads of the Party and State, government
and the *Stasi*, are disgraced and expelled from the SED ... Top officials,
including Günter Mittag, in charge of economic policy in the GDR and
Harry Tisch, head of East German trade unions, are arrested on suspicion
of embezzlement of public funds ... A warrant is issued for the arrest

of the Secretary of State Alexander Schlack-Golodkowski, a key figure in East German exports, currency dealings, but also covert weapons export. With close contacts to West German firms, politicians and secret service, Schalck-Golodkowski escapes to the West ... A human chain, consisting of hundreds of thousands of East Germans, is organised right across the territory of the GDR in protesting against corruption and calling for a democratic renewal.

44. Mass demonstrations against SED abuses of power

Hunderttausende DDR-Bürger haben am Sonntag Menschenketten von insgesamt rund 1400 Kilometern Länge gebildet, um für eine radikale demokratische Erneuerung von Staat und Gesellschaft zu demonstrieren. Entlang von fünf Fernstraßen standen die Menschen von Rügen über Ostberlin bis nach Thüringen und von der Oder bis zur deutsch-deutschen Grenze.[1] Die Aktion Sühnezeichen,[2] das Neue Forum und andere Oppositionsgruppen hatten dazu aufgerufen, sich während der viertelstündigen Aktion von 12 bis 12.15 Uhr einzureihen.

Die bisher einmalige Demonstration richtete sich auch gegen Amtsmißbrauch und Korruption hochrangiger SED-Parteifunktionäre. Auf vielen Plakaten stand zu lesen: 'SED ade' oder 'Schluß mit dem SED-Schlaraffenland'. Mit Texten wie 'Staatsverbrecher vor Gericht', 'Volksbetrüger und Waffenhändler ins Gefängnis' oder 'Egon, gib uns unsere Milliarden wieder' wurde die aufwendige Lebensführung der Spitzenleute verurteilt.

In Ostberlin, wo sich auf der Fernstraße 96 die Nord-Süd- und Ost-West-Kette in der Schönhauser Allee trafen, kam kurzfristig der Verkehr in der Innenstadt zum Erliegen. Straßenbahn-, Bus- und Autofahrer reihten sich spontan in die Menschenschlange ein.

Viele Demonstranten trugen Transparente oder hatten Kerzen in den Händen. Auf Spruchbändern stand zu lesen: 'Gehaltskürzung für Egon Krenz', 'Betrogene aller Bezirke, vereinigt euch',[3] 'Alle Staatsverbrecher vor Gericht, sonst vertrauen wir der Wende[4] nicht'.

'Wir wollen unsere Hoffnung auf eine Umgestaltung ausdrücken und Veränderungen durchsetzen', sagte die Ostberliner Lehrerin

Rita Keil. 'Die Protestbewegung darf nicht nachlassen', meinte die Studentin Bärbel Schröder.

Die Teilnehmer der Demonstration kamen aus allen Bevölkerungsschichten der DDR. Sogar Kleinkinder in Kinderwagen waren mitgebracht worden. Immer wieder hoben die Menschen die Hand mit dem 'V'-Zeichen für Victory (Sieg). Einige trugen die Deutschlandflagge. Andere hielten Transparente hoch, auf denen unter anderem zu lesen war: 'Deutschland einig Vaterland − Wir sind ein Volk'.

In Dresden folgten Zehntausende dem Aufruf, von einem zentralen Platz aus mehrere Ketten zu benachbarten Orten und Städten zu bilden. An der Dresdner Zentrale der Staatssicherheit hinterließen die Demonstranten unzählige brennende Kerzen am Eingangstor und an der angrenzenden Mauer.

An der bayerisch-thüringischen Grenze beteiligten sich rund 1000 Menschen an einer vom Neuen Forum Eisfeld (DDR) organisierten Reihe von Thüringen ins Coburger Land.[5] Mit Kerzen und grünen Bändern in den Händen bildeten sie eine dichte Kette zwischen den beiden Schlagbäumen der Kontrollstellen in Eisfeld (DDR) und Rottenbach (Landkreis Coburg). Auf der DDR-Seite hatte man dazu eigens einen Durchgang geöffnet, durch den zunächst auch Bürger aus Bayern nach drüben gelangten. Später ließen die DDR-Grenztruppen nur noch Bürger der DDR passieren.

Süddeutsche Zeitung, 4. Dezember 1989.

Vocabulary
    sich ein.reihen join
der Amtsmißbrauch abuse of office
das SED-Schlaraffenland SED dolce vita, life of luxury
der Volksbetrüger swindler of the people
der Waffenhandel arms dealing
    die aufwendige Lebensführung luxurious life-style
das Spruchband banner
die Gehaltskürzung cut in salary
der Staatsverbrecher state criminal
die Wende turning-point
die Umgestaltung reorganisation
    nach.lassen let up
die Bevölkerungsschicht section of the population
das Transparent banner
    angrenzend adjoining
der Schlagbaum barrier

die **Kontrollstelle** checkpoint
gelangen reach

Notes

1 **Rügen** (north), **Thüringen** (south), **Oder** (eastern border), **deutsch–deutsche Grenze** (western border).
2 **Aktion Sühnenzeichen:** An organisation founded by the Protestant church to carry out works of atonement in countries which suffered at the hands of the Nazis.
3 **Betrogene ... euch:** A play on the communist slogan, 'Proletarier aller Länder, vereinigt euch!'
4 **die Wende:** The change of course which the SED was claiming to have carried out voluntarily.
5 **von Thüringen ins Coburger Land:** From East Germany across into North Bavaria in West Germany.

4 December. A further large demonstration takes place in Leipzig.

45. Slogans at the 4 December Leipzig demonstration

Kopfgeld und Steckbrief für den Verbrecher Golodkowski![1] Holt ihn und die geraubten DM-Milliarden zurück! *** Macht die Betriebe frei von Stasi und Partei! *** Bestraft die Volksbetrüger! *** Besetzt das Stasi-Gebäude! *** Wir fordern die sofortige Entmachtung und Auflösung der Stasi! *** ZK-Mafia in U-Haft! *** Gegen Neofaschismus und Ausländerhaß! *** Bonzen vor Gericht! *** Gegen Stalinismus und Kapitalismus! Stop den Bonzen in Ost und West! Für Autonomie! *** Haftbefehl: Krenz, Honecker – von Wahlbetrug zum geplanten Massenmord, und nun illegaler Waffenhandel! *** Enteignung und Bestrafung der Parasiten des Volkes! *** Mafiosi aller Länder, vereinigt Euch! *** Mittag, Stoph und Tisch – die Schmarotzer der Nation! U-Haft für die Wandlitz-Bande![2] *** Die SED stinkt vor Korruption, sie gehört auf den Misthaufen der Geschichte! *** Gib der SED keine Chance – Deutschland, einig Vaterland! *** Macht die Gefängnisse von den Politischen frei, wir brauchen Platz für die Partei! *** Zwei Staaten, eine Nation – Konföderation! *** Wiedervereinigung? Und wo bleibt der aufrechte Gang?[3] *** Der Schoß ist fruchtbar noch, aus dem das kroch![4] Wiedervereinigung? Wir wollen kein Viertes Reich! *** Wir lassen uns nicht einverleiben, die Kapis sollen drüben bleiben![5] *** Kein 4. Reich! *** Jetzt keine Wiedervereinigung, sondern neuen Sozialismus! *** Denkt über die Gefahren der Wiedervereinigung nach! *** Gegen ein widervereinigtes Deutschland! *** Mit "Deutschland, einig Vaterland!" fängt es an. Habt Ihr vergessen, wo es aufhört? Bedenkt die braune Gefahr![6] *** Nie wieder Großdeutschland![7] Kein 4. Reich! *** Für unser Land! Wir lassen uns nicht verkohlen![8] *** Ja zur Volksherrschaft, Nein zur Einverleibung der DDR! *** Macht Euch nicht zur Nutte des Westens! *** Gegen braune Wiedervereinigung! *** Über Konföderation zur Einheit! *** Einigkeit und Recht und Freiheit – wir sind ein Deutschland! *** Kein neues Experiment, sondern Wiedervereinigung!

Vocabulary

das Kopfgeld reward for the arrest of
der Steckbrief warrant
die Milliarde thousand million
der Volksbetrüger swindler of the people
die Entmachtung removal of power
die Auflösung disbanding
die U-Haft (Untersuchungshaft) detention (awaiting trial)
der Ausländerhaß xenophobia
die Enteignung confiscation
die Bestrafung punishment
der Schmarotzer parasite
    gehört auf den Misthaufen der Geschichte should be thrown on the garbage-heap of history
die Wiedervereinigung reunification
die Einverleibung annexation
die Nutte whore

Notes

1 **Alexander Schalck-Golodkowski:** The Secretary of State in the East German Ministry of Foreign Trade responsible for official and covert international commercial transactions and the procurement of foreign currency. Schalck-Golodkowski, who was also reported to have contacts with West German politicians and the secret service, fled to the Federal Republic.
2 **die Wandlitz-Bande:** The Wandlitz gang. The name given to the leading members of the SED with their villas in the political 'ghetto' in Wandlitz.
3 **der aufrechte Gang:** Walking upright, like a man, not crawling like an animal, 'on all fours', to West Germany.
4 **'Der Schoß ist fruchtbar noch, aus dem das kroch!'** – Bert Brecht on Nazism in the 'Epilog zu Arturo Ui', his parable on the rise of Hitler.
5 **Wir lassen ... bleiben:** 'No annexation! Tell the capitalists to stay over there.'
6 **die braune Gefahr:** The threat of Nazism.
7 **Großdeutschland:** Greater Germany; the German Reich incorporating Central European areas with ethnic German populations annexed in the Third Reich.

8 **verkohlen:** to make fool of someone. A play on *Kohl*, the West German Chancellor.

Clear calls are now heard for a rapid reunification of the two German states. These are rejected by those wishing to retain the sovereignty of the GDR and to reform East German socialism. The demonstrations rapidly polarise into two camps. Those calling for a renewal of democratic socialism in East Germany are increasingly abused and threatened.

46. Fears of growing nationalist sentiment

Ich habe Angst. Diese Montags-Demo war zum Fürchten. Nicht etwa die Forderungen nach lückenloser Aufdeckung aller Ungesetzlichkeiten in diesem Land – dahinter stehe ich voll und ganz –, nein, ich habe Angst vor einer Zukunft, einer großdeutschen.

Es fällt mir schwer, besonnen zu reagieren, wenn Zehntausende ihr 'Deutschland einig Vaterland' skandieren. Also brüllte ich dagegen, 'Kohlköpfe', 'Rechte raus' und versuchte vergeblich, mit den Leuten ins Gespräch zu kommen. Denn mein Vaterland heißt DDR. Und gemeinsam mit den 'Helden von Leipzig' wollte ich eigentlich in diesem Land einen unabhängigen, antifaschistischen, demokratischen, einen wahrhaft sozialistischen Staat aufbauen.

Aber wo sind denn heute diese Helden? ...

Vor allem, so mein Eindruck, schwammen junge Leipziger am Montag fast allein gegen den Strom. Dafür mußten sie sich vieles anhören: 'Geh erst mal arbeiten' oder 'Ihr seid noch zu jung, um eine eigene Meinung zu haben' waren noch harmlos. Bei 'Von Moskau bezahlt' oder 'Bonzenkinder' konnte ich nicht mehr lachen. Ich will beileibe nicht alle Demonstranten, die sich für die Wiedervereinigung aussprachen, in einen Topf werfen. Nur ein Einwurf: Um wessen Zukunft geht es eigentlich?

Um unser aller Zukunft wohl, besonders um eine hoffnungsvolle für die Jugend. Deshalb blieben mir folgende Montagsbilder wohl besonders schmerzlich haften: Eltern, die, ihre Kinder an der Hand, ein geeintes Deutschland forderten und alle Andersdenkenden niederbrüllten. Hatten sie vorher einmal ihre Töchter und Söhne befragt? Hatten sie wirklich lange genug nachgedacht?

Es geht um unser Land. Es steht mir nicht zu, über Leute zu richten, die dazu ihre Meinung auf der Straße kundtun. Aber auch ich möchte gehört werden, mit meiner Angst und der Hoffnung, daß sich an den Montagen in Leipzig mehr Menschen zur neuen DDR bekennen.

Junge Welt (Organ des Zentralrats der FDJ), 6. Dezember 1989.

Vocabulary
  die lückenlose Aufklärung complete clarification
  der Kohlkopf nerd
  gegen den Strom schwimmen swim against the current
  das Bonzenkind child of the party big-wigs
  in einen Topf werfen, i, a, o lump together
  der Einwurf objection
  haften bleiben stick in one's mind
  der Andersdenkende someone with a different opinion
  nieder.brüllen shout down
  es steht mir nicht zu I am not entitled to
  sich bekennen (zu + dat.) declare one's support for

47. The calls for unification grow louder

Das kann doch nicht die Demonstration sein, von der eben noch auf dem Karl-Marx-Platz behauptet worden war, sie habe Deutschland erstmals nach dem Zweiten Weltkrieg überall wieder Sympathien eingebracht! Das ist doch nicht jener friedliche Volksaufstand, von dem eine ehemalige Bürgerin der DDR, die vor zwei Jahren wegen einer Demonstration für Rosa Luxemburg ausgewiesen worden war, berichtet, er sei inzwischen selbst für Protestbewegungen in Großbritannien ein Modell geworden. Jetzt stehen wir vor dem Neuen Rathaus am Martin-Luther-Ring neben einer verloren wirkenden Gruppe von jungen Leuten und können die Angst nachempfinden, die einigen dieser jungen Menschen im Gesicht geschrieben steht. Hundertfach, tausendfach schlägt den jungen Leuten die Aggression der Demonstranten entgegen: 'Wir sind Deutsche, was seid ihr?' 'Faules Pack, faules Pack!', ertönen die Sprechchöre. Ein Mann in den Vierzigern ruft: 'Geht doch nach Rußland!' ...
Es ist nur eine Gruppe von Studenten an der Leipziger Karl-Marx-Universität, von denen sich die meisten einem losen

Zusammenschluß namens 'Die Linke' zurechnen. Ihre Sprüche und Transparente weichen kaum von den Aufrufen und Forderungen ab, wie sie die Oppositionsgruppen seit Anbeginn, gerade auch hier in Leipzig, formuliert haben. Die Studenten haben auf ein Plakat geschrieben, daß sie sich nicht 'BRDigen'[1] lassen wollen, sie schwenken die Fahne der DDR und plädieren für einen selbstbestimmten Staat.

Doch diese Gemeinplätze der Bürgerbewegung entsprechen nicht mehr der Stimmung und den Wünschen der meisten Menschen, die nun schon zum zehnten Male den breiten Straßenring rund um die Leipziger Altstadt füllen. ...

Die Montagsdemonstration ist zum unerbittlich ausgetragenen Meinungsstreit geworden, der das große Fest der Freiheit gründlich verdorben hat. An bedrohlichen Vorwarnungen, an bösen Vorahnungen hat es in Leipzig nicht gefehlt. Erschrocken mußten die Repräsentanten der Bürgerbewegung schon in den letzten zwei Wochen bei den Auftaktkundgebungen beobachten, wie die Stimmung umzuschlagen drohte, weil immer mehr Demonstranten mit schwarz-rot-goldenen[2] Fahnen und der Losung auf den Lippen: 'Deutschland, einig Vaterland'[3] erschienen. ...

Alle begründen ihr Eintreten für die Wiedervereinigung allein mit der Hoffnung, so schnell es nur irgendwie geht in den Genuß jenes Wohlstandes zu kommen, den sie bei ihren Besuchen in der Bundesrepublik erlebt haben. Eine ältere Frau bringt es in der Diskussion mit einem Anhänger des Demokratischen Aufbruchs auf den Nenner: 'Ich geh' bald in Rente, ich will doch auch noch was vom Leben haben.' Kein Einwand kann diesem Wunsch standhalten: Sie wolle kein Versuchskaninchen für einen neuen Sozialismus werden, sagt die Arbeiterin.

Süddeutsche Zeitung, 13. Dezember 1989.

Vocabulary
  der **Volksaufstand** people's uprising
    aus.weisen, ei, ie, ie expel
    verloren wirkend looking isolated
    faules Pack idle riff-raff
    ertönen sound
  der **Sprechchor** chorus
    plädieren für advocate
    selbstbestimmt sovereign

der **Gemeinplatz** platitude
der **unerbittlich ausgetragene Meinungsstreit** implacably waged controversy
die **Vorahnung** presentiment
die **Auftaktkundgebung** initial meeting
    um.schlagen, ä, u, a turn ugly
die **Losung** slogan
der **Wohlstand** affluence
    auf den Nenner bringen get to the essence of the problem
    in Rente gehen draw a pension
der **Einwand** objection
    stand.halten resist, prevail against
das **Versuchskaninchen** 'guinea-pig'

Notes
1 **BRDigen:** A play on BRD (die Bundesrepublik Deutschand) and beerdigen = to bury.
2 **schwarz-rot-gold:** The emblematic colours of the German flag.
3 **Deutschland, einig Vaterland:** The unsung line of the GDR national anthem, dating from a time when German unification was still officially an East German goal.

5 December. Erich Honecker is placed under house arrest together with other leading members of the Politburo ... The works' militia are ordered to turn in their weapons to allay fears of a wave of armed repression by the still powerful organs of the state ... In many East German towns citizens occupy *Stasi* offices to prevent documents from being removed or destroyed as incriminating evidence ... West Germany's Foreign Minister Hans-Dietrich Genscher visits Moscow for consultations with Mikhail Gorbachev. Gorbachev categorically rejects Kohl's ten-point plan for an eventual reunification of Germany. West Germany is warned that the Soviet people will react critically to any attempt to alter the outcome of the Second World War ... 6 December. Public outrage after the disclosure of corruption in the SED forces Egon Krenz to resign from his position of *Staatsratsvorsitzender* after forty-four days in office ... As the disintegration of the GDR gathers pace, the National Defence Council, responsible for military and defence policy, resigns ... President Gorbachev of the Soviet Union and President Mitterand of France meet in Kiev for consultations in view of the dramatic international implications of events in East Germany. They warn against unilateral actions by Germany in the question of the relationship between the two German states ... The continuing flood of East Germans leaving for West Germany increasingly jeopardises economic and social life in the GDR ... 7 December. The first meeting of the 'Round Table' takes place, in which representatives of the SED, the 5 former 'Block Parties' and opposition groups debate the future of the GDR. The first free elections

are planned for May 1990 ... 8 December. At an emergency meeting of the SED the lawyer Gregor Gysi is unanimously elected as the new Party chairman. Gysi has established a reputation while defending former critics of the regime. The SED breaks with the past by rejecting Stalinism. It issues a public apology for the crisis into which the former party leadership has led the country ... 9 December. At a European Community summit in Straßburg the leaders of the European states accept the German policy on reunification, which is to be embedded in the general process of European integration ... Before the Central Committee in Moscow Mikhail Gorbachev states that the Soviet Union will not intervene in the developments within the Warsaw Pact, in East Germany, Poland, Czechoslovakia, Hungary, Bulgaria and Romania, which he describes as a democratisation and renewal of socialism. In the case of Germany he emphasises that East Germany will not be abandoned and that the realities created by the Second World War, the existence of two sovereign German states, must be accepted ... 11 December. There is a further large demonstration in Leipzig.

48. Slogans at the 11 December Leipzig demonstration

Keine Experimente, SED und Sozialismus sind am Ende – wir sind *ein* Volk!***Erneuerte DDR: ökologisch, demokratisch, sozial!***Nazis raus!***Wider Vereinigung![1]***Wir danken Dir, Gorbi! Geh nicht weg!***Wir sind *ein* Volk, wir fordern Wiedervereinigung beider deutscher Staaten!***Soll Konsumrausch uns BRDigen?***Kein Haß und keine Selbstjustiz!*** Wiedervereinigung ja, sozialistische Armut nein!***Gegen Aufkommen von Faschismus!***Ein vereintes Deutschland im vereinten Europa!***Demonstration bis zur Einheit der Nation!***Konföderation jetzt – mit Helmut Kohl in eine bessere Zukunft!***Kein Wohlstand auf Kosten der Dritten Welt!***Wiedervereinigung statt sozialistischem Experiment!

Vocabulary
der Konsumrausch consumerist intoxication
die Selbstjustiz lynch law

Notes
1 **wider Vereinigung:** Against unification – a play on Wiedervereinigung = reunification.

49. The continued mass exodus from the GDR

Es sind die 'Weggeher', die die Schlagzeilen und die Köpfe und Herzen der Menschen in der DDR füllen, weniger die zahlreichen personellen Veränderungen in den politischen Gremien des Landes. Ungewohntes zum Thema 'Warum geht Ihr weg?' gab es am Dienstagabend in einer Diskussion im DDR-Fernsehen, in der Vertreter der Blockparteien und des Innenministeriums über den Exodus sprachen. Das Thema war lange tabu gewesen, wie auch die Teilnehmer des TV-Gespräches befanden. ...

Vor nicht allzu langer Zeit noch wurden alle die in den Medien beschimpft, die sich zum Gehen entschlossen hatten oder tatsächlich gingen; niemand nannte genaue Zahlen. Inzwischen bringt die Nachrichtensendung Aktuelle Kamera in jeder ihrer Ausgaben die neuesten Ausreisezahlen sowie Informationen über die Aufnahmefähigkeit der bayerischen Auffanglager. Berichte darüber, daß sich in der Bundesrepublik wegen der Ausreise-Welle angeblich das Gefühl entwickle, in einen nationalen Notstand zu geraten, sollen ebenso abschrecken wie die Erklärung, daß die Flüchtlingsmassen mit schwindender Sympathie und Gastfreundschaft aufgenommen würden. In der Fernsehdiskussion war man sich über die Gründe für die Abwanderung weitgehend einig, weniger jedoch über konkrete Wege, sie aufzuhalten. Fehlende Hoffnung auf einen bevorstehenden Wandel in der DDR sei für viele Übersiedler bislang der Grund gewesen zu gehen; jetzt jedoch hätten sich die Umstände geändert. Fehlendes Vertrauen in die Reformierbarkeit des Systems und die Reformbereitschaft der politischen Führung seien ausschlaggebend dafür, daß stündlich Hunderte die Grenze überquerten.

Die Vorschläge zur Abhilfe gingen auseinander; einig war man sich nur darüber, daß fehlendes Vertrauen durch Verläßlichkeit und Ehrlichkeit wiederhergestellt werden müßten. Superintendent Krusche nannte den Entwurf des Reisegesetzes als Beispiel dafür, daß auch 20 Tage nach dem, was in der DDR 'Wende' genannt wird, die Massen dennoch das Land verlassen: 'Das Reisegesetz ist mit seiner bürokratischen Überfrachtung eine Fortschreibung des Bestehenden;[1] nötig wäre ein völlig anderer, ein ganz neuer Entwurf gewesen. Ich bin dafür, daß man jedem Bürger der DDR einen Paß in die Hand drückt und sagt: Nun mal los!'[2] ...

Die SED erklärt im *Neuen Deutschland*, sie schaffe Garantien für die Unumkehrbarkeit der Wende. Was viele im Land inzwischen schon belächeln, die Behauptung der SED nämlich, sie habe die Wende letztlich bewirkt, das führen die Demonstranten auf der Straße, die neuen Gruppierungen und Parteien ad absurdum, das stellen die Vertreter anderer Blockparteien in Frage. Der stellvertretende Vorsitzende der Liberalen Partei, Hans-Dieter Raspe, äußert sich in einem scharfen Leitartikel in der Parteizeitung *Der Morgen* zur Überheblichkeit der SED. Überhaupt kämpfen alle Zeitungen am Mittwoch mit harten Bandagen, die Führungsrolle und der Machtanspruch der bisherigen Machthaber wird lauter und aggressiver denn je in Frage gestellt. Raspe fordert die ganze Macht für das Volk: 'Auf dem Papier hatten wir die Macht längst. Da war sie festgeschrieben und festgesetzt, im Gewahrsam der Worthülse. Im Leben hat sie uns gefehlt. Manchem so sehr, daß er ihrer Abwesenheit kaum noch gewahr wurde, im Trott der Selbstherrlichkeit, der Arroganz und Ignoranz, im bleiernen Frieden der Sturheit.'[3]

Starke Worte, traurige Worte. In der *Berliner Zeitung* wird von Wissenschaftlern der DDR ein neues Gesellschaftsmodell gefordert, um 'mit dem Modellwechsel dem Systemwechsel zuvorzukommen'. Die Nationaldemokratische Partei will radikale Erneuerungen in Kunst und Kultur, die Liberalen ein neues Wahlgesetz. Die FDJ, wilden Gerüchten vom Dienstag zufolge kurz vor der Selbstauflösung, stellt eine Latte von Forderungen auf, so lange wie eine ganze Seite ihrer Zeitung *Junge Welt*. Von einer singbaren Nationalhymne über eine Neugestaltung der Jugendweihe,[4] die Fünf-Tage-Woche und Mitbestimmung in der Schule bis zur Bestrafung schlechter Arbeit durch Lohnkürzung reicht die Palette. ...

In dem Maße, in dem der Führungsanspruch der SED wackelt, erstarken die Bündnispartner, zumindest verbal.

Den Bürgern scheint es derzeit noch egal, wer stark oder schwach ist, wer sich auf dem aufsteigenden Ast befindet oder aber den, auf dem er sitzt, eigenhändig absägt. Man wartet ab, schimpft, mißtraut allem und jedem – oder man geht einfach. Das Verständnis für diejenigen, die das Land verlassen, ist auf der Straße nicht sonderlich groß, viele fühlen sich ein wenig im Stich gelassen. Schließlich bricht hier und da die Versorgung mit dem Nötigsten zusammen, weil es an Arbeitskräften mangelt, schließlich verschlechtern sich die Arbeitsbedingungen in den Betrieben mit jeder Hand, die fehlt. In einem Ostberliner Bauunternehmen sind in den vergangenen Monaten 60 von insgesamt rund tausend Mitarbeitern in den Westen gegangen. Das klingt zunächst nicht dramatisch, hat aber den Kollegen viel Mehrarbeit gebracht; sie sind sauer.

Süddeutsche Zeitung, 9. November 1989.

Vocabulary
die 'Weggeher' those leaving
das Gremium committee, body
   beschimpfen abuse
die Ausgabe programme
die Ausreisezahlen the emigration figures
die Aufnahmefähigkeit capacity
das Auffanglager reception camp
   ab.schrecken deter
die Flüchtlingsmassen mass of refugees
   auf.nehmen, i, a, o receive
   bevorstehend imminent
die Reformfähigkeit reformability
die Reformbereitschaft readiness to reform
   ausschlaggebend decisive
die Verläßlichkeit dependability
der Superintendant dean
die Überfrachtung top-heaviness
   eine Fortschreibung des Bestehens a prolongation of the status quo
die Unumkehrbarkeit irreversibility
   mit harten Bandagen kämpfen fight with the gloves off
   im Gewahrsam der Worthülse enshrined in empty phrases
   im Trott der Selbstherrlichkeit in the humdrum routine of autocratic rule
   zuvor.kommen, o, a, o forestall
   Gerüchten zufolge according to rumour
die Selbstauflösung self-dissolution
   eine Latte von Forderungen a catalogue of demands
die Mitbestimmung democratic participation
die Palette spectrum
   auf dem aufsteigenden Ast on the way up, their stock is rising
   im Stich gelassen left in the lurch
die Mehrarbeit extra work

Notes
1 **Das Reisegesetz ... Bestehenden:** The law on travel, so bureaucratically top-heavy, is a prolongation of the *status quo*.
2 **Nun mal los!:** Off you go!

157

3 **Auf dem Papier ... der Sturheit:** 'We had already had the power for a long time on paper. It was formulated and codified there, enshrined in empty words. In real life we lacked any power. Some to such an extent that we hardly noticed its absence in the daily routine of autocracy, arrogance and stupidity, in the leaden calm of intransigence.'

4 **eine Neugestaltung der Jugendweihe:** A reorganisation of the Youth Initiation ceremony. *Jugendweihe* was introduced to the GDR as a secular alternative to religious confirmation.

12 December. Willy Brandt, the Honorary Chairman of the West German SPD and the architect of 'Ostpolitik' issues a thanks to Soviet officers for preventing a bloodbath on 9 October by warning the GDR military authorities against the use of force ... 16 December. To signal its break with the past the SED changes its name to SED-PDS (*Partei des Demokratischen Sozialismus*) – later to simply PDS ... 18 December. Opposition groups participating in the Round Table consultations demand a right to veto decisions by the government. The GDR government rejects the demand ... 19 December. West German Federal Chancellor Helmut Kohl arrives in Dresden for a two-day working visit. He consults with GDR leader Hans Modrow. They agree on the formation of a Contractual Community to work jointly on areas of common interest. It is announced that West Germans will be allowed to visit the GDR from Christmas onwards without a visa and without having to change currency. The Brandenburg Gate dividing East and West Berlin is to be opened. Economic co-operation is agreed. Kohl speaks to a huge crowd in Dresden. He reiterates the aim of an eventual reunification of Germany but he cautions the need to take account of the security interests of neighbouring states.

50. Kohl's speech to East Germans in Dresden

Mein Ziel bleibt – wenn die geschichtliche Stunde es zuläßt – die Einheit unserer Nation.

Liebe Freunde, ich weiß, daß wir dieses Ziel erreichen können und daß diese Stunde kommt, wenn wir gemeinsam dafür arbeiten – und wenn wir es mit Vernunft und mit Augenmaß tun, mit Sinn für das Mögliche. Es ist ein schwieriger Weg, aber es ist ein guter Weg; es geht um unsere gemeinsame Zukunft.

Ich weiß auch, daß dies nicht von heute auf morgen zu erreichen ist. Wir, die Deutschen, leben nun einmal nicht allein in Europa und in der Welt. Ein Blick auf die Landkarte zeigt, daß alles, was

sich hier bei uns verändert, Auswirkungen auf unsere Nachb.
haben muß, auf die Nachbarn im Osten und auf die Nachbarn im
Westen. Es hat keinen Sinn, nicht zur Kenntnis zu nehmen, daß
uns auf unserem Weg viele mit Sorge und manche auch mit Ängsten
beobachten. Aus Ängsten aber kann nichts Gutes erwachsen.
Wir müssen als Deutsche unseren Nachbarn sagen: Angesichts
der Geschichte dieses Jahrhunderts haben wir Verständnis für
manche dieser Ängste. Wir werden sie ernst nehmen.
Natürlich wollen wir unsere Interessen als Deutsche vertreten.
Wir sagen 'ja' zum Selbstbestimmungsrecht, das allen Völkern
dieser Erde zusteht – auch den Deutschen. Aber wenn wir dieses
Selbstbestimmungsrecht für die Deutschen verwirklichen wollen,
dann dürfen wir auch die Sicherheitsbedürfnisse der anderen nicht
außer acht lassen. Wir wollen eine Welt, in der es mehr Frieden
und mehr Freiheit gibt, die mehr Miteinander und nicht mehr
Gegeneinander kennt.

Helmut Kohl

Vocabulary

    zu.lassen, ä, ie, a allow
  das Augenmaß sense of proportion
    von heute auf morgen overnight
    nicht zur Kenntnis nehmen ignore
  das Selbstbestimmungsrecht right of self-determination
  die Sicherheitsbedürfnisse security requirements

22 December. The Brandenburg Gate is opened by Modrow and Kohl.
Modrow describes the opening of the Gate as a sign for the renewal of
the GDR ... 24 December. West Germans are allowed to travel to the
GDR without visa formalities ... 27 December. The increasing frequency
of extreme right-wing incidents and neo-Nazi slogans in East Germany
leads the fourth session of the Round Table to issue a warning against
the rise of neo-fascism in the GDR ... 31 December. Celebrations take
place on New Year's Eve on both sides of the Berlin Wall ... During 1989
a total of 343,854 East Germans have left their country to settle in the
West ... As the social and economic fabric of the GDR disintegrates,
West Germans begin to move into East Germany seeking quick profits
and future business opportunities.

Geschäftemacher oder seriöse Kaufleute – sie alle
on dem Konsumschub, den die Öffnung des Eisernen
usgelöst hat. Hunderttausende von DDR-Bürgern
strömen. t dem 9. November durch die Innenstädte von Lübeck
und Hof, von Bayreuth[1] und West-Berlin. Selbst in Hamburg,
50 Kilometer von der deutsch-deutschen Grenze entfernt, belegen
die Trabis inzwischen die Parkplätze und Gehwege.

In Kaufhäusern und Billig-Läden ist bisweilen kein Durchkommen
mehr. Sonderangebote sind schnell ausverkauft, vor den Kassen
der Obst- und Süßwarenabteilungen bilden sich lange Schlangen.

In Deutschland-West wirkt die Öffnung der Grenze, kurzfristig
zumindest, wie ein kleines Konjunkturprogramm.

Die bundesdeutsche Börse feierte, ganz konsequent, das historische
Ereignis gleich am Tag nach dem Hochziehen der Schlagbäume
mit einer kleinen DDR-Hausse: Die Kurse von Kaufhaus- und
anderen konsumnahen Aktien zogen sprunghaft an.[2]

Doch schon drei Börsen-Tage später kam der Rückschlag, stärker
und kräftiger als erwartet. Die Begeisterung verflog, Unsicherheit
machte sich breit.

Den Börsianern und Kleinanlegern, den Managern und den
Politikern dämmerte, daß mit der plötzlichen Öffnung der bislang
hermetisch verriegelten DDR eine ökonomische Situation einge-
treten war, für die es keine historische Parallele gibt; für die sich
auch in keinem Lehrbuch der Volkswirtschaft eine Handlungsanweisung finden läßt. Es ist eine Situation voller Risiken.

Die nun für alle durchlässige Ost-West-Grenze ließ über Nacht zwei
Wirtschaftswelten aufeinanderprallen, die unterschiedlicher nicht
sein könnten.

Im Westen eines der am höchsten entwickelten Länder der
Industriewelt, vollgestopft mit allen Gütern blühender Wohlstands-
gesellschaften, ausgewiesen als Exportweltmeister, ausgestattet
mit einer der härtesten Währungen des Globus, weltoffen und
hochgradig wettbewerbsfähig.

Im Osten eine Mangelwirtschaft, deren Automobile mit Motoren
fahren, die vor dem Krieg konstruiert wurden; deren Telefonnetz
so dürftig ist, daß die Wartezeiten für private Neuanschlüsse oft
zehn Jahre überschreiten; deren Außenhandelsprodukte im Westen

160

weit unter den Gestehungskosten verschleudert werden müssen, damit sie überhaupt Abnehmer finden.

Entblößt hat sich ohne jede Anpassungsfrist eine Wirtschaft, die ihre Währung genau wie ihre Bürger unter Verschluß gehalten hat. Ostmark durfte und darf nicht aus der DDR heraus- und nicht hineingebracht werden.

Nun auf einmal wird das Geld hin- und hergeschafft, Kontrollen sind, zumindest bei den gegenwärtigen Besuchermassen, nicht möglich. Nun auf einmal wird die Ostmark in den West-Städten gehandelt, als sei sie eine Währung wie jede andere.

Nur: Sie ist es nicht. Für eine Ostmark erhielt der DDRler auf dem Ku'damm[3] Mitte vergangener Woche noch zehn Pfennig, am Freitag nur noch fünf. Doch für eine Ostmark, also für fünf Pfennig West, kann der West-Berliner im Ostteil der Stadt ein ganzes Kilo subventioniertes Brot kaufen. Keine Volkswirtschaft kann solche Mißverhältnisse zwischen dem Außenwert ihrer Währung und den Preisen im Inneren dauerhaft verkraften, wenn die Devisengrenzen offen bleiben.

Pleite war, gemessen an den Maßstäben modernen Industrie-nationen, das östliche Murks-Unternehmen schon lange; die bisherigen Geschäftsführer hatten allerdings den Konkurs über Jahre mit getürkten Bilanzen verschleppt. Die Öffnung der Grenze, vom Volk erzwungen, zwingt das Regime nun zum Offenbarungseid. Die Zeit des Verschleierns ist vorbei.

Karl Marx hat endgültig ausgedient. Die von ihm konzipierte Wirtschafts- und Gesellschaftsordnung, in der die Produktions-mittel allein dem Volk gehören, in der ein staatlicher Plan das Chaos des Markts ersetzen soll – sie hat sich als eine untaugliche Utopie erwiesen.

Die Marx-Wirtschaft verhalf den Menschen nicht zu mehr Freiheit, sondern sie zwang zur totalen Unterwerfung. Die politische Unfreiheit wurde nicht mal durch materielle Gewinne ausgeglichen: Die Plan-Ökonomie blieb in der Warenproduktion uneinholbar hinter dem marktwirtschaftlichen Konkurrenzmodell zurück.[4]

Was nun, Herr Modrow?

Abschotten kann sich die DDR nicht mehr – sie muß sich anpassen: Der Öffnung der Grenzen wird irgendwann die Reform der Währung folgen und die Reform des gesamten Wirtschaftssystems.

Der Spiegel, Nr. 47/1989.

Vocabulary

windige Geschäftemacher dubious profiteers
der **Konsumschub** boost to consumer spending
kein Durchkommen packed out
das **Sonderangebot** special offer
das **Konjukturprogramm** programme of economic expansion
die **Börse** stock exchange
die **Hausse** stock exchange boom
die **Kurse** stock exchange quotations
an.ziehen, ie, o, o rise
der **Rückschlag** setback
verfliegen, ie, o, o dissipate
sich breit.machen spread
der **Börsianer** stock exchange speculator
der **Kleinanleger** small investor
dämmern (+ dat.) dawn on
hermetisch verriegelt hermetically sealed off
die **Handlungsanweisung** instruction
durchlässig permeable
aufeinander.prallen collide
die **Wohlstandsgesellschaft** affluent society
ausgewiesen als acknowledged to be
aus.statten equip
weltoffen open to the world
hochgradig wettbewerbsfähig highly competitive
die **Mangelwirtschaft** clapped-out economy
unter Gestehungskosten below production cost
verschleudern dump
der **Abnehmer** buyer
entblößen expose
die **Anpassungsfrist** period of adjustment
unter Verschluß under lock and key
subventionieren subsidise
das **Mißverhältnis** disproportion
der **Außenwert** external value
verkraften cope with
pleite bankrupt
das **Murks-Unternehmen** economic shambles, ruined firm
der **Konkurs** bankruptcy
mit getürkten Bilanzen with rigged balance-sheets
verschleppen delay
der **Offenbarungseid** declaration of bankruptcy
verschleiern cover up
hat ausgedient has outlived its usefulness, failed
sich erweisen als turn out to be
untauglich impracticable
die **Unterwerfung** subjugation
aus.gleichen, ei, i, i balance out
uneinholbar lagging behind

162

sich ab.schotten seal itself off
sich an.passen adapt

Notes

1 **Lübeck,** in the North of Germany, Hof and Bayreuth further south close to the East German border.
2 **Die Kurse ... an:** 'There was a sudden leap in the quotations for shares of department stores and other retail branches.'
3 **Ku'damm:** The popular name for the Kurfürstendamm, the prestige shopping boulevard in West Berlin.
4 **Die Plan-Ökonomie ... zurück:** 'In the production of goods the planned economy trailed hopelessly behind the competitive model of the market economy.'

3 January 1990. 200,000 take part in a demonstration against neo-Nazi activities before the monument to the Soviet soldiers who fell in the Second World War in the struggle against German fascism ... It is revealed by the East German Minister of Economics, Christa Luft, that the GDR has debts to western countries amounting to $20 thousand million, a major factor in the collapse of the East German economy ... 8 January. At the weekly Monday demonstrations in Leipzig ever louder calls are heard for immediate German unification. 'Deutschland einig Vaterland' becomes the central demand of subsequent demonstrations ... 11 January. The *Volkskammer* passes legislation allowing foreign investment in the GDR ... Leading former members of the SED, including Egon Krenz and Günter Schabowski, lay down their parliamentary mandates ... 12 January. The recently formed East German SDP changes its name to SPD, in line with the West German SPD, in time for the election campaign which is under way; it advocates a 'socially and ecologically oriented market economy' and a gradualist policy towards German unification ... 13 January. Prices in East Germany begin to rise dramatically as subsidies are removed from key commodities ... 14 January. Hans Modrow holds discussions with the head of the West German concern Daimler-Benz, Eduard Reuter ... Modrow issues a declaration in favour of a 'social market economy'; he advocates co-operation between Eastern European countries and the European Community ... 15 January. It is announced that with the gradual dissolution of the *Stasi* 30,000 former employees have been re-employed in industry out of a total staff of 85,000 ... Neues Forum calls for demonstrations against surviving *Stasi* structures as more and more is revealed about the vast scope of its surveillance activities. In Lichtenberg, East Berlin, demonstrators occupy *Stasi* headquarters ... Warning strikes break out against the *Stasi*, the continuing influence of former SED functionaries in political life and in industry, and in support of a referendum on German unification ... There is a demonstration of 150,000

163

in Leipzig and a further 150,000 in Dresden and Karl-Marx-Stadt ...
16 January. GDR citizens continue to pour into West Germany at a rate
of 1,500 to 2,000 per day. To discourage further emigration and the
imminent collapse of East Germany with unforeseeable consequences
the Bonn government cuts its generous support for those emigrating to
the West ... 17 January. Strikes continue against the SED's continued
hold on power and against the *Stasi* ... 18 January. In a debate in the
West German *Bundestag* all political parties, with the exception of the
Grünen, support the idea of German unification ... In the GDR Hermann
Axen, the former Central Committee Secretary is arrested ... 19 January.
Criminal investigations are begun against Heinz Keßler, the former GDR
Defence Minister, for corruption and abuse of office ... 20 January.
In the GDR a DSU is formed – a sister party of the Bavarian CSU –
for the coming election ... 21 January. The former President of the
Volkskammer, Horst Sindermann, is arrested, accused of embezzlement
and abuse of office ... The GDR begins officially to sell pieces of the
Berlin Wall. Offers of over DM 100,000 per section are reported ...
22 January. Egon Krenz describes the *Stasi* as a 'Staat im Staat' which
kept even leading members of the SED under surveillance.

52. The Stasi. A state-within-the state

Die Deutschen, so heißt es oft im Ausland, seien besonders
gewissenhaft, fleißig und ordentlich. Ginge es nach diesen
Attributen, müßte die ehemalige Staatssicherheit der DDR
nachträglich für ihre Arbeit einen Orden erhalten. Denn wohl
kaum anders ist zu beschreiben, was nach dem Abgang des alten
SED-Regimes aus dem Hause des Stasi-Chefs Erich Mielke an
deutscher Gründlichkeit der staunenden Öffentlichkeit präsentiert
wurde. Ob es dabei um die Bespitzelung der eigenen Bevölkerung,
Auslandsspionage oder die Unterbringung einer ganzen Terro-
ristengeneration der RAF[1] ging – die Arbeit des 'Ministeriums
für Staatssicherheit' (MfS) war sprichwörtlich umfassend.
1950 offiziell als 'Schild und Schwert der Partei' gegründet, wurde
die Stasi im Laufe der Jahre immer weiter ausgebaut, zu einem
unübersehbaren Machtfaktor im SED-Staat, zum 'Staat im Staate'.
Im September 1990 zog das Regierungskomitee zur Auflösung des
MfS und dessen Nachfolgebehörde Amt für Nationale Sicherheit
Bilanz: 85 000 hauptamtliche Mitarbeiter hatten nahezu das

gesamte öffentliche Leben der DDR wie mit den Tentakeln einer Krake durchzogen. Hinzu kamen die nebenberuflichen Mitarbeiter, über deren Zahl selbst der Leiter des Regierungskomitees, Günter Eichborn, nur spekulieren konnte: 100 000 bis 500 000. Insgesamt stand diesem imposanten Ministerium ein Jahresetat von rund vier Milliarden D-Mark zur Verfügung. Zum Vermögen gehörten unter anderem auch 836 Wohnhäuser mit 18 000 Wohnungen sowie 1819 Dienst-, Sport- und Erholungseinrichtungen. Der Stasi war damit, wie das Regierungskomitee abschließend feststellte, der 'am besten organisierte Geheimdienst der Welt'.

Die Sammelwut der Stasi kannte keine Grenzen: mehr als 168 Kilometer Aktenbestände kamen zusammen. Was sich darunter befand, konnte die Öffentlichkeit im Sommer 1990 in einer Ausstellung bewundern, die unter dem Titel 'Die Banalität des Bösen' in Leipzig lief. Hier wurde dokumentiert, mit welcher Pedanterie die Stasi bei ihrer täglichen Arbeit vorgegangen war. Keine Spitzelaktion, die nicht mit bürokratischer Genauigkeit beantragt wurde. Dazu dienten fein säuberlich hergestellte Vordrucke, die Bezeichnungen wie 'Auftragsersuchen Beobachtung' oder – in schönstem Amtsdeutsch– 'Sammel-Suchauftrag zur Überprüfung von DDR-Bürgern' trugen.[2] Was ein Geistlicher bei einem Rentnerfasching getrunken hatte, welche Vorzüge der Schüler einer 9. Klasse beim bundesdeutschen VW-Polo vor dem Trabi erkannte – alles fand Eingang in den Aktenwust, nichts schien banal genug.

Selbst ein 'Geruchskataster' wurde extra angelegt, in denen konservierte Geruchsproben von Oppositionellen lagerten. Zu ihrer Identifizierung ließ man speziell ausgebildete Hunde abrichten. Die Stasi konnte innerhalb der DDR nach Gutdünken schalten und walten. Telefone wurden überwacht, Post mit speziellen Geräten geöffnet und fachmännisch wieder geschlossen, wobei die Stasi nicht selten, zumeist wenn es sich um Währung aus dem Westen handelte, den Inhalt gleich selbst einbehielt. Aber auch Briefe wurden zurückgehalten – viele Empfänger erhielten sie erst nach der Zerschlagung der Stasi-Strukturen, Jahre später. Die Opposition war der Stasi ein besonderer Dorn im Auge, hierfür war sie ja geschaffen worden, hier konnte sie ihre Effektivität beweisen. ...

Auch die Kirche, die ihr oft als schützendes Dach diente, blieb nicht verschont. Gezielt wurden durch Erpressung und Bestechung Pfarrer zur Mitarbeit gezwungen, Gemeindemitglieder angeworben, Beichtstühle abgehört. So verfügte auch im kirchlichen Kreis die Stasi über ein engmaschiges Netz von festen und sogenannten inoffiziellen Mitarbeitern. Für den Ernstfall – sprich bei inneren Unruhen – hatte die Stasi ebenfalls vorgesorgt. Internierungslager sollten Tausende von Systemgegnern aufnehmen. Mehrfach wurde die Einsatzbereitschaft dieser Lager erprobt. Dabei war an alles gedacht worden, wie ein Beiblatt zu einer 1984 durchgespielten Übung 'Schild' verdeutlichte. Es schlüsselte den 'persönlichen Bedarf' der 'zu isolierenden Personen' auf: '2 Paar Socken, 2 Handtücher, 2 Taschentücher, 2 mal Unterwäsche, 1 Nähzeug, 1 Zahnputzzeug, 1 Schuhputzzeug.'

Das Mißtrauen der Stasi beschränkte sich keinesfalls nur auf die Opposition. Die gesamte DDR-Gesellschaft wurde zum Objekt ihrer Arbeit. Ob Blockparteien, Massenorganisationen, Nationale Volksarmee (NVA), Volkspolizei, Rechtsanwälte – überall hatte die Stasi ihre Zuträger. Gefürchtet war die Stasi nicht nur innerhalb der DDR. Auch im Ausland agierte sie – und zwar sehr erfolgreich. Insbesondere die Bundesrepublik diente der 'Hauptverwaltung Aufklärung' (HVA), dem Auslandsspionagedienst der Stasi, als bevorzugtes Ziel. Unter ihrem Chef Markus Wolf, der die HVA von 1952 bis 1987 führte, brach der DDR-Geheimdienst in allerhöchste Positionen der Bundesrepublik ein. Günther Guillaume,[3] der MfS-Spion, der als Kanzlerberater Willy Brandts 1973 dessen Sturz einleitete, war nur die Spitze des Eisbergs. Nach der Vereinigung am 3. Oktober 1990 mußten die westdeutschen Geheimdienste entdecken, daß die HVA jahrelang mit ihnen Katz und Maus gespielt hatte. 'Kundschafter für den Frieden', wie die Stasi-Spione vom Regime genannt wurden, saßen beim Bundesamt für Verfassungsschutz, beim Bundesnachrichtendienst und im Militärischen Abschirmdienst.[4] An der innerdeutschen Grenze im Thüringer Wald und auf dem Brocken[5] im Harz führte die Stasi hochmoderne Anlagen, mit denen die gesamte Bundesrepublik und Westeuropa abgehört wurden. Witz der Geschichte: Die Technik stammte überwiegend vom 'Klassenfeind' – aus der Bundesrepublik. Die Stasi-Strukturen zu zerschlagen – dies war (und ist) eine der Hauptforderungen der DDR-Bürgerbewegungen.

Doch die Arbeit erwies sich schwieriger, als zunächst angenommen. Nicht nur, daß die völlig überlasteten Bürgerrechtler im Aktenmaterial schier versanken − auch von Seiten der letzten DDR-Regierung kam kaum Unterstützung. Im Gegenteil: DDR-Innenminister Peter-Michael Diestel[6] sorgte − gewollt oder ungewollt − dafür, daß alte Stasi-Strukturen weiterhin unangetastet blieben. Den Bürgerkomitees entzog er die Kontrollrechte, verhinderte die Überprüfung aller Kandidaten der Kommunalwahlen auf eine mögliche Stasi-Vergangenheit und verschleppte schließlich die Überprüfung der Volkskammerabgeordneten. Bei der Auflösung des MfS wurde − so die Überzeugung vieler Bürgerrechtler − mehr verdunkelt als erhellt. Bestes Beispiel war im September 1990 die Entdeckung von 57 'Offizieren im besonderen Einsatz'[7] (OibE) in mehereren DDR-Ministerien. Einer davon war Dieter Stein − Büroleiter des staatlichen Komitees zur Auflösung der Stasi.

Daß die Stasi auch im vereinten Deutschland ein brisantes Thema bleiben würde, zeigten schon die Verhandlungen zum Staatsvertrag. Erst die Besetzung der ehemaligen Stasi-Zentrale in Ostberlin durch Bürgerrechtler im September 1990 verhinderte, daß die Stasi-Akten in die Hände des Bundesarchivs[8] übergingen. Die Forderung nach Einsicht in ihre persönliche Stasi-Akte wurde allerdings abgewiesen. Schließlich bestimmte die Bundesregierung den ehemaligen Volkskammerabgeordneten Jochen Gauck zum Sonderbeauftragten für das Stasi-Erbe. Der Rostocker Pfarrer vom Bündnis 90[9] ist sich sicher, daß auch in Zukunft die ehemalige Stasi viel Arbeit bringen wird. 'Der Drache scheint besiegt, wird schon ausgestellt und verhöhnt − aber er atmet noch.'

Severin Weiland, *9. November. Das Jahr danach* (Munich, 1991), 79−82.

Vocabulary
- **so heißt es** it is said
- **ging es nach diesen Attributen** judged by these attributes
- **nachträglich** belatedly
- **die Bespitzelung** spying on
- **die Unterbringung** accommodation
- **sprichwörtlich** proverbially
- **die Auflösung** dissolution
- **die Nachfolgebehörde** the subsequent authority

die **Tentakeln einer Krake** the tentacles of an octopus
  durch.ziehen, ie, o, o penetrate
die **Sammelwut** mania for collecting
die **Aktenbestände** store of dossiers
die **Spitzelaktion** surveillance operation
der **Vordruck** printed form
der **Rentnerfasching** old age pensioners' party
der **Vorzug** advantage
  Eingang finden be entered
der **Aktenwust** mass of dossiers
das **Geruchskataster** registry of odours
  konservierte Geruchsproben preserved samples of odours
  ab.richten lassen have trained
  nach Gutdünken schalten und walten run things at its own discretion
  ein.behalten, ä, ie, a confiscate
die **Zerschlagung** breaking up
  ein Dorn im Auge a thorn in the flesh
  nicht verschont bleiben, ei, ie, ie not to be spared
die **Erpressung** blackmail
die **Bestechung** bribery
das **Gemeindemitglied** member of the congregation
  an.werben, i, a, o hire
der **Beichtstuhl** confessional
  ab.hören bug
  sprich that is
  vor.sorgen make provision
das **Internierungslager** internment camp
die **Einsatzbereitschaft** operational readiness
das **Beiblatt** instruction
  auf.schlüsseln list, break down
- der **Zuträger** informant
die **Aufklärung** intelligence
der **Kanzlerberater** Chancellor's adviser
der **Kundschafter** spy, scout
  sich erweisen turn out to be
  überlastet overburdened
  versinken, i, a, u drown
  unangetastet untouched, unharmed
die **Überprüfung** clearance, checking
  verdunkeln obscure
  erhellen illuminate
  im besonderen Einsatz special operations
  ein brisantes Thema a controversial topic
die **Einsicht in** access to
  ab.weisen, ei, ie, ie reject
der **Sonderbeauftragte** special commissioner

Notes
1 **RAF: Die Rote Armee Fraktion:** A left−anarchist group (the Baader-Meinhof

group) responsible for attacks on West German industrialists and politicians, particularly during the 1970s. While many were imprisoned, some fled to the GDR where they were given new identities.

2 **Dazu dienten ... trugen:** 'For this they used meticulously produced forms classified as "Surveillance Application" or – in finest officialese – "Group Observation Warrant to Monitor Citizens of the GDR".'

3 **Günter Guillaume:** The aide close to the West German Chancellor Willy Brandt, who resigned when Guillaume was revealed to be an East German 'mole'.

4 **Bundesamt für Verfassungsschutz, Bundesnachrichtendienst, Militärischer Abschirmdienst:** The West German agencies responsible for inner security, foreign intelligence and military intelligence.

5 **Brocken:** The highest mountain in the Harz region on the German–German border.

6 **Peter-Michael Diestel:** A member of the East German CDU, briefly Minister of the Interior in Modrow's coalition.

7 **Offiziere im besonderen Einsatz:** special operations officers.

8 **Bundesarchiv:** The Federal Archives in Koblenz.

9 **Bündnis 90:** The electoral alliance formed in February 1990, comprising *Neues Forum, Demokratie Jetzt* and the *Initiative Frieden und Menschenrechte*.

23 January. The first meeting takes place of the German–German Economic Commission to plan co-operation between the two countries ... 25 January. Free commercial activity becomes legal for all craft, trading and service firms in the GDR ... 50,000 East Germans cross the border to West Germany. They threaten to leave East Germany for good unless SED power structures locally and centrally are dismantled ... 27 January. After a fierce controversy Neues Forum votes to remains an action group and not to stand as a political party in the coming election. It is agreed that the question of unification, to which many activists are opposed, should be left to a referendum ... 28 January. In view of the growing social and economic instability in the GDR Hans Modrow agrees with the Round Table to bring forward the date of the planned elections to the *Volkskammer* from May to 18 March ... 29 January. After leaving hospital Erich Honecker is placed under arrest. This step is widely criticised in East and West. He is released a day later as unfit to be kept in prison due to his bad health ... 30 January. Hans Modrow confers with Mikhail Gorbachev in Moscow. Gorbachev shifts his position on German unification significantly. Having previously insisted that 'history will decide', he now states that 'basically, no one casts doubt' upon the idea of a unified German state. He insists that the process of *rapprochement* between East and West and the interests of the four Allied Powers in the Second World War must be respected.

1 February. Accepting the inevitability of German unification, Hans Modrow submits a three-stage plan for a Confederation of the two German states.

53. Modrow's plan for a German confederation

'Europa tritt in eine neue Etappe seiner Entwicklung ein. Das Nachkriegskapitel wird abgeschlossen. Voraussetzungen für eine friedliche und gutnachbarliche Zusammenarbeit aller Völker bilden sich heraus. Die Vereinigung der beiden deutschen Staaten rückt auf die Tagesordnung.

Das deutsche Volk wird seinen Platz beim Aufbau der neuen Friedensordnung finden, in deren Ergebnis sowohl die Teilung Europas in feindliche Lager als auch die Spaltung der deutschen Nation überwunden werden. Es ist die Stunde gekommen, einen Schlußstrich unter den Zweiten Weltkrieg zu ziehen, einen deutschen Friedensvertrag abzuschließen. Durch ihn würden alle Probleme geregelt, die mit der Aggression Hitlerdeutschlands und dem Scheitern des 'Dritten Reiches' verbunden sind.

Eine endgültige Lösung der deutschen Frage kann nur in freier Selbstbestimmung der Deutschen in beiden Staaten erreicht werden, in Zusammenarbeit mit den vier Mächten und unter Berücksichtigung der Interessen aller europäischen Staaten. Sie muß den gesamteuropäischen Prozeß fördern, der unseren Kontinent ein für allemal von militärischen Gefahren befreien soll. Die Annäherung beider deutscher Staaten und ihre nachfolgende Vereinigung darf durch niemanden als Bedrohung betrachtet werden.

In diesem Sinne schlage ich einen verantwortungsbewußten nationalen Dialog vor. Sein Ziel sollte es sein, konkrete Schritte zu bestimmen, die zu einem einheitlichen Deutschland führen, das ein neuer Faktor der Stabilität, des Vertrauens, des Friedens in Europa zu werden bestimmt ist.

Die Vertreter der DDR und der BRD könnten mit einem solchen Dialog und in gleichberechtigten Verhandlungen bestmögliche Antworten auf die Fragen nach der Zukunft der deutschen Nation finden.

Die Schritte auf dem Weg zur deutschen Einheit könnten sein:

- Abschluß eines Vertrages über Zusammenarbeit und gute Nachbarschaft als eine Vertragsgemeinschaft, die bereits wesentliche konföderative Elemente enthalten sollte wie Wirtschafts-, Währungs- und Verkehrsunion sowie Rechtsangleichung.

- Bildung einer Konföderation von DDR und BRD mit gemeinsamen Organen und Institutionen, wie z. B. parlamentarischer

Ausschuß, Länderkammer, gemeinsame Exekutivorgane für bestimmte Bereiche.

– Übertragung von Souveränitätsrechten beider Staaten an Machtorgane der Konföderation.[1]

– Bildung eines einheitlichen deutschen Staates in Form einer Deutschen Föderation oder eines Deutschen Bundes durch Wahlen in beiden Teilen der Konföderation, Zusammentreten eines einheitlichen Parlaments, das eine einheitliche Verfassung und einheitliche Regierung mit Sitz in Berlin beschließt.

Notwendige Voraussetzungen für diese Entwicklung:

– Jeder der beiden deutschen Staaten trägt dafür Sorge, die Schritte zur Einheit Deutschlands mit seinen Verpflichtungen gegenüber anderen Ländern und Ländergruppen sowie mit notwendigen Reformen und Veränderungen in Übereinstimmung zu bringen. Hierzu gehört der Übergang der DDR zur Länderstruktur. Wahrung von Stabilität, Recht und Gesetz im Innern gehören ebenso zu den unabdingbaren Voraussetzungen wie die strikte Erfüllung früher abgeschlossener Verträge zwischen der DDR und der BRD, die unter anderem vorsehen, sich gegenseitig nicht in innere Angelegenheiten einzumischen.

– Wahrung der Interessen und Rechte der vier Mächte sowie der Interessen aller Völker Europas an Frieden, Souveränität und sicheren Grenzen. Die vier Mächte sollten ihre Absicht erklären, nach Bildung eines einheitlichen deutschen Staates alle aus dem Zweiten Weltkrieg und der Nachkriegsperiode entstandenen Fragen abschließend zu regeln, einschließlich der Anwesenheit ausländischer Truppen auf deutschem Boden und der Zugehörigkeit zu Militärbündnissen.

– Militärische Neutralität von DDR und BRD auf dem Weg zur Föderation.

Hans Modrow, Ministerpräsident der Deutschen Demokratischen Republik.

Vocabulary

die Voraussetzung precondition
sich heraus.bilden emerge
die Friedensordnung system of peace
einen Schlußstrich ziehen, ie, o, o make a clean break
unter Berücksichtigung having regard to
ein für allemal once and for all

die **Annäherung** *rapprochement*
  verantwortungsbewußt aware of our responsibility
der **Abschluß eines Vertrags** the conclusion of a treaty
  eine Vertragsgemeinschaft contractual community
die **Wirtschafts-, Währungs- und Verkehrsunion** economic, currency and transport
    union
die **Rechtsangleichung** standardisation of law
die **Landeskammer** parliamentary chamber of federal states
  gemeinsame Exekutivorgane joint executive institutions
die **Übertragung von Souveränitätsrechten** transference of sovereign rights
der **Bund** federation
  dafür Sorge tragen make sure that
die **Verpflichtung** obligation
  in Übereinstimmung bringen harmonise
die **Wahrung** preservation
  unabdingbar indispensable
  innere Angelegenheit internal affair
  sich ein.mischen interfere
  abschließend regeln finally settle
die **Zugehörigkeit zu Militärbündnissen** membership of military alliances

Notes
1 **parlamentarischer Ausschuß ... Konföderation:** Parliamentary Commission
  (second) Parliamentary Chamber (*Länder*), joint executive bodies for designated
  areas, the transfer of sovereignty rights of both states to the political institutions
  of the Confederation.

4 February. An East German liberal party, FDP, is founded ... 5 February.
The Round Table criticizes interference by West German political parties
in support of the corresponding parties in the East German *Volkskammer*
election campaign. Prominent West German politicians and speakers
continue to appear at election meetings in the GDR ... The radical
right-wing West German party, die *Republikaner*, is banned in the GDR ...
An electoral alliance, '*Allianz für Deutschland*' is formed between the
East German CDU, DSU and *Demokratischer Aufbruch* ... 100,000
demonstrate in Leipzig for a referendum on the future of Germany.

54. The East German revolution changes direction

Wie war es möglich, daß das DDR-Volk, das doch allen Grund
hatte, auf seine erfolgreiche und unblutige demokratische Revolution stolz zu sein, so plötzlich zur Selbstaufgabe bereit war?
Daß die aufbegehrende Phantasie und der subversive Witz der
bisherigen Demonstrationen so rasch dem schrillen und bettelnden

Dauerton 'Deutschland, einig Vaterland!' weichen mußte? Woher kam dieser abrupte Wechsel von der eigenen, originären zur geborgten Sprache der CDU-importierten Parolen, zur Stumpfsinnigkeit des Fahnenschwenkens und der 'Helmut! Helmut!'[1]-Rufe? Was hat diese Demokratiebewegung, die doch im Oktober so grandios als antistalinistische Volkserhebung aufgebrochen war, so plötzlich um ihr Selbstbewußtsein und um ihre Courage gebracht?

Und wie kam es zu diesem gehässigen Umschlag in die Intoleranz, in das neue Feindbild-Denken, ins Auspfeifen jedes Redners, der andere Prioritäten setzte als die der Wiedervereinigung? Wer im Januar in Leipzig oder Magdeburg noch mit Plakaten demonstrieren ging, die auf der Eigenstaatlichkeit der DDR bestanden und gegen den raschen Anschluß votierten, mußte Spießruten laufen und war − nicht selten − tätlichen Angriffen ausgesetzt. Die wenige Monate vorher noch von der Staatspartei als 'Konterrevolutionäre' ausgegrenzt und verfolgt worden waren, wurden nun von den schwarz-rot-goldenen Fahnenträgern niedergeschrien: 'Ihr seid das letzte!', 'Rote und Juden raus!', 'Ihr roten Schweine!'. Was als 'sanfte Revolution' begonnen hatte, endete in Lynch- und Pogromstimmung gegen diejenigen, die ihr den Weg bereitet hatten.

Nicht nur bei den Demonstrationen, auch in der politischen Arena, in der Parteienlandschaft und den DDR-Medien, hatte das Personal gewechselt und gaben auf einmal ganz andere Leute den Ton an als jene, von denen die Novemberrevolution ausgegangen war. Solange sie einen gemeinsamen Feind hatte, den SED- und Stasi-Staat, war sich die Opposition einig, hatte die intellektuelle Avantgarde aus den Menschenrechts-, Friedens- und Umweltgruppen die Massen hinter sich. Doch kaum war der Machtkampf mit der Staatspartei und ihrem Apparat gewonnen, zerbrach diese 'Einheitsfront', die Opposition zersplitterte sich in bald gegeneinander rivalisierende Gruppen und Parteien, und die Mitläufer von gestern, den Blick nun nicht mehr auf Ostberlin, sondern auf Bonn gerichtet, gaben den Ton an.

Aus dem einjährigen Abstand von heute sieht man es deutlicher: Das Ende des SED-Regimes war schneller besiegelt, die Wende in der DDR früher unumkehrbar geworden, als es damals, im Herbst 1989, den Anschein hatte, als die Akteure es selbst für

173

möglich gehalten hatten. Mit beidem hatten sie nicht gerechnet: mit dem stupenden Erfolg der Bürgerbewegung und mit der Hilflosigkeit des Regimes, dessen inneres Machtgefüge schon vor der Wende so morsch und ausgehöhlt war, daß schon der erste Ansturm der Massen es umblies. So waren sie gleichsam durch ihren eigenen Erfolg paralysiert.

Das 'Neue Forum' und die kritischen Genossen an der Basis hatten ja nie im Traum daran gedacht, die Staatspartei zu stürzen; sie wollten mit der Führung in einen Dialog treten, von ihr anerkannt und als Partner in dem gemeinsam zu vollziehenden Reformprozeß ernstgenommen werden.

Michael Schneider, *Die abgetriebene Revolution* (Berlin, 1990), 79–80.

Vocabulary
die **Selbstaufgabe** capitulation
die **aufbegehrende Phantasie** insubordinate imaginativeness
der **Dauerton** monotone
    weichen (+ dat.), ei, i, i give way to
die **Stumpfsinnigkeit** tediousness
das **Fahnenschwenken** flag-waving
    gehässig vicious
der **Umschlag** change in mood
die **Eigenstaatlichkeit** national autonomy
das **Spießrutenlaufen** running the gauntlet
    aus.setzen (+ dat.) expose to
    aus.grenzen ostracise
das **Letzte** scum
die **Lynch- und Pogromstimmung** lynching and pogrom mood
den **Ton angeben** here: run the show
der **Mitläufer** collaborator
    aus einem einjährigen Abstand after an interval of one year
    besiegeln set the seal on
die **Wende** turning-point
    stupend amazing
    morsch rotten
    aus.höhlen erode
    um.blasen, ä, ie, a blow down
    vollziehen, ie, o, o complete

Notes
1 **Helmut** = Helmut Kohl

10 February. At a historic meeting in Moscow Gorbachev and Kohl agree that the Germans have the right to determine the time and route to unification.

55. Gorbachev accepts German self-determination

Ich habe heute abend an alle Deutschen eine einzige Botschaft zu übermitteln. Generalsekretär Gorbatschow und ich stimmen darin überein, daß es das alleinige Recht des deutschen Volkes ist, die Entscheidung zu treffen, ob es in einem Staat zusammenleben will. Generalsekretär Gorbatschow hat mir unmißverständlich zugesagt, daß die Sowjetunion die Entscheidung der Deutschen, in einem Staat zu leben, respektieren wird, und daß es Sache der Deutschen ist, den Zeitpunkt und den Weg der Einigung selbst zu bestimmen. ... Sie (die deutsche Frage; ed.) muß eingebettet sein in die gesamteuropäische Architektur.

Bundeskanzler Helmut Kohl

Vocabulary
 die Botschaft message
   übermitteln deliver
   unmißverständlich unmistakably
   zu.sagen promise
   Sache der Deutschen the Germans' affair
   ein.betten embed

175

VI. Elections and unification

12, 13 February. A meeting takes place in Bonn between Kohl and Modrow. Kohl rejects Modrow's request for immediate economic assistance. Negotiations are to begin on currency union. This means, in effect, that East Germany abandons sovereignty as an economic unity and independent state, as the D-Mark replaces the GDR's own currency.

56. Bonn's aim: unification

Die nötige Soforthilfe von fünfzehn Milliarden DM, um die die Regierung Modrow im Januar vergeblich gebeten hatte, wurde von der Bundesregierung strikt abgelehnt. In ein 'Faß ohne Boden' wolle und könne man sein 'gutes Geld', die DM, nicht werfen, erklärten der Finanz- und Wirtschaftsminister einmütig. Dabei ging es gar nicht darum, das marode Wirtschaftssystem der DDR zu stützen, sondern nur darum, im Bereich der Dienstleistungen und der medizinischen Versorgung die größten Löcher zu stopfen, die durch den Exodus von Zehntausenden von Facharbeitern und von über 4 000 ÄrztInnen und KrankenpflegerInnen entstanden waren. Schließlich profitierte auch die bundesdeutsche Industrie von diesem Exodus: Sie konnte ihren eigenen Facharbeiter-Mangel, den sie selbst verschuldet hatte, nun mit DDR-Facharbeitern kompensieren, ohne einen Pfennig für deren Ausbildungskosten bezahlt zu haben. Und da letztere froh waren, überhaupt Arbeit zu finden, konnte man sie billig, oft zu außertariflichen Bedingungen einkaufen.

Immer wieder erklärte die Bundesregierung, die Regierung Modrow sei nicht demokratisch legitimiert, deshalb sei das Verhandeln so schwierig. Mit anderen garantiert selbst ermächtigten Regierungen, sei es das frühere Schah-Regime im Iran, das

Apartheid-Regime in Südafrika oder Pinochets Diktatur in Chile, hatte man nicht solche Schwierigkeiten.

Dabei hatte die Regierung Modrow längst die Vertreter der verschiedensten Oppositionsgruppen an der Regierung beteiligt und mit dem Runden Tisch ein Organ geschaffen, das, wenn auch nicht aus freien Wahlen, so doch aus der Demokratiebewegung des Herbstes hervorgegangen war.

Vor allem durch gezielte Entwürdigungs- und Demütigungsrituale sollten die Übergangsregierung Modrow und die Vertreter des Runden Tisches in den Augen der Ostdeutschen delegitimiert werden. So wurden die Beschlüsse des Runden Tisches – vom Verfassungsentwurf bis zur Sozialcharta, vom neuen Gewerkschaftsgesetz bis zu Ullmanns Konzept, die DDR-Bürger über Anteilsscheine am Volkseigentum zu beteiligen – von den Bonner Politikern und ihren medialen Verstärkern stets mit spöttischer Herablassung kommentiert oder lächerlich gemacht, als handele es sich um die Vorschläge und Konzepte von dilettierenden Sonntags-Politikern oder weltfremden Spinnern, die keine Ahnung haben, wie man Politik macht.

Als die Vertreter des Runden Tisches, zusammen mit Hans Modrow, im Januar nach Bonn kamen, wurden sie nicht etwa wie Revolutionäre, sondern wie Bittsteller auf dem Sozialamt behandelt. Der noch amtierende Ministerpräsident der DDR wurde nicht etwa von Kohl, sondern von dessen Kanzleramtssekretär empfangen; er mußte buchstäblich den Hintereingang benutzen. 'Wir sitzen hier bei den reichen Brüdern im Westen und haben nichts zu sagen', klagte Rainer Eppelmann,[1] der mit zur Delegation gehörte. So reichliches Lob die Bundesregierung der demokratischen Volkserhebung in der DDR gespendet hatte, deren legitimierten Vertretern wurde rasch deutlich gemacht, daß sie keine Bedingungen zu stellen haben, im Klartext: daß die Einheit nur als Akt der Unterwerfung unter die Konditionen Bonns zu haben sei. 'Hilfe, wirkliche Hilfe', schrieb Günter Grass, 'Wird nur nach westdeutschen Konditionen gegeben. Eigentum ja, heißt es, aber kein Volkseigentum, bitte. Die westliche Ideologie des Kapitalismus, die jeden anderen Ismus ersatzlos gestrichen hat, spricht sich wie hinter vorgehaltener Pistole aus: entweder Marktwirtschaft oder ... Wer nicht spurt, kriegt nix. Nicht mal Bananen.'[2]

Um bei der abschließenden Pressekonferenz in Bonn nicht mit ganz leeren Händen dazustehen, sprach Modrow davon, daß die DDR in das künftige vereinte Deutschland neben einem gewissen Anlagevermögen auch 'Werte einzubringen hat, geistige und kulturelle Werte, die in Jahrzehnten trotz alledem gewachsen sind'. Das kaum unterdrückte Hohngelächter des anwesenden Publikums verriet schon den Preis, zu dem solche Werte in Zukunft gehandelt werden würden. ...

Dem Bonner Ruf nach der 'Wiedervereinigung' – dies läßt sich an der gezielten Destabilisierungspolitik ebenso ablesen wie an den verweigerten Sofort-Hilfen und den erpresserischen Bedingungen, die die Bundesregierung mit ihnen verknüpfte – lagen jedenfalls nicht die gleichen Motive zugrunde wie dem der Leipziger Montags-läufer.[3] Was für die einen, die Ostdeutschen, primär ein Hilferuf, der Wunsch nach der D-Mark und die Hoffnung war, der real-sozialistischen Misere zu entkommen, dies war für die anderen, für die politisch-ökonomische Führungsriege der Bundesrepublik und ihre Gründergeneration, die Einlösung des alten, nie über-wundenen Traumes von einem (wieder) großen und mächtigen Deutschland, die endliche Aufhebung der tiefen nationalen Kränkung, die das Superversailles[4] von 1945 und die deutsche Teilung für sie bedeutet hatte, und vor allem die konkret sich bietende Chance, den verhaßten deutschen Staat jenseits der Elbe, den man nie anerkannt und niemals toleriert hatte, nun endlich liquidieren und zugleich das eigene Wirtschaftsgebiet, den eigenen Markt bis an die Grenzen von Oder und Neiße (und darüber hinaus) vorschieben zu können. Wo das Kapital hilft, will es erfahrungs-gemäß auch gleich verfügen und in Besitz nehmen. Eben darum hat Kohl so aufs Tempo gedrückt und so rasch die Weichen für die staatliche Einheit gestellt.

Eben weil diese Motive hinter der patriotischen Tarnschicht so mächtig waren, durfte das Für und Wider einer deutsch-deutschen Konföderation, d. h. einer nicht nationalstaatlichen Lösung der deutschen Frage, gar nicht erst zum Gegenstand einer öffentlichen Verhandlung werden.

Michael Schneider, *Die abgetriebene Revolution* (Berlin, 1990), 100–1.

Vocabulary
der **Faß ohne Boden** endless drain
einmütig unanimous
marod clapped out
die **Löcher stopfen** repair the holes
der **Facharbeiter** skilled worker
verschulden be to blame for
die **Ausbildungskosten** training costs
zu außertariflichen Bedingungen below agreed rates
selbst ermächtigt self-appointed
hervor.gehen (aus + dat.) develop out of
die **Entwürdigungs- und Demütigungsrituale** undiginified and humiliating rituals
die **Übergangsregierung** transitional government
delegitimieren rob of their legitimacy
der **Verfassungsentwurf** draft constitution
die **Sozialcharta** social charter
die **Anteilsscheine** share vouchers
die **medialen Verstärker** media amplifiers
spöttische Herablassung mocking, patronising tone
dilettierend amateurish
weltfremde Spinner unrealistic loonies
der **Bittsteller** supplicant
das **Sozialamt** social security office
die **Volkserhebung** people's revolution
im Klartext in plain language
die **Unterwerfung** submission
der **Ismus** '-ism'
ersatzlos streichen here: completely displace
das **Anlagevermögen** assets
ein.bringen, i, a, a contribute
das **Hohngelächter** mocking laughter
die **Montagsläufer** Monday demonstrators
die **realsozialistische Misere** the disaster of 'real socialism'
die **Führungsriege** ruling elite
die **Einlösung des Traums** the attainment of a dream
überwinden, i, a, u overcome
die **Aufhebung** ending, suspension
die **Kränkung** humiliation
liquidieren liquidate
erfahrungsgemäß experience shows
verfügen control
aufs Tempo drücken speed things up
die **Weichen stellen** set the course
die **Tarnschicht** camouflage covering

Notes
1 **Rainer Eppelmann:** An opposition pastor in the GDR; under Modrow Eppelmann was Minister for Peace and Disarmament.
2 **Wer nicht ... Bananen:** 'If you don't do as you're told, you don't get a thing, not even bananas.'

179

3 **Dem Bonner Ruf ... Montagsläufern:** 'As is clear both from the calculated policy of destabilization and the refusal to give immediate assistance and the extortionate conditions to which the Federal government linked assistance, Bonn's call for 'reunification' was not based on the same motivation as that of the Monday demonstrators in Leipzig.'

4 **Superversailles:** The conditions dictated by the Allies at the end of the Second World War (Potsdam) were, in the view of German nationalists, an even greater humiliation than the conditions laid down at Versailles after the defeat of Germany in the First World War.

14 February. At the 'Open Skies' Conference in Ottawa the Foreign Ministers of the GDR, the Federal Republic, the USA, the USSR, the United Kingdom and France (the four Allied Powers) agree on '2 + 4 talks' to discuss the international and security aspects of German unification... The constitutional, economic and social questions of unification will be left to the two German states ... No agreement is reached on whether a united Germany be a member of NATO, an idea still adamantly rejected by the USSR.

57. The GDR economy on the verge of collapse

Die Wirtschaft der DDR steht am Rande des Zusammenbruchs. Streiks, Arbeitsniederlegungen, mangelnde Kooperation und Auswanderung haben erhebliche Produktionsausfälle verursacht, klagte der Leiter des Wirtschaftskomitees des Ministerrats, Karl Grünheid. Im Januar (1990) erreichte die Produktion der Industrie nicht das Dezember-Niveau, im ersten Quartal 1990 wird die Industrie der DDR nicht mehr Waren produzieren als in der gleichen Zeit 1985. Auf das ganze Jahr gerechnet, dürfte die Produktion um vier bis fünf Prozent sinken. Die Exportziele werden verfehlt, gleichzeitig sind höhere Importe nötig, um die Versorgung zu sichern und dringend erforderliche Ausrüstungen für den Umweltschutz zu beschaffen. ...

Statt zu helfen, bedienen sich die Kapitalisten erst einmal. Vor allem in grenznahen Gebieten und in Ost-Berlin gehen Bundesbürger auf Einkaufstour, hamstern DDR-Waren und bevölkern Restaurants und Kneipen. Besonders begehrt bei Bundesbürgern sind Fleisch, Wurst, Fisch, Butter, Käse, Teigwaren. All diese Produkte sind für Bundesbürger dank des (damaligen) Wechselkurses von eins zu drei (legal) oder gar eins zu sechs (illegal) und der horrenden staatlichen Subventionen unglaublich billig. Selbst Wein, Sekt, Zigaretten, Photoapparate, Glas, Porzellan und Straßenschuhe, die seit 1977 nach Vorgaben von Salamander[1] in der DDR produziert werden, landen in den Einkaufstaschen von Bundesbürgern. Im Bezirk Schwerin fallen Mitarbeiter bundesdeutscher Firmen in Gaststätten und Restaurants ein, um Betriebsfeiern zu veranstalten.

In grenznahen Gebieten machen DDR-Unternehmen fünfzig Prozent ihres Umsatzes mit Bundesbürgern; in vielen Gaststätten, wo ein Glas Bier bei offiziellem Umtauschkurs knapp zwanzig Pfennig (West) kostet, sind die Umsätze dank der trinkfreudigen und hungrigen Bundesdeutschen um hundert Prozent gestiegen. Dieser Boom, der Händler und Wirte im Westen fröhlich stimmen würde, schafft in der DDR Unruhe. Denn das Land produziert zu wenig, um dem Käuferansturm aus dem Westen auf Dauer gewachsen zu sein. ...

Der Niedergang der Ökonomie (Wirtschaft) beschränkt sich nicht auf Industrie und Handel. Vor allem das Gesundheitswesen leidet unter der Übersiedlung vieler DDR-Bürger in die Bundesrepublik – in diesem Jahr (1990) schon rund 70 000. Das Südstadtkrankenhaus in Rostock verliert pro Woche fünf bis sieben Schwestern. In Berlin kann das Krankenhaus Mitte nur noch dank der Unterstützung anderer Krankenhäuser weiterarbeiten. In etlichen Kliniken haben ganze Abteilungen dichtgemacht.

Peter Christ, "Alles Schrott", in *Die Zeit*, 9. Februar 1990.

Vocabulary
>**am Rand des Zusammenbruchs** on the verge of collapse
>
>**die Arbeitsniederlegung** walk-out
>
>**die Auswanderung** emigration
>
>**der Produktionsausfall** loss of production
>
>**das Quartal** quarter
>
>**verfehlen** miss, not reach
>
>**die Versorgung** supply
>
>**die Ausrüstung für den Umweltschutz** equipment for environmental protection
>
>**beschaffen** obtain
>
>**sich bedienen** help oneself
>
>**auf Einkaufstour gehen** go on a shopping spree
>
>**hamstern** hoard
>
>**die Teigwaren** pasta
>
>**horrend** extortionate

ein.fallen, ä, ie, a invade
eine Betriebsfeier veranstalten hold an office party
der **Umsatz** turnover
der **Umtauschkurs** exchange rate
trinkfreudig fond of drinking
das **Gesundheitswesen** health system
die **Übersiedlung (in + acc.)** emigration to
dicht.machen close down

Notes
1 **nach Vorgaben ... Salamander:** using patterns from the West German shoe
company Salamander.

15 February. In the *Bundestag* Kohl rejects the Soviet proposal for a
neutralised, demilitarised united Germany which belongs neither to NATO
nor to the Warsaw Pact. This idea, which has been widely canvassed
both within East and West Germany and abroad, is criticised for leaving
Germany as a politically unattached and potentially threatening major
power in central Europe ... In a declaration from his temporary accommodation provided by the church Erich Honecker accepts political
responsibility for the crisis in the GDR.

58. Honecker accepts political responsibility
(Lobetal, 14. Februar 1990)

Entsprechend meinen früheren Erklärungen gegenüber der damaligen SED bekenne ich mich zu der politischen Verantwortung
für die Krise, in die der Staat und die Bevölkerung der DDR
geraten ist. Das betrifft auch die Umstände, die letzlich zu der
Fälschung der Wahlergebnisse vom 7. Mai 1989 führten. Gleichzeitig möchte ich betonen, daß ich nie in meinem Leben politische
Entscheidungen aus egoistischen Motiven getroffen habe und
daß ich mich frei von jeder Schuld im strafrechtlichen Sinne
fühle.

Erklärung des ehemaligen Staats- und Parteichefs Erich Honecker.[1]

Vocabulary
    entsprechend in correspondence with
die **Fälschung** rigging
    im strafrechtlichen Sinn in terms of criminal law

Notes

1 Erich Honecker was later flown to Moscow in a clandestine operation. After the collapse of the Soviet Union he sought refuge in the Chilean Embassy in Moscow. Ordered to leave by the Russian authorities, he returned to Berlin to face trial. He was charged with manslaughter, being held responsible for the shooting of escapees crossing the border. Due to his declining health the trial was abandoned in 1993. He flew to Chile, where he died in 1994.

17 February. The systematic dismantling of the Berlin Wall begins ... 20 February. An enormous depository of Western goods confiscated by the *Stasi* is discovered, from which leading East German politicians have helped themselves freely ... 20 February. It is announced that 5 million dossiers have been gathered from Stasi archives. As many as one family in two in the GDR has been under surveillance ... 28 February. There are reports of East German soldiers and officers reporting for service at the West German Ministry of Defence.

2 March. The Round Table submits a 'Social Charter' containing wide-ranging social and constitutional guarantees to be incorporated in future negotiations on German unification ... 3 March. Both Modrow and Gorbachev reject the idea of membership of NATO by a united Germany ... The West German SPD, initially against immediate German unification, abandons its previous policy of a Confederation of two independent German states. It accepts the idea of an accession of the GDR to the Federal Republic under Article 23 of the Basic Law (Federal Constitution) ... In March dispossessed East German landowners from the Federal Republic begin to survey their former property and holdings in the GDR with a view to re-establishing a claim to ownership ... 14 March. Shortly before the *Volkskammer* elections Wolfgang Schnur, the Chairman of the *Demokratischer Aufbruch* admits to having collaborated with the *Stasi* and resigns. This is the first of many subsequent accusations, confessions and revelations involving politicians, churchmen and sportsmen and women ... 18 March. The first free elections for the *Volkskammer* are held.

59. Volkskammer elections in the GDR

Ob die Wahl klare Mehrheitsverhältnisse in der DDR schaffen würde, war im Verlauf des Wahlkampfes noch sehr unklar. Ängste und Unsicherheit der Bevölkerung prägten den Wahlkampf und die Themenstellung der Parteien bis zum letzten Tag. Noch bis kurz vor den Wahlen erwartete man ein sehr knappes Ergebnis für die beiden größten Parteien, SPD und CDU, die sich stark an die Strukturen ihrer bundesdeutschen Schwesterparteien anlehnten. Doch die Wähler votierten anders. Stärkste Partei wurde die CDU mit fast 41 Prozent, während die Sozialdemokraten nicht einmal 22 Prozent auf sich vereinen konnten. Katastrophal war das Ergebnis für die Bürgerbewegungen, die die 'friedliche Revolution' in der DDR im Herbst 1989 auf den Weg brachten: Nur zwölf Mandate und einen Stimmenanteil von 2,9 Prozent konnten Neues Forum, Demokratie Jetzt und die Initiative Freiheit und Menschenrechte, die sich im Bündnis 90 zusammengeschlossen hatten, nach dem Urnengang der DDR-Bürger verbuchen. Eine mögliche Ursache für das Versagen der Bürgerbewegungen wird wohl die Polarisierung der Wahlthemen gewesen sein. Während sich die SPD und CDU stark an bundesdeutsche Vorgaben orientierten, trafen sich die Bürgerbewegungen mit der PDS, der Nachfolgeorganisation ihres ehemaligen Gegners SED, bei der Einschätzung, daß die DDR sich doch eine gewisse Eigenständigkeit bewahren sollte. Für viele DDR-Wähler war diese Position, in einer vor allem wirtschaftlich unsicheren Lage, jedoch nicht tragbar. Zudem war für viele DDR-Bürger die Frage der Zugehörigkeit schon vor der Wahl gelöst: Bei einer Umfrage gaben 52 Prozent der Befragten an, sie fühlten sich als 'Deutsche' und nur 37 Prozent bezeichneten sich als 'DDR-Bürger'. ...

Zwei Tage nach der Wahl veröffentlichte das Meinungsforschungsinstitut infas die Analyse zur Volkskammerwahl: 'Der Wahlkampf ... bezog seine Dynamik und seine Akzente weitgehend aus den Aktivitäten der bundesdeutschen Parteien, die mit Wahlwerbung und Auftritten von Spitzenpolitikern die Wähler in Massenkundgebungen mobilisierten. Die zahlreichen Parteien, die sich nach dem Umbruch in der DDR gebildet haben, zeigten wenig eigenes Profil, obgleich sich die Debatte im wesentlichen um ein Thema drehte: weniger das Ob, als vielmehr das Wie und Wann der Vereinigung Deutschlands und ihre Folgen standen zur Frage. Dabei rückten die zentralen Akteure der 'friedlichen Revolution' und ihre politischen Gruppierungen immer weiter in den Hintergrund.' So war es eigentlich auch nicht überraschend, daß die bundesdeutsch orientierten Parteien über zwei Drittel der Wählerstimmen bekamen. Drei überwiegende Trends im Wählerverhalten wurden deutlich: In der DDR herrscht ähnlich wie in der Bundesrepublik ein Nord-Süd-Gefälle: der Süden wählte konservativer (Stimmenanteile der Allianz[1] bis zu 62 Prozent). Hingegen zeigte sich, daß die großen Städte der DDR ein besseres Pflaster für Sozialdemokraten, Bürgerbewegungen und der SED-Nachfolgepartei PDS waren. Auch in Ausbildung, Berufszugehörigkeit und Wahlverhalten zeigten sich starke Unterschiede. Akademische Wähler legten ein ähnliches Wahlverhalten wie die Bevölkerung der großen Städte an den Tag. Wohingegen auf die Allianz in südlichen Landkreisen mit überwiegender Arbeiterbevölkerung bis zu zwei Drittel der Stimmen entfielen. Dieser Trend ist wohl auch am auffallendsten: Gerade in hochindustrialisierten Gebieten mit einem sehr hohen Arbeiternehmeranteil – einer Klientel, die historisch eigentlich sozialdemokratisch orientiert ist – fanden die konservativen Parteien einen enormen Anhang. Dazu infas: 'CDU und CSU sind hier weit im Terrain vorgedrungen, das ihnen soziologisch verschlossen zu sein schien. Eine gewisse Parallele hat es nur einmal auch in der Bonner Wahlgeschichte gegeben, nämlich 1983, als große Teile der Arbeiterschaft für die konservative Wende[2] gestimmt hatten.' Ein Wählerverhalten, das nicht umsonst dazu führte, daß von einer 'Wahl zugunsten der D-Mark' gesprochen wurde.

Bernhard Michalowski, "Die erste freie Wahl", in Weiland *et al.*, *9. November. Das Jahr danach* (Munich, 1990), 94–8.

Vocabulary

    klare Mehrheitsverhältnisse schaffen produce a clear majority
    ein knappes Ergebnis a close result
    sich an.lehnen (an + acc.) be oriented to
das Mandat mandate, seat in parliament
    sich zusammen.schließen, ie, o, o unite
der Urnengang ballot
    verbuchen win, score
die Vorgaben guidelines
die Einschätzung evaluation, judgement
    tragbar tolerable
die Zugehörigkeit here: national identity
das Meinungsforschungsinstitut opinion poll organisation
    beziehen obtain, derive
die Wahlwerbung election propaganda
das Auftreten von Spitzenpolitikern appearances by leading politicians
die Massenkundgebung mass rally
das Profil identity

in den **Hintergrund rücken** recede into the background
überwiegend predominant
ein **Nord-Süd-Gefälle** a North-South differential
ein **besseres Pflaster** a more favourable (electoral) territory
die **Berufszugehörigkeit** type of job
an **den Tag legen** display
entfallen, ä, ie, a (auf + acc.) be allotted to
auffallend striking
die **Klientel** clientele, here: electorate
der **Anhang** support
im **Terrain vorgedrungen** encroached on ground
verschlossen closed to
nicht umsonst not for nothing

Notes

1 **Allianz: Allianz für Deutschland** − the electoral alliance formed in February 1990 between the *CDU* (*DDR*), *Demokratischer Aufbruch* and *Deutsche Soziale Union.*

2 **die konservative Wende:** The Social Democratic Chancellor, Helmut Schmidt, was defeated in 1982 when the Social–Liberal coalition (SPD–FDP) was replaced by the Christian–Liberal coalition (CDU–CSU–FDP) under Helmut Kohl.

19 March. At a meeting in Prague Warsaw Pact ministers affirm Germany's right to unification. While Hungary, Poland and Czechoslovakia accept the principle of NATO membership by a united Germany, the Soviet Union continues to insist on German neutrality. This is the clearest possible indication of the radical political differences now emerging in the Eastern bloc and the coming disintegration of the Warsaw Pact as a political and military alliance.

5 April. The first assembly is held of the freely elected *Volkskammer*. The Chairman of the East German CDU, Lothar de Maizière, forms a government ... 6 April. The Soviet Foreign Minister, Eduard Shevardnadze, states that for a transitional period Germany could be a member of both NATO and the Warsaw Pact, until a joint European security system is worked out. This is a major shift in the Soviet position ... 12 April. Lothar de Maizière heads a coalition. The main task of the new government is to negotiate the planned Social and Currency Union with West Germany followed by the unification of the two German states.

60. De Maiziere's government statement

Die Erneuerung unserer Gesellschaft stand unter dem Ruf 'Wir sind das Volk!' Das Volk ist sich seiner selbst bewußt geworden. zum ersten Mal seit vielen Jahrzehnten haben sich die Menschen in der DDR als Volk konstituiert. Die Wahlen, aus denen dieses Parlament hervorgegangen ist, waren Wahlen des Volkes. Zum ersten Mal trägt die Volkskammer ihren Namen zu Recht. Und aus dem Ruf 'Wir sind das Volk!' erwuchs der Ruf 'Wir sind ein Volk!'. Das Volk in der DDR konstituierte sich als ein Teil eines Volkes, als Teil des einen deutschen Volkes, das wieder zusammenwachsen soll. ...

Der Neuanfang unserer Gesellschaft soll auch ein ehrlicher Neuanfang sein: In dem großen historischen Prozeß unserer Befreiung haben wir einem Politiker die wirksame Bündelung vieler positiver Impulse besonders zu danken: Michail Gorbatschow. Wir ahnen die schwere Last, die er in der Sowjetunion zu tragen hat. Wir bitten die Bürger der Sowjetunion, die Politik der DDR und ihr Streben nach der Einheit Deutschlands nicht als bedrohlich anzusehen. Wir sind uns unserer historischen Schuld gegenüber der Sowjetunion bewußt, und wir möchten als freier Staat mit einer Sowjetunion, in der das neue Denken gesiegt hat, freundschaftlich zusammenarbeiten. Glasnost und Perestroika haben der Welt neue, lange Zeit nicht für möglich gehaltene historische Horizonte erschlossen.

Sie förderte auch in der DDR eine Bürgerbewegung, die alle gesellschaftlichen Sektoren erfaßte. Eine entscheidende Kraft dieses Prozesses waren die neuen demokratischen Gruppen, in denen sich Menschen zusammenfanden, die die Fesseln der Vergangenheit sprengten. Die Träger der friedlichen Revolution im Herbst 1989 verdienen einen herausragenden Platz in der deutschen Geschichte. ...

Die Menschen des Widerstandes erinnern uns an unsere Verantwortung für unsere Geschichte. Es ist nicht die PDS allein, die unsere DDR-Vergangenheit zu verantworten hat. Auch meine Partei[1] muß sie verantworten. Wir alle müssen sie verantworten. Es waren immer nur ganz wenige, die etwa bei Wahlen wagten, Gegenstimmen abzugeben oder der Wahl fernzubleiben. Jeder frage sich selbst, ob er immer alles richtig gemacht und welche

Lehren er zu ziehen hat. Es sind nicht immer die Mutigen von einst, die heute am lautesten die Bestrafung anderer fordern. ...

Nach Jahrzehnten der Unfreiheit und der Diktatur wollen wir Freiheit und Demokratie unter der Herrschaft des Rechts gestalten. Dazu brauchen wir einen prinzipiellen Ansatz.

Nicht die Staatssicherheit war die eigentliche Krankheit der DDR, sie war nur eine ihrer Auswüchse. Die eigentliche Erbkrankheit der sozialistischen Gesellschaft war der diktatorische Zentralismus, der aus stalinistischer Verblendung an die Stelle der Demokratie, an die Stelle der Selbstbestimmung der Menschen gesetzt worden war. Dieser Zentralismus war es, der eine alles gesellschaftliche Leben vergiftende Atmosphäre des gesellschaftlichen Drucks erzeugte. Zwang und Druck vernichteten Initiative, Verantwortungsbereitschaft, eigene Überzeugung und machten es zu einer menschlichen Leistung, dem eigenen Gewissen zu folgen. Deshalb genügt es heute nicht, ein Problem aufzugreifen, sondern wir müssen viel tiefer ansetzen. Wir müssen uns unsere seelischen Schäden bewußtmachen, die sich in Haß, Unduldsamkeit, in neuem, nun antisozialistischem Opportunismus, in Müdigkeit und Verzweiflung äußern. Wir müssen uns gegenseitig helfen, freie Menschen zu werden. ...

Es geht um vier Dinge: die Freiheit des Andersdenkenden, Gerechtigkeit für alle, Frieden als Gestaltungsaufgabe nach innen und nach außen, Verantwortung für das Leben in allen seinen Gestalten.

Seit dem Sommer des vorigen Jahres haben wir viele schöne Zeichen der Freundschaft, der Hilfsbereitschaft und der Offenheit der Bundesbürger erlebt. Aber wir sehen mit Sorge auch Tendenzen schwindender Bereitschaft, abzugeben und solidarisch zu sein. Daher eine herzliche Bitte an die Bürger der Bundesrepublik: Bedenken Sie, wir haben 40 Jahre die schwere Last der deutschen Geschichte tragen müssen. Die DDR erhielt bekanntlich keine Marshall-Plan-Unterstützung, sondern sie mußte Reparationszahlungen erbringen. Wir erwarten von ihnen keine Opfer. Wir erwarten Gemeinsamkeit und Solidarität. Die Teilung kann tatsächlich nur durch Teilen aufgehoben werden. ...

Wir werden gefragt: Haben wir gar nichts einzubringen in die deutsche Einheit? Und wir antworten: Doch, wir haben! Wir bringen ein unser Land und unsere Menschen, wir bringen geschaffene Werte und deren Fleiß ein, unsere Ausbildung und unsere Improvisationsgabe. Not macht auch erfinderisch. Wir bringen die Erfahrungen der letzten Jahrzehnte ein, die wir mit den Ländern Osteuropas gemeinsam haben. Wir bringen ein unsere Sensibilität für soziale Gerechtigkeit, für Solidarität und Toleranz. In der DDR gab es eine Erziehung gegen Rassismus und Ausländerfeindlichkeit, auch wenn sie in der Praxis wenig geübt werden konnte. Wir dürfen und wollen Ausländerfeindlichkeit keinen Raum geben. Wir bringen unsere bitteren und stolzen Erfahrungen an der Schwelle zwischen Anpassung und Widerstand ein. Wir bringen unsere Identität ein und unsere Würde.

Unsere Identität, das ist unsere Geschichte und unsere Kultur, unser Versagen und unsere Leistungen, unsere Ideale und unsere Leiden. Unsere Würde, das ist unsere Freiheit und unser Menschenrecht auf Selbstbestimmung.

Regierungserklärung vom Ministerpräsident der DDR, Lothar de Maizière.

Vocabulary

sich konstituieren constitute itself
erwachsen, ä, u, a, (aus + dat.) grow out of
bedrohlich threatening
die **Fesseln sprengen** break the shackles
herausragend pre-eminent
zu verantworten haben to be held responsible for
die **Gegenstimme** dissenting vote
ein **prinzipieller Ansatz** a beginning from basics
die **Staatssicherheit** state security apparatus
die **Auswüchse** unhealthy excrescences
die **Verblendung** blindness
die **Verantwortungsbereitschaft** readiness to take responsibility
die **Leistung** achievement
auf.greifen, ei, i, i tackle
an.setzen begin
die **seelischen Schäden** psychological damage
der **Andersdenkende** someone with a different opinion
die **Gestaltungsaufgabe** creative task
ab.geben, i, a, e make sacrifices
die **Reparationszahlung** payment of reparations
auf.heben, e, o, o overcome
die **Improvisationsgabe** talent for improvisation
die **Sensibilität** sensitivity
die **Ausländerfeindlichkeit** xenophobia
die **Schwelle** threshold

die **Anpassung** conformity
die **Selbstbestimmung** self-determination

Notes
1 **meine Partei:** the East German CDU, one of the Blockparteien.

61. The effects of planned economic union

Seit dem 7. Februar mißt das Kabinett Kohl der Herstellung einer
Währungsunion zwischen der BRD und der DDR höchste
Bedeutung bei. Ziel ist, daß auch in unserem Land die D-Mark als
gesetzliches Zahlungsmittel eingeführt wird und die Mark der DDR
ablöst. Dieser 'kürzere' Weg zur D-Mark würde unsere Wirtschaft
schlagartig dem Kosten- und Preisdruck des Weltmarktes
aussetzen. Verbunden damit wären sicherlich ein bestimmter
Produktivitätszuwachs, die schnelle Überwindung von Vorsor-
gungsengpässen und erweiterte Reisemöglichkeiten.
Doch gegenwärtig beträgt nach BRD-Angaben das Produktivitätsgefälle zwischen der BRD und der DDR in den einzelnen Wirt-
schaftsbereichen 35 bis 60 Prozent. Ein solches Gefälle führt bei
einer Einführung der D-Mark unweigerlich zu einem massenhaften
Ruin von Betrieben, aber auch Genossenschaften und Privat-
unternehmen, die der Konkurrenz aus der BRD nicht gewachsen
sind. Bei diesem Produktivitätsgefälle ist es auch nicht möglich,
annähernd gleiche Löhne wie in der BRD zu zahlen. Das Lohngefälle, und damit ein entscheidender Übersiedlungsgrund, wären
also nach wie vor vorhanden. Ungeklärt ist auch die Frage, was
mit den Spareinlagen und dem Bargeld der DDR-Bevölkerung
passiert, da die Einführung der D-Mark ja gleichbedeutend mit
einer Währungsreform wäre (daß 172 Milliarden DDR-Mark im
Verhältnis 1:1 umgetauscht werden, ist wohl kaum durchführbar).
Schließlich auch das Problem, woher die Renten für DDR-Bürger
kommen sollen, die ja auch in D-Mark gezahlt werden müssen.
Nicht zuletzt müßten auch die Grundfonds (Betriebsausstattung)
und Immobilien umbewertet werden, was vor allem zu Preis-
erhöhungen für Boden-, Wohn- und Gewerberäume führen
würde.
Deshalb sollte man nicht auch die Möglichkeit eines 'längeren'
Weges zur D-Mark aus dem Auge verlieren, der über die

schrittweise Konvertierbarkeit (Austauschbarkeit gegen andere Währungen) der DDR-Mark führt. Zwar würden Betriebe und Bevölkerung dann nur schrittweise in den Genuß von D-Mark gelangen, doch wären die sozialen und wirtschaftlichen Risiken überschaubarer. Außerdem wäre die Währungsunion dann nicht Ausgangspunkt von Wirtschatsreformen und dem Zusammenwachsen der beiden deutschen Staaten, sondern integrierter Bestandteil dieser Prozesse, wodurch ökonomische und soziale Härten begrenzbarer wären.

Gerald Nowak, "Die von vielen erwünschte Währungsunion hat ihre Haken", in *Leipziger Volkszeitung*, 10./11. February 1990.

Vocabulary
dem Kosten- und Preisdruck aus.setzen expose to cost and price pressures
 die Überwindung von Versorgungsengpässen the overcoming of shortages
 das Produktivitätsgefälle the discrepancy in productivity
 die Genossenschaft co-operative
 der Konkurrenz gewachsen a match for competition
 das Lohngefälle wage differentials
 die Spareinlage savings
 die Währungsreform currency reform
 der Grundfonds capital base
 die Betriebsausstattung firm's capital
 die Immobilien property
  um.bewerten convert
 die Gewerberäume commercial property sites
 die Konvertierbarkeit convertibility
 die Austauschbarkeit convertibility
  überschaubar foreseeable, calculable
 ein integrierter Bestandteil an integral component part
  begrenzbar containable

18 April. There are no further border controls between East and West Germany. Espionage activity between the two countries is officially ended ... 19 April. De Maizière demands a currency exchange rate of 1:1 in the coming currency union ... 24 April. The *Bundesbank* recommends an exchange rate of 2:1. This marks the beginning of a bitter and prolonged controversy on the exchange-rate conditions of currency union ... 29 April. After a meeting with Gorbachev, de Maizière declares that a continued membership of NATO by a united Germany must be conditional on a basic change in the confrontational character and military posture of the alliance.

2 May. Agreement is reached on the details of the currency union. Wages, rent and pensions are to be converted at a rate of 1:1. Bank savings are to be converted at varying rates according to age groups in order not to disadvantage older and poorer people. The general exchange rate is 2:1 ... 4 May. After previous major disarmament concessions by the Soviet Union the USA declares that it is ready to forego a modernisation of nuclear short-range weapons in Europe. This marks a further stage in radical disarmament measures carried out by East and West in Europe ... 5 May. The '2 + 4 talks' begin in Bonn to discuss border questions, political and strategic problems, questions relating to international law and the residual Allied presence in Berlin ... 6 May. The first free local elections are held in the GDR ... 8 May. The FDGB, the East German trade-union organisation, is disbanded ... The managing directors of the industrial *Kombinate* of East Germany are dismissed prior to reorganisation, later privatization or closure ... 16 May. A German Unity Fund, initially of DM 115 billion, is set up to finance modernisation in the GDR ... 18 May. The *Staatsvertrag* on Economic, Currency and Social Union between the two German states is signed.

62. The signing of the Treaty of Economic Union. Kohl's speech

Die Unterzeichnung des Staatsvertrages ist ein denkwürdiges Ereignis für alle Deutschen und Europäer. Was wir hier erleben, ist die Geburtsstunde des freien und einigen Deutschland: vor den Augen der Welt bekunden die Vertreter der frei gewählten Regierungen beider Teile Deutschlands ihren Willen, als ein Volk, als eine Nation gemeinsam ihre Zukunft in einem freiheitlichen und demokratischen Staat zu gestalten.

Mit diesem historischen Tag der Unterzeichnung des Vertrages über die Wirtschafts-, Währungs- und Sozialunion beginnt auch ein neuer Abschnitt der europäischen Geschichte. Wir stellen uns damit gleichzeitig einer großen Gestaltungsaufgabe. Ihr Gelingen ist weit über die Grenzen Deutschlands hinaus von größter Bedeutung für die Zukunft ganz Europas.

Wir haben uns mit dem Übergang von der sozialistischen Kommandowirtschaft zur Sozialen Marktwirtschaft in der DDR wahrlich keine leichte Aufgabe gestellt. Wir betreten in vieler Hinsicht Neuland und mußten als gleichberechtigte Partner nach Lösungen suchen für eine Fülle von neuen Problemen, ja einer bisher beispiellosen Herausforderung begegnen. ...

Der Staatsvertrag über die Währungs-, Wirtschafts- und Sozialunion bedeutet einen ersten entscheidenden Schritt auf dem Weg zur Einheit. Für die Menschen in Deutschland wird damit – in wichtigen Bereichen ihres täglichen Lebens – die Einheit erlebbare Wirklichkeit.

Unseren Landsleuten in der DDR eröffnet sich – nach einer sicherlich nicht einfachen Zeit des Übergangs – die Chance auf eine rasche, durchgreifende Besserung ihrer Lebensbedingungen. Auch in diesem Sinne ist der heutige Tag für sie ein Tag der Hoffnung und der Freude.

Mit der Unterzeichnung des Staatsvertrages verbindet sich gleichzeitig noch eine andere Botschaft: Es ist ein starkes Zeichen der Solidarität unter den Deutschen: Die Geschicke der Deutschen in der Bundesrepublik und in der DDR werden dadurch unauflöslich miteinander verwoben. Von nun ab ist klar: Wir gehen in eine gemeinsame Zukunft, in einem vereinten und freien Deutschland. Nationale Solidarität wird auch in Zukunft gefordert sein. Ich bin sicher, daß Bund und Länder mit ihrer Einigung über den Fonds zur Finanzierung der deutschen Vereinigung[1] eine gute Lösung gefunden haben.

Ich bin mir bewußt, daß der Weg schwierig sein wird – aber das Ziel lohnt die Anstrengungen. Die Einheit und Freiheit Deutschlands zu vollenden – das ist ein großartiges Werk, an dem alle mitarbeiten müssen. Ich weiß, daß sich in diesen Tagen hüben wie drüben viele Menschen fragen, was dieser beispiellose Vorgang für sie ganz persönlich bedeutet – für ihren Arbeitsplatz, ihre soziale Sicherheit, für ihre Familien. Ich habe Verständnis für solche Sorgen. Doch meine Landsleute in der Bundesrepublik möchte ich fragen: Wann je waren wir wirtschaftlich besser gewappnet für diese nationale Gemeinschaftsaufgabe der deutschen Einheit als heute?

Und meinen Landsleuten in der DDR rufe ich zu: Die Einführung der Sozialen Marktwirtschaft bietet Ihnen alle Chancen, ja die Gewähr dafür, daß Mecklenburg/Vorpommern und Sachsen-Anhalt, daß Brandenburg, Sachsen und Thüringen bald wieder blühende Landschaften in Deutschland sein werden, in denen es sich für jeden zu leben und zu arbeiten lohnt.

Wir Deutschen müssen jetzt zusammenstehen und mit Zuversicht eine gemeinsame Zukunft gestalten. Ich bitte deshalb die Menschen in der Bundesrepublik, auch weiterhin Solidarität mit unseren Landsleuten in der DDR zu zeigen. Bleiben wir uns stets bewußt, daß den Menschen in der DDR vierzig Jahre lang gewaltsam verwehrt wurde, so zu leben, wie die Deutschen in der Bundesrepublik.

Auch an die Menschen in der DDR habe ich eine Bitte: Denken Sie daran, daß der Wohlstand in der Bundesrepublik hart erarbeitet werden mußte. Millionen von Menschen haben über viele Jahre hinweg durch ihren Fleiß und ihre Leistungsbereitschaft dazu beigetragen. Nichts wurde ihnen geschenkt.

Auch in der DDR geht es jetzt nicht um Geschenke, es geht um Hilfe zur Selbsthilfe. Dabei dürfen wir einander nicht überfordern. Und es darf auf dem Weg zur Einheit auch niemand auf der Strecke bleiben. Die Menschen in Ost und West können sich darauf verlassen. Niemandem werden unbillige Härten zugemutet.[2]

Zur Vereinigung Deutschlands gehört auch, daß die Menschen in gegenseitigem Verständnis zusammenfinden. Dabei hat jeder etwas einzubringen: Die Deutschen in der Bundesrepublik außer ihrer harten Währung und ihrer erfolgreichen Wirtschaftsordnung eben auch noch anderes: vor allem eine bewährte freiheitliche Verfassung und die Ideale einer Demokratie, mit der wir vierzig Jahre Erfahrungen sammeln durften.

Die DDR wiederum bringt den Fleiß, die Ideen und die Hoffnungen ihrer Menschen ein, nicht zuletzt auch das Selbstbewußtsein jener, die sich in einer friedlichen Revolution mutig gegen eine Diktatur durchgesetzt haben. Und vielleicht können unsere Landsleute aus der DDR mit ihrem unverstellten Sinn für den Wert der Freiheit auch dem einen oder anderen bei uns den Blick dafür schärfen, welch kostbares Gut das ist: eine deutsche Demokratie in einem einigen Vaterland. ...

Am Ende dieses Jahrhunderts, das so viel Leid über die Menschen gebracht hat, bietet sich uns Deutschen eine einzigartige Chance – die Chance, 'in freier Selbstbestimmung die Einheit und Freiheit Deutschlands zu vollenden' und 'in einem vereinten Europa dem Frieden der Welt zu dienen'. So lautet der Auftrag des Grundgesetzes. Das erwarten auch unsere Nachbarn von uns. Wir wollen deutsche Europäer sein und europäische Deutsche.

Nutzen wir diese Chance, stellen wir uns unserer Pflicht. Ich rufe die Deutschen in Ost und West dazu auf: Schaffen wir das vereinte

Deutschland in einem vereinten Europa. Gehen wir gemeinsam in eine glücklichere Zukunft — für alle Deutschen. Der heutige Tag ist ein Markstein auf diesem Weg.

Erklärung von Bundeskanzler Helmut Kohl.

Vocabulary

denkwürdig memorable
ein neuer Abschnitt a new chapter
die Gestaltungsaufgabe creative task
der Übergang transition
die sozialistische Kommandowirtschaft the socialist command economy
die soziale Marktwirtschaft social market economy
Neuland betreten enter unknown territory
beispiellos unprecedented
erlebbar which can be experienced
durchgreifend thoroughgoing
unauflöslich verwoben inseparably interwoven
der Fonds fund
gewappnet equipped
die Gemeinschaftsaufgabe joint task
blühend thriving
die Zuversicht confidence
verwehrt denied
die Leistungsbereitschaft readiness to work
einander überfordern demand too much of each other
sich durch.setzen assert oneself
unverstellt genuine
die Selbstbestimmung self-determination
der Markstein milestone

Notes

1 **Fonds zur Finanzierung der deutschen Vereinigung:** The initial amount agreed upon to modernise the East German economy and infrastructure, DM 115 thousand million, proved to be totally inadequate. The question of subsequent financial transfer from the 'old' Federal *Länder* to the 'new' *Länder* in East Germany remained a fundamental controversial issue.

2 **Niemandem werden ... zugemutet:** The pledge that German unification would be carried out without economic sacrifices, in the form of tax increases and unemployment, proved to be an empty promise, which soon resulted in disaffection in East and West.

63. The signing of the Treaty of Economic Union. De Maizière's speech

Dies ist heute für uns ein wichtiger Tag. Es beginnt die tatsächliche Verwirklichung der Einheit Deutschlands. Die Währungs-, Wirtschafts- und Sozialunion macht den Einigungsprozeß unumkehrbar. Was wir heute tun, ist ein entscheidender Schritt auf unser Ziel hin: in Freiheit die Einheit Deutschlands in einer europäischen Friedensordnung zu vollenden. ...

Die Einführung der D-Mark, die Einführung der dynamischen Rente[1] und einer Arbeitslosenversicherung sowie die Hilfen für den Staatshaushalt der DDR sind eine großzügige politische Geste der Bundesrepublik Deutschland. Niemand soll vergessen, was die Mark der DDR heute auf einem freien Markt wirklich wert wäre. Und niemand soll sich über die tiefe Krise der DDR-Wirtschaft Illusionen machen. Wir konnten und können nicht so weitermachen wie bisher. Nicht alle Blütenträume, die manche mit dem Staatsvertrag verbunden haben, konnten in Erfüllung gehen. Aber niemandem wird es schlechtergehen als bisher. Im Gegenteil. Welches Land bekommt eine solch gute Startposition wie wir mit diesem Vertrag?

Jetzt sind wir in der DDR am Zuge, das Beste daraus zu machen. Ausgehend von einem realistischen Bild der Lage müssen wir mit einem neuen Gründergeist, mit Engagement, mit Zuversicht und mit dem Vertrauen in die eigene Kraft an die Arbeit gehen. Dabei werden wir die soziale Gerechtigkeit nie aus den Augen verlieren. In unserem sozialen Engagement lassen wir uns so schnell von niemandem übertreffen.[2]

Den Bürgerinnen und Bürgern in der Bundesrepublik Deutschland möchte ich sagen:

Meine Regierung trägt Verantwortung zuerst für die Deutschen in der DDR und deren Interessen. Das entspricht dem Wählerauftrag in unserer neugewonnenen Demokratie.

Zugleich aber stehen wir mit der Bundesregierung in einer gemeinsamen Verantwortung für eine ungeteilte Zukunft. Die Stabilität der D-Mark und die Wahrung eines gesamtwirtschaftlichen Gleichgewichts in der Bundesrepublik und in der DDR, also in dem neuen gemeinsamen Wirtschaftsraum, sind auch unser Ziel in der DDR. Ich sage zu, daß wir nach Kräften dafür sorgen werden, daß die Mittel aus der Bundesrepublik Deutschland bei uns gut angelegt werden.

Ihre Hilfe aus dem Westen verstehen wir als Hilfe zur Selbsthilfe. Auf Dauer wollen wir nichts geschenkt haben. Wir wollen uns unsere Zukunft selbst erarbeiten.

Angesichts der Größe des Vorhabens einer Währungs-, Wirtschafts- und Sozialunion ist es natürlich, daß es in beiden Staaten in Deutschland Diskussionen gibt. Ich finde nur erstaunlich, daß es in Deutschland mancherorts mehr Sorgen gibt als Hoffnungen. Bei uns werden zu viele vor dem unbestrittenen Berg von Problemen, den wir vor uns haben, kleinmütig.

Vielleicht sollten wir Deutschen auch in dieser Frage nicht zu sehr auf uns selbst bezogen sein, sondern nach Europa schauen. Ich bin davon überzeugt, daß im Ergebnis des Einigungsprozesses kein Deutscher ärmer wird, sondern daß es uns allen gemeinsam bessergehen wird. Und dies nicht zu Lasten Europas, sondern zum Nutzen einer gesamteuropäischen Entwicklung in Frieden, Freiheit, Wohlstand und sozialer Gerechtigkeit.

Die Einheit Deutschlands sollte daher nicht in einem neidischen Gegeneinander, sondern in einem fruchtbaren Miteinander wachsen. Wir und Ihr, Hüben und Drüben, Wessis und Ossis,[3] diese und ähnliche Vokabeln sollten bald aus dem Sprachgebrauch verschwinden.

Erklärung des Ministerpräsidenten der DDR Lothar de Maizière.

Vocabulary
der Einigungsprozeß process of unification
    unumkehrbar irreversible
die Arbeitslosenversicherung unemployment insurance
die Blütenträume Utopian dreams
    am Zuge sein to be now up to someone
der Gründergeist spirit of the founders of the nation
das Engagement commitment
die Zuversicht confidence
der Wählerauftrag the mandate of the voters
    an.legen invest
    unbestritten undisputed
    kleinmütig faint-hearted
    auf uns selbst bezogen preoccupied with ourselves
    aus dem Sprachgebrauch verschwinden lose their currency

Notes
1 **dynamische Rente:** The system of index-linked pension increases.
2 **In unserem ... übertreffen:** 'We shall not allow anyone to outdo us in our social commitment.'
3 **Ossis, Wessis:** The half-affectionate, half-derisive way of describing East and West Germans, illustrating the differences in attitude and character.

19 May. The SPD candidate for the Chancellorship, Oskar Lafontaine, recommends the rejection of the *Staatsvertrag*. After controversial and protracted discussions the SPD demands improvements in the negotiated terms of the treaty and then signals acceptance ... 31 May. In Washington Gorbachev again rejects membership of NATO by a united Germany.

7 June. There is the first in a number of arrests in East Germany of former members of the RAF (the *Rote Armee Fraktion*, West German left-anarchists responsible for political assassinations and bank-raids during the 1970s and 1980s.) They have been allowed to assume a new identity in the GDR ... The Warsaw Pact countries agree to change the character of their alliance and to overcome the division of Europe into hostile blocs during the Cold War ... 7 June. Responding, NATO foreign ministers offer Warsaw Pact countries 'friendship and co-operation' ... 9 June. The three western Allied Powers give up their residual legal rights in Berlin dating from the end of the Second World War ... 17 June. The term 'socialism' is officially removed from the Constitution of the GDR by the *Volkskammer* ... 21 June. The *Bundestag* and the *Volkskammer* pass resolutions recognising the Oder-Neiße-line, the Eastern border with Poland.

1 July. The Staatsvertrag and Currency Union come into force. The GDR gives up its own currency and adopts the D-Mark.

64. The GDR adopts the D-Mark

'Kommt die D-Mark nicht hierher, gehen wir zu ihr', hatte es auf einer der Leipziger Montags-Demonstrationen geheißen. Nun wollen Tausende dabeisein, wenn es soweit ist, wenn das, was DDR-Bürger über 40 Jahre lang als 'etwas besonders Heiliges' (so ein Bekannter) angesehen haben, für jedermann zugänglich wird. 'Richtiges Geld', 'Währung', 'Valuta' oder kurz 'Bunte',[1] so haben die Menschen aus der DDR die D-Mark schon früher genannt und damit deutlich gemacht, was sie vom eigenen Geld hielten. Die DDR-Mark wurde für reine Willkürpreise in Zahlung genommen. ...

'Ich freue mich riesig', sagt eine Frau kurz vor Mitternacht auf dem Alexanderplatz. 'Gleich sind wir alle Wessies', meint eine andere. Mit der D-Mark-Ausstattung[2] hat die sozialistische Mangelwirtschaft für die Menschen in der DDR ein Ende. ...

'Um null Uhr geht die Tür auf', verkündet 15 Minuten vor Mitternacht der eigens aus Frankfurt an die Spree[3] geeilte Chef der Deutschen Bank, Hellmut Hartmann. 'Wir haben genügend Geld. Sie kriegen alle Ihr Geld.' Erster Kunde ist Hans-Joachim Corsalli, ein 41jähriger Kohlenfahrer. Sieben Stunden hat er gewartet, bis ihm die Bediensteten die vorher beantragten 2000 D-Mark auszahlen. Er erhält von der Bank ein Sparbuch über 100 D-Mark und einen Präsentkorb zusätzlich. Die meisten Kunden begnügten sich freilich mit Summen zwischen 500 und 1000 Mark. Reichen muß die Abschlagszahlung vom eigenen Konto bis zum 9.Juli, wenn Banken und Sparkassen den normalen Zahlungsverkehr wiederaufnehmen. Viele der Wartenden wollten freilich noch in der Nacht im Westen Berlins 'ein paar Scheine auf den Kopp hauen'.

Walter Momper, noch Regierender Bürgermeister des Berliner Westens, signiert verfallende Ostmarkscheine über 100 Mark. 'Das ist der Gipfel', sagt er denen, die sie ihm hinhalten. Gegen 0.30 Uhr wird die Lage vor der Deutschen Bank, die als einzige zu dieser Zeit D-Mark in Ost-Berlin anbietet, kritisch. Immer mehr Menschen drängen gegen die Glastür. Eine Frau wird ohnmächtig und über die Köpfe der anderen in die Bank gehoben. Fensterscheiben gehen zu Bruch. ...

'Nun haben wir 30 Jahre gewartet, und das ist heute der letzte Tag der sozialistischen Wartegemeinschaft',[4] versucht Uwe, ein Kranwagenfahrer, die Menschen zu beruhigen.

Karl-Heinz Baum, "Sekt und Feuerwerk für die Bunten", in *Frankfurter Rundschau*, 2. Juli 1990.

Vocabulary
> **zugänglich** accessible, available
> **die Valuta** foreign currency
> **der Willkürpreis** arbitrary price
> **die Abschlagszahlung** interim payment
>> **auf den Kopp (Kopf) hauen** to blue one's money, go on a spending spree
>> **verfallen** expire (here: as legal tender)

Notes
1 **Bunte:** Coloured paper – a colloquial term for West German bank-notes.
2 **D-Mark Ausstattung:** being issued with D-Marks.
3 **Spree:** The river in Berlin.
4 **die sozialistische Wartegemeinschaft:** The socialist community of queuers' –
a sarcastic play on the East German 'sozialistische Wertegemeinschaft' – the
socialist community of shared values.

15 July. At a historic meeting in the Caucasus Gorbachev and Kohl reach
agreement on Germany's continued membership of NATO and the
continued presence of Soviet troops in East Germany for a transitional
period. West Germany offers the Soviet Union considerable economic
assistance to deal with its mounting problems. A sum of DM 12 billion
is agreed. Kohl returns to Bonn having achieved all of West Germany's
goals.

23 August. The *Volkskammer* approves the accession of the GDR to
the Federal Republic to come into force in October 1990 ... 31 August.
In East Berlin the two chief negotiators, Minister of the Interior Wolfgang
Schäuble and Secretary of State Günther Krause sign the *Einigungsvertrag*
for the Federal Republic and the GDR.

20 September. The two German parliaments approve the *Einigungsvertrag*.

2 October. The troops of the *Nationale Volksarmee* are placed under
the command of the *Bundeswehr* ... The *Volkskammer* holds its last
session ... 3 October 1990. The GDR ceases to exist. East Germany is
united with the Federal Republic.

65. Germany's new role in the world after unification

Der deutsche Kanzler richtete eine Botschaft an die Nachbarn.
'Wir sind dann', verkündete Helmut Kohl im Deutschlandfunk
über die Wiedervereinigung der Deutschen am 3. Oktober, 'nicht
nur nach der Zahl, sondern nach allen anderen Daten das stärkste
Land in Europa.'
Schon die Bundesrepublik allein verstand sich als *eine* europäische
Vormacht. Kohls Sicherheitsberater Horst Teltschik: 'Es ist in der
Vergangenheit in der EG nichts gegen uns gelaufen.' Nun soll
Deutschland *die* europäische Vormacht werden. Teltschik:
'Künftig geht es erst recht nur mit, nicht gegen uns.'[1]
Nicht als Schmeichelei, sondern als Tatsachenfeststellung nahm

der Bonner Kanzler das Wort des amerikanischen Präsidenten George Bush, die Deutschen seien 'partners in leadership' der Supermacht USA. Bestätigte doch der sowjetische Präsident Michail Gorbatschow ein ums andere Mal den Deutschen, sie spielten im großen Ausgleich zwischen Ost und West 'die Schlüsselrolle'. Kohl mochte auch nicht widersprechen, als der französische Präsident Francois Mitterand zu ihm sagte: 'Helmut. Sie haben die Fäden in Europa in der Hand.'

Ungarns früherer Außenminister Gyula Horn, Vorsitzender der Sozialistischen Partei, sieht das vereinte Deutschland mit der Sowjetunion und den USA gleichziehen: Die Einheit lasse Deutschland zur dritten Großmacht in der Welt werden.

Das neue Deutschland — eine Großmacht, gleichen Rangs mit den beiden Supermächten und ein Mittler zwischen ihnen? Eine Weltmacht, die Europa dominiert und, in seiner Mitte gelegen, den Westen mit dem Osten verknüpft?

Viele Lorbeerkränze wurden da jüngst gewunden. Die Deutschen dürfen sich schmeicheln lassen — übertrieben ist die Beweihräucherung allemal.[2]

Weltmacht: Ohne atomare Waffen, ohne nennenswerte Rohstoffe, in schlechter strategischer Lage, abhängig von Exporten, auf Jahrzehnte durch die milliardenteure Renovierung der ehemaligen DDR belastet — bleibt da der neue Staat nicht, was der westliche Teil war: eine gewichtige Mittelmacht?

'Bis zum Status einer Supermacht', urteilte die *International Herald Tribune* über das vereinte Deutschland, 'wird es noch eine Weile dauern.' Es darf dauern. Außenminister Hans-Dietrich Genscher behagt es nicht, daß Deutschland neben die vier Siegermächte und China als ständiges Mitglied in den Weltsicherheitsrat komplimentiert werden könnte, wie es der sowjetische Deutschlandexperte Nikolai Portugalow vorgeschlagen hat; Genscher hält Deutschland, nicht zuletzt wegen seiner NS-Vergangenheit, in der Rolle als Weltpolizist für überfordert. Allenfalls als gelegentlicher Hilfssheriff, der seine beschränkten Möglichkeiten durch Zahlungsbereitschaft kompensiert, sind die Deutschen vorstellbar.

Allerdings gefiel es Genscher durchaus, als am vorigen Mittwoch in den Vereinten Nationen die Außenminister und Botschafter, vor allem aus der Dritten Welt, Schlange standen, um ihm zu seiner Rede zu gratulieren. Hohe Erwartungen richten Ägypter,

Inder oder Lateinamerikaner an das reiche Deutschland, die westliche Macht ohne große koloniale Vergangenheit, die bislang keine Zeichen neuer Machtpolitik gesetzt hat – vermutlich zu hohe Erwartungen.

Auch Teltschik gibt zu, daß Deutschland nach den wirtschaftlichen Daten oder der Bevölkerungszahl 'gar nicht so überwältigend' dasteht. Aber: Politisch entscheidend sei, welches Bild sich die anderen von Deutschland machten. Und da erscheine es als zentrale Kraft zumindest in Europa. Teltschiks Chef geht weiter: Das wiedervereinigte Deutschland werde von 1992 an im europäischen Binnenmarkt mit seinem einheitlichen Wirtschaftsgebiet von 336 Millionen Verbrauchern ein von Amerikanern wie Sowjets umworbener Partner. Also doch mehr als bloß eine Mittelmacht?

Daß es überhaupt soweit gekommen ist, konnten manche, denen diese Deutschen unheimlich sind, nicht aufhalten. Nicht Mitterand auf seiner Blitzvisite in Kiew, um Michail Gorbatschow zu größerem Widerstand gegen die Wiedervereinigung aufzustacheln. Nicht Margaret Thatcher mit ihrem öffentlichen Aufruf, die Wiedervereinigung könne noch 10, 15 Jahre auf sich warten lassen. Nicht die Polen mit ihrer Angst vor dem unheimlichen Nachbarn, die durch Kohls Torheiten[3] lange genährt wurde.

Fast schon wieder vergessen: Dem Umschwärmen ging passiver Widerstand voraus, nicht zu knapp.

Die Deutschen haben es aller Welt mit ihrem Eilmarsch in die Einheit wieder einmal gezeigt. Sie sind auf der Siegerseite des Kalten Krieges. Sie haben die Ergebnisse des von ihnen begonnenen und verlorenen Zweiten Weltkriegs zu ihren Gunsten revidiert, auch wenn sie im Osten auf fast ein Viertel des einstigen Reichsgebiets verzichten mußten.

Die Teilung des Landes und des Kontinents ist mit dem Zusammenbruch des kommunistischen Experiments aufgehoben. Deutschland beherrscht wieder, so Geopolitiker Genscher, 'die Herzlage Europas', zu der sich die anderen westeuropäischen Völker eben in 'Randlage' befänden: die Briten auf ihrer Insel, die Franzosen am Atlantik, die Italiener und Spanier auf ihren Halbinseln; Dänen, Niederländer, Belgier, Luxemburger finden keine Erwähnung. Der Schwerpunkt Europas: verlagert zugunsten der Deutschen nach Osten.

Was die Deutschen in zwei Weltkriegen nicht bekommen haben –

es fällt ihnen wohl bald friedlich zu, ihrer wirtschaftlichen Tüchtig-keit wegen: die Führung in Europa, jedenfalls in EG-Europa, das auf alle noch Draußenstehenden ungemein anziehend wirkt. An der Spitze des einigen Vaterlandes kann sich Helmut Kohl, von der Harvard University als 'German Hercules' gefeiert, nun auch noch zu jenem Staatsmann mausern, der den alten Kontinent einigt.

Trotz aller Einbindung in die EG, trotz der grenzüberschreitenden Regionalisierung Europas wächst nach klassischen Großmacht-Kategorien die Einflußzone der Deutschen. Kleinere Staaten haben sich anzupassen. Fest verankert in der Europäischen Gemeinschaft, kann Deutschland, sobald der Aufbau der ehemaligen DDR in Schwung gekommen ist, seinem traditionellen Drang nach Osten folgen. Und diesmal sind die Deutschen den östlichen Nachbarn höchst willkommen; ihre Wirtschaftskraft soll die allgemeine Not lindern helfen.

So sehen die anderen den deutschen 'Koloß' (Kohl), lassen bei einem Ausfuhrvolumen von rund 700 Milliarden Mark alle anderen Staaten hinter sich, finanzieren mit 28 Prozent den größten Anteil des EG-Budgets.

Der Spiegel, Nr. 40/1990.

Vocabulary
die Vormacht dominant power
die Tatsachenfeststellung statement of fact
der Ausgleich balance
die Fäden in der Hand haben to hold the reins, be in overall control
  gleich.ziehen ie, o,o (mit + dat.) catch up with
der Mittler mediator
die Beweihräucherung adulation
die Renovierung modernisation
  jemandem nicht behagen someone feels uneasy about
der Weltsicherheitsrat UNO Security council
der Hilfssheriff deputy sheriff
die Zahlungsbereitschaft willingness to pay
der europäische Binnenmarkt the single European market
  umworben sought-after
die Mittelmacht medium-size power
die Blitzvisite lightning trip
  auf.stacheln incite
  unheimlich unnerving, scary
das Umschwärmen admiring attention
der Eilmarsch forced march

die **Randlage** peripheral position
    jemandem zu.fallen, ä, ie, a to fall into someone's lap
    sich mausern (zu + dat.) blossom into
    grenzüberschreitend cross-border
die **Not lindern** alleviate suffering

Notes

1 **Künftig ... uns:** 'In the future, all the more, things will only be possible *with* us, not *against* us.'

2 **Viele Lorbeerkränze ... allemal:** 'Many laurel wreaths have recently been woven [for us] in this connection. The Germans can feel flattered – but the adulation is exaggerated by any standards.'

3 **Kohls Torheiten:** Kohl's stupidities. This refers to Kohl's protracted refusal to issue an explicit and binding recognition of the inviolability of Poland's borders with Germany.

4 **ein Viertel des einstigen Reichsgebietes:** cf. p. 43, n. 3.

66. Günter Grass's sceptical footnote

Schon jetzt ist abzusehen, daß es auf lange Zeit Deutsche erster und zweiter Klasse geben wird. Das neue Unrecht, das auf altem fußt, trifft eine Bevölkerung, die dem anhaltenden Unrecht nach zwölf Jahren nationalsozialistischer Herrschaft weitere fünfundvierzig Jahre lang untertan war. Diese siebzehn Millionen Ostdeutschen sind es gewesen, denen stellvertretend die Hauptlast des von allen Deutschen begonnenen und verlorenen Krieges aufgebürdet wurde. Geschwächt von Anbeginn durch Demontage und Reparationsleistungen in Milliardenhöhe, hatten sie nie freie Wahl; den Westdeutschen hingegen wurde von den Siegern Freiheit geschenkt und Marshallplanhilfe zugestanden. Die Bewohner der SBZ,[1] des Staates in Gänsefüßchen,[2] blieben 'die armen Brüder und Schwestern', an die man sich, anläßlich Weihestunden, zu erinnern bemühte. Jahrzehntelange Herablassung und unverbindliche Wiedervereinigungsrhetorik waren kränkend genug. Die Deutschen zweiter Wahl trugen allzu geduldig die Kleider ihrer reichen Verwandten auf.

Und nun sind sie abermals zweitklassig. Anstelle kommunistischer Mangelwirtschaft wird ihnen unter dem Etikett 'Soziale Marktwirtschaft' rüde Ausbeutung geboten. Häßlich sieht diese Einheit aus. Das ohnehin Ungeschlachte des Kanzlers aller Deutschen hat sich zur Überlebensgröße ausgewachsen und wirft seinen Schatten.

Ihm ist es gelungen, der Teilung Deutschlands, wenngleich die Mauer gefallen ist, Bestand zu sichern. Die Einheit nach seinem Maß spaltet. Den ohnehin Verletzten kränkt sie, dem Schwachen zeigt sie seine Härte. Nicht nur um sich greifende Arbeitslosigkeit, auch die wachsende Erkenntnis, daß später, wenn für Billiglohn Arbeit wieder angeboten sein wird, die Besitzverhältnisse eindeutig zugunsten des westdeutschen Kapitals geregelt sein werden. Diese schon jetzt festgeklopfte Gewißheit legt Treibbeete an für sozialen Neid, der sich in der Regel zu Haß auswächst. Den wieder einmal Zukurzgekommenen, den abermals Angeschmierten, den ewigen Underdogs verspricht Haß in emotionalen Schüben immerhin Stärke.[3]

Schon haben sich die soeben noch zerstrittenen westdeutschen Rechtsradikalen mit den ostdeutschen vereinigt: ihnen ist Konjunktur angesagt. Und da sich Haß nur in Einzelfällen (die literarisch ergiebig sein mögen) als Selbsthaß verzehrt, wird er Ziele außerhalb seines eigenen völkischen Dunstkreises suchen: Westlich der Oder ist Polenhaß alltägliche Gegebenheit. ...

Günter Grass, *Ein Schnäppchen namens DDR* (Frankfurt/Main, 1990), 45–7.

Vocabulary

    fußen (auf + dat.) be based on
    stellvertretend as representatives
  die Demontage dismantlement of industry
  die Reparationsleistungen reparation payments
    zu.gestehen, e, a, a grant, concede
  die Weihestunde commemorative ceremony
  die Herablassung condescension
    unverbindliche Wiedervereinigungsrhetorik noncommittal rhetoric of reunification
    kränkend offensive
  die Mangelwirtschaft economy of scarcity
  das Etikett label
    rüde rough
  die Ausbeutung exploitation
  das Ungeschlachte crudely dominant manner
    überlebensgroß larger than life
  der Bestand continuation
    um sich greifend spreading
  die Besitzverhältnisse property relations
    festgeklopft final, categorical
    Treibbeete an.legen prepare fertile ground

der Zukurzgekommene someone who has lost out in life
der Angeschmierte someone who has been conned
der Schub wave, burst
der völkische Dunstkreis ethnic miasma

Notes

1 **SBZ: sowjetische Besatzungszone** – Soviet Zone of Occupation. Grass ironically uses the term employed for many years to refer to the GDR.
2 **Staat in Gänsefüßchen:** 'The state in quotation marks.' The custom practised particularly by the Axel Springer press (*Bildzeitung*, *die Welt*, etc.) of referring to the GDR as the so-called 'DDR', to deny its final recognition as a state.
3 **Diese schon ... Stärke:** The finality of these facts, which have already been firmly established, is sowing the seeds of social envy, which, as a rule, grows into hatred. For those who are again going to be the losers, those who have been conned once more, for the eternal underdogs, emotional waves of hatred at least provide a semblance of power.

Arbeitsteil

Beantworten Sie folgende Fragen:

Text 1

[1] Charakterisieren Sie die 'Epoche', die mit dem Abbau des 'Eisernen Vorhangs' zu Ende ging.

[2] In welchem Sinne waren die Sperranlagen zwischen Ungarn und Österreich 'historisch und politisch überholt'? Wie kommt der ungarische Politiker zu dieser Einschätzung?

Text 2

[1] Beschreiben Sie mit eigenen Worten den Ablauf der Ereignisse anläßlich des internationalen Treffens an der österreichisch-ungarischen Grenze.

[2] Wie vermittelt der Text die Dramatik der geschilderten Ereignisse?

Text 3

[1] Welche Rolle schreibt das *Neue Deutschland* den westlichen Medien zu?

[2] Was bezweckt das *Neue Deutschland* mit diesem Kommentar?

Text 4

[1] Beschreiben Sie mit eigenen Worten die Gründe für die Unzufriedenheit der DDR-Bürger, die der Stasibericht anführt.

[2] Inwiefern war Ihrer Ansicht nach die DDR-Führung informiert über die öffentliche Meinung im Lande?

Text 5

[1] Welche kritische Haltung nimmt das *Neue Forum* gegenüber der Gesellschaftsordnung im Osten bzw. im Westen ein?

[2] Läßt sich der Ton der Erklärung des *Neuen Forums* als radikal oder eher als moderat bezeichnen?

Text 6

[1] Wie unterscheidet sich dieser Aufruf des *Neuen Forum* von seiner ersten Erklärung? (Text 5)

[2] Welche Reformen hätten Ihrer Ansicht nach noch zu diesem Zeitpunkt in der DDR durchgeführt werden können, ohne das politische System grundsätzlich in Frage zu stellen?

Text 7

[1] Wie stellt das *Neue Deutschland* das weitere Schicksal der Flüchtlinge dar, die nach Westen geflohen sind?

[2] Das *Neue Deutschland* kritisiert die Einflußnahme der westlichen Medien. Welche Rolle spielten Ihrer Meinung nach überhaupt die Medien – West u n d Ost – im Laufe der Revolution in der DDR?

Text 8

[1] Das *Neue Deutschland* unterstellt 'Kräften der Bundesrepublik' eine aktive Teilnahme an der sich zuspitzenden Krise. Welcher Art könnte die Rolle des Westens bei den Ereignisse in der DDR gewesen sein?

Text 9

[1] Wie begründen die Mitarbeiter des *Berliner Ensembles* die Notwendigkeit einer öffentlichen Diskussion zwischen Volk und Regierung?

Text 10

[1] Wie wird in dem Zeitungsbericht die Dramatik der Ereignisse veranschaulicht?

Text 11

[1] Wie versucht die DDR-Führung, ihre Politik im Hinblick auf die Ausreisenden zu begründen?

[2] Welche Überlegungen bewogen die Menschen Ihrer Meinung nach, aus der DDR wegzugehen bzw. in der DDR zu bleiben?

Text 12

[1] Vergleichen Sie die Forderungen des *Staatsschauspiels Dresden* mit der Erklärung des *Berliner Ensembles* (Text 9) hinsichtlich Ton und Inhalt. Welche Unterschiede fallen auf?

Text 13

[1] Inwieweit unterscheiden sich die Erwartungen des Taxifahrers von denen des Autors?

Text 14

[1] Geben Sie die Hauptgedanken Honeckers in dieser Passage wieder.

Text 15

[1] Welche konkrete Kritik kommt in der Stellungnahme des Gerhart-Hauptmann-Theaters zum Ausdruck?

[2] Warum standen Ihrer Meinung nach Schauspieler, Künstler, Musiker und Schriftsteller bei den kritischen Stellungnahmen in vorderster Reihe?

Text 16

[1] Warum rufen die Demonstranten: 'Wir bleiben hier'; 'Gorbi, hilf' uns'?

[2] Fassen Sie die Forderungen der oppositionellen Gruppen zusammen.

[3] Warum nennt sich die neugegründete Partei zu diesem Zeitpunkt noch 'SDP' (später SPD)? Welche sind die Ziele der SDP?

Text 17

[1] Was bezwecken die Sicherheitskräfte mit ihrer Vorgehensweise gegenüber den Demonstranten?

[2] Wo lag Ihrer Einschätzung nach bei den Sicherheitskräften der DDR die Grenze zwischen Überzeugung und Gehorsam?

Text 18

[1] Woran erkennt man die Vorsicht bzw. die Besonnenheit der Demonstranten?

[2] Wie sind die Parolen der Demonstranten zu bewerten? Vergleichen Sie auch die Texte 19 und 20.

Text 21

[1] Welche Bedeutung wird der von Honecker verfaßten Textstelle zugemessen?

[2] Welche Differenzen werden anhand dieses Berichtes innerhalb des Politbüros deutlich?

Text 22

[1] Welchen Kurs verfolgt Krenz in dieser Rede hinsichtlich Reformbereitschaft auf der einen Seite und Stabilität auf der anderen?

[2] Welche Faktoren im Inland bzw. im Ausland mußte Krenz in dieser Phase berücksichtigen?

[3] Wie schätzen Sie die Gefahr internationaler Spannungen bzw. Konfrontationen in dieser Phase der Revolutionen in Osteuropa ein?

Text 23

[1] Inwiefern haben sich die Forderungen bis Ende Oktober 1989 in Ton und Inhalt verändert?

Text 24

[1] Fassen Sie die Mißstände zusammen, die in den öffentlichen Versammlungen kritisiert werden.

[2] Wie reagieren die Verantwortlichen in Politik und Verwaltung auf die Kritik?

Text 25

[1] Inwieweit wird durch die Forderungen der Demonstranten zu diesem Zeitpunkt das Weiterbestehen der DDR als Staat in Frage gestellt?

Text 26

[1] Welche Unterschiede fallen zwischen der großen Kundgebung in Berlin und den früheren Demonstrationen auf?

Text 27

[1] Wie charakterisiert Christa Wolf den Stimmungswandel in der Bevölkerung?

[2] Wie ist dieser Ihrer Meinung nach zu erklären?

Text 28

[1] In welchen historischen Zusammenhang stellt Heym die Demonstration am Alexanderplatz?

[2] Warum unterstreicht er die Macht des Volkes?

Text 29

[1] Wie deutet Hein die Rolle Erich Honeckers? Warum geht er auf diese Frage ein?

[2] Bewerten Sie die Reden Wolfs, Heyms und Heins rhetorisch.

Text 30

[1] Wird die veränderte Zusammensetzung der Demonstrationen bzw. Kundgebungen bis Anfang November anhand der Parolen erkennbar?

Text 31

[1] Was fällt Ihnen stilistisch auf bei dieser Beschreibung der Maueröffnung?

Text 32

[1] Mit welchen Stilmitteln gibt die Autorin die Stimmung in Westberlin nach Öffnung der Mauer wieder?

Text 33

[1] Beschreiben Sie in eigenen Worten die Reaktionen der Menschen angesichts der Konsummöglichkeiten, der Verkehrssituation bzw. der Ausgabe des Begrüßungsgeldes in Westberlin.

Text 34

[1] Welche politischen und historischen Hintergründe gibt der *Spiegel*-Text über die Maueröffnung an?

[2] Was ist hier die Absicht des *Spiegels*?

Text 35

[1] In welchem Licht stellt der Bericht der DDR-Zeitung die Besuche von DDR-Bürgern im Westen dar?

Text 36

[1] Was beabsichtigen die Autoren dieses Aufrufes?

[2] Was wird nach Ihrer Einschätzung der Aufruf für eine Wirkung auf die DDR-Bevölkerung in dieser Phase gehabt haben?

Text 37

[1] Wie sind die Parolen am 13. November zu deuten?

[2] Inwieweit wird das Weiterbestehen der DDR als sozialistischer Staat hier in Frage gestellt?

Text 38

[1] Wie wird hier die politische Position Hans Modrows charakterisiert?

[2] Welches sind die Anzeichen für den fortschreitenden Zusammenbruch der DDR als Staat?

Text 39

[1] Wie werden die führenden oppositionellen Gruppen in der DDR gekennzeichnet?

[2] Welches sind die organisatorischen und politischen Schwierigkeiten, mit denen sich diese Gruppen konfrontiert sehen?

Text 40, 41

[1] Fassen Sie die wesentlichen Forderungen der Demonstration zusammen.

[2] Welche Parolen stehen noch im Gegensatz zu den immer lauter werdenden Forderungen nach Wiedervereinigung?

Text 43

[1] Wie verhalten sich zu diesem Zeitpunkt die Staatsorgane bzw. die Volkskammer gegenüber der SED?

[2] Welches sind die Gründe für die Schwächung der Position Modrows?

Text 44

[1] Wie bewerten Sie das Kräfteverhältnis zwischen denjenigen, die die DDR reformieren wollten und denjenigen, die eine Wiedervereinigung befürworten?

[2] Wie schätzen Sie die Chancen der SED ein, in dieser Phase ihre Macht aufrechtzuerhalten bzw. zurückzuerobern?

Text 45

[1] Woran läßt sich das zunehmende Selbstbewußtsein der Demonstranten erkennen?

[2] Warum werden Stimmen laut gegen eine Wiedervereinigung Deutschlands?

Text 46

[1] Wie stellt sich der Verfasser des Briefes an die *Junge Welt* die 'neue' DDR vor?

Text 47

[1] Welche Gegensätze werden zwischen den Demonstrantengruppen anhand dieses Textes erkennbar?

[2] Geben die in den Demonstrationen gerufenen Parolen ein realistisches Bild von der Stimmungslage in der DDR wieder?

Text 48

[1] Welche bekannten und welche neuen Forderungen erkennen Sie in den Parolen und Transparenten vom 11. Dezember?

Text 49

[1] Welche Veränderungen gibt es in der Rolle der Medien der DDR in dieser Phase?

[2] Welche Mißstände werden in den öffentlichen Diskussionen in den Medien angesprochen?

[3] Warum gelingt es nicht, den Massenexodus aus der DDR aufzuhalten?

Text 50

[1] Charakterisieren Sie die Reaktionen anderer Länder zu diesem Zeitpunkt angesichts der Entwicklungen in Deutschland.

[2] Skizzieren Sie die Haltung bzw. die Strategie des Bundeskanzlers Helmut Kohl im Hinblick auf die Entwicklungen in der DDR.

212

Text 51

[1] Welche unmittelbaren bzw. längerfristigen Auswirkungen auf die Wirtschaft der DDR hat die Öffnung der Grenze?

[2] Was kritisiert der *Spiegel* an der Planwirtschaft der DDR?

Text 52

[1] Wodurch ist die Arbeit der Stasi gekennzeichnet?

[2] Was ist mit einem 'Staat im Staat' gemeint?

Text 53

[1] Was versteht Modrow unter einer 'Konföderation'?

[2] Warum war es Ihrer Meinung nach nicht möglich, das Modell einer schrittweisen Vereinigung der zwei deutschen Staaten zu realisieren?

Text 54

[1] Warum spricht Schneider von einer 'Selbstaufgabe' der Revolution?

[2] Wie beurteilen Sie Schneiders Einschätzung der Ziele der Revolution in der DDR?

Text 55

[1] Was ist konkret gemeint mit 'eingebettet in die gesamteuropäische Architektur'?

[2] Welche institutionellen, sicherheitspolitischen bzw. wirtschaftspolitischen Aspekte sind angesprochen?

[3] Warum werden diese Aspekte gerade von deutschen Politikern immer wieder betont?

Text 56

[1] Was kritisiert Schneider an der Haltung der Bundesregierung? Warum spricht er von einer 'Destabilisierungspolitik'?

[2] Was ist seiner Meinung nach der Grund für die Strategie der schnellen Schritte in Richtung Wiedervereinigung?

Text 57

[1] Mit welchen wirtschaftlichen und sozialen Schwierigkeiten sieht sich die DDR in dieser Phase konfrontiert?

[2] Wäre es Ihrer Meinung nach möglich gewesen, ohne die Wiedervereinigung die wirtschaftliche Lage der DDR zu stabilisieren?

Text 58

[1] Warum fühlt sich Erich Honecker frei von Schuld 'im strafrechtlichen Sinne'? Kann man Ihrer Meinung nach die Schuldfrage moralisch, historisch-politisch und strafrechtlich unterschiedlich bewerten?

Text 59

[1] Wie ist nach Ansicht des Autors das schwache Abschneiden der Bürgerbewegung bei der Wahl zu erklären?

[2] Was ist unter einer 'Wahl zugunsten der D-Mark' zu verstehen?

Text 60

[1] Was kritisiert de Maizière an dem alten Machtsystem der DDR?

[2] Was meint er mit 'seelischen Schäden', 'antisozialistischem Opportunismus', 'Sensibilität für soziale Gerechtigkeit'?

Text 61

[1] Fassen Sie die Vorteile bzw. Nachteile der Währungsunion zusammen.

[2] Welche Prognosen des Autors erwiesen sich als zutreffend?

Text 62

[1] Wie ist Kohls Ansprache aus der historischen Perspektive zu bewerten?

[2] Was fällt Ihnen bei Kohls Ansprache auf im Hinblick auf Stil und Rhetorik?

Text 63

[1] Welche Sorgen und Probleme spricht de Maizière als Folge der Wiedervereinigung an?

[2] Warum spricht er von 'Illusionen und Blütenträumen'?

Text 64

[1] Was war gemeint mit der Parole: 'Kommt die D-Mark nicht hierher, gehen wir zu ihr'?

[2] Inwieweit lassen sich das Streben nach Demokratie und der Wunsch nach westlichem Wohlstand in der DDR trennen?

Text 65

[1] Wie bewertet der *Spiegel* die Vorstellung von Deutschland als neuer Weltmacht infolge der Wiedervereinigung?

[2] Wie ändert sich die politisch-strategische Lage Deutschlands infolge des Zusammenbruchs der DDR und des Warschauer Paktes?

Text 66

[1] 1. Warum befürchtet Grass eine erneute Spaltung der deutschen Gesellschaft?

[2] Inwiefern waren seine Ängste begründet?

Select bibliography

I. The revolution in the GDR

Eckhard Bahr, *Sieben Tage im Oktober. Aufbruch im Oktober* (Leipzig, 1990).

Hannes Bahrmann and Christoph Links, *Wir sind das Volk. Die DDR zwischen 7. Oktober und 17. Dezember 1989. Eine Chronik* (Berlin, Weimar, 1990).

Bernhard Baule, ' "Wir sind das Volk!" Politische Bedingungsfelder der Freiheitsrevolution in der DDR', in *Ursachen und Verlauf der deutschen Revolution 1989*, ed. Konrad Löw (Berlin, 1991).

Peter Behnen, Albrecht Pohle and Julius Wöppel, *Revolution in der DDR. Informationen – Materialien – Fragen* (Hanover, 1990).

— Albrecht Pohle and Julius Wöppel, *Lösung der deutschen Frage. Von der Revolution in der DDR bis zur ersten gesamtdeutschen Wahl* (Hanover, 1991).

Wolfgang Bialas, 'DDR Identität im Umbruch', *das Argument*, 186 (1991), 257–64.

Thomas Blanke and Rainer Erd (eds.), *DDR – ein Staat vergeht* (Frankfurt/Main, 1990).

Phillip J. Bryson and Manfred Melzer, *The End of the East German Economy from Honecker to Reunification* (London, 1991).

William Carr *et al.*, 'Panel Discussion: What has been the driving force behind German unification and reunification: cultural identity, power politics or economic necessity?', *German History*, 9,2 (1991), 152–72.

Karl Cordell, 'The Role of the Evangelical Church in the GDR', *Government and Opposition*, 25,1 (winter 1990), 48–59.

Robert Darnton, *Berlin Journal, 1989–1990* (New York, 1991).

Peter Decker and Karl Held, *DDR kaputt, Deutschland ganz. Eine Abrechnung mit dem 'Realen Sozialismus' und dem Imperialismus deutscher Nation* (Munich, 1989).

Klaus von Dohnanyi, *Brief an die Deutschen Demokratischen Revolutionäre* (Munich, 1990).

Hans Endlich and Harm Mögenburg, *Deutschland einig Vaterland. Abgang einer Diktatur, Chancen eines Neuanfangs* (Frankfurt/Main, 1991).

Fischer Weltalmanach (ed.), *Sonderband DDR* (Frankfurt/Main, 1990).

J. Fitzmaurice, 'Elections in Eastern Europe: Eastern Germany', *Electoral Studies*, 9/4 (December 1990), 327–36.

K. W. Fricke, 'Das Ende der DDR-Staatssicherheit?', *Deutschland Archiv*, 12 (1989), 1340–44.

— 'Zur Abschaffung des Amtes für Nationale Sicherheit', *Deutschland Archiv*, 1 (1990), 59–62.

Joachim Gauck, *Die Stasi-Akten – Das unheimliche Erbe der DDR.* bearbeitet von Margarethe Steinhausen und Hubertus Knabe (Reinbek and Hamburg, 1991).

Gesamtdeutsches Institut – Bundesanstalt für gesamtdeutsche Aufgaben (ed.), *Dokumentation zur Entwicklung der Blockparteien der DDR von Ende September bis Anfang Dezember 1989* (Bonn, 1990).

— *Analysen, Dokumentationen und Chronik zur Entwicklung in der DDR von September bis Dezember 1989* (Bonn, 1990).

— *Dokumentation zur Entwicklung der neuen Parteien und Bürgerrechtsgruppen in der DDR* (November 1989 – Februar 1990) (Bonn, 1990).

— *Dokumentation zur Entwicklung der neuen Parteien in der DDR* (Februar 1990 – April 1990) (Bonn, 1990).

— *Dokumentation zur politischen Entwicklung in der DDR und zu den innerdeutschen Beziehungen April 1990* (Bonn, 1990).

— *Dokumentation und Chronik der innerdeutschen Beziehungen* (1.1.1990 – 31.3.1990) (Bonn, 1990).

— *Dokumentation und Chronik der innerdeutschen Beziehungen* (1.4.1990 – 30.6.1990) (Bonn, 1990).

— *Dokumentation zur Wiederherstellung der 5 Länder in der DDR* (Bonn, 1990).

Gert-Joachim Glaeßner, *Der schwierige Weg zur Demokratie. Vom Ende der DDR zur deutschen Einheit* (Opladen, 1991).

Gert-Joachim Glaeßner (ed.), *Eine deutsche Revolution. Der Umbruch in der DDR, seine Ursachen und Folgen* (Frankfurt/Main, 1991).

Dieter Golombek and Dietrich Ratzke (eds.), *Dagewesen und Aufgeschrieben. Reportagen über eine deutsche Revolution* (Frankfurt/Main, 1990).

— *Facetten der Wende. Reportagen über eine deutsche Revolution*, Bd. II (Frankfurt/Main, 1991).

Jürgen Grabner *et al.* (eds.), *Leipzig im Oktober. Kirchen und alternative Gruppen im Umbruch der DDR. Analysen zur Wende* (Berlin, 1990).

Eduard Grimme, 'Medienmacht und Schweigespirale – der revolutionäre Umbruch in der DDR', *Materialien zur politischen Bildung*, 1 (1990), 18–22.

Gruppe Linkswende, *Ein Staat. Ein Volk?* (Darmstadt, 1990).

Gregor Gysi, *Wir brauchen einen dritten Weg. Selbstverständnis und Programm der PDS* (Hamburg, 1990).

Dan Hamilton, *The East German Opposition: A Primer for the March Elections*, American Institute for Contemporary German Studies (Washington DC, March 1990).

Rolf Henrich, *Der vormundschaftliche Staat. Vom Versagen des real existierenden Sozialismus* (Reinbek, 1989).

Helmut Herles and Ewald Rose (eds.), *Vom Runden Tisch zum Parlament* (Bonn, 1990).

Hans-Hermann Hertle, 'Der Weg in den Bankrott der DDR-Wirtschaft. Das Scheitern der 'Einheit von Wirtschafts- und Sozialpolitik' am Beispiel der Schürer/Mittag Kontroverse im Politbüro 1988', *Deutschland Archiv*, 2 (1991).

Stefan Heym, *Sieben Geschichten aus der ummittelbaren Vergangenheit* (Munich, 1990).

Peter Hoff, 'Continuity and Change: Television in the GDR from autumn 1989 to summer 1990', *German History*, 9,2 (1991), 184–96.

Christa Hoffmann, 'Die Entwicklung in der DDR 1989/1990', *Informationen zur politischen Bildung*, 4,229 (1990), 11–19.

A. Holzschuh, 'Die Medien proben die Pressefreiheit', *Deutschland Archiv*, 2 (1990).

216

G. Holzweißig, 'DDR-Presse im Aufbruch', *Deutschland Archiv*, 2 (1990).

Andreas Huyssen, 'After the Wall: The Failure of German Intellectuals', *New German Critique*, 52 (winter 1991).

Infratest Kommunikationsforschung, *Die Meinung der DDR-Bürger im deutschen Vereinigungsprozeß von Mai bis August 1990* (Munich, 1990).

Cordula Kahlau (ed.), *Aufbruch: Frauenbewegung in der DDR. Dokumentation* (Munich, 1990).

Hubertus Knabe (ed.), *Aufbruch in eine andere DDR. Reformer und Oppositionelle zur Zukunft ihres Landes* (Reinbek, 1990).

Helga Königsdorf, *Adieu DDR. Protokolle eines Abschieds* (Reinbek, 1990).

Egon Krenz, *Wenn Mauern fallen, die friedliche Revolution: Vorgeschichte – Ablauf – Auswirkungen* (Vienna, 1990).

Jürgen Kuczynski, *Probleme der Selbstkritik* (Cologne, 1991).

Kursbuch, *Abriß DDR* (September 1990).

Günter Kusch *et al.*, *Schlußbilanz-DDR. Fazit einer verfehlten Wirtschafts- und Sozialpolitik* (Berlin, 1991).

Karin and Karlheinz Lau, *Deutschland auf dem Weg zur Einheit. Dokumente einer Revolution* (Braunschweig, 1990).

Christiane Lemke, *Die Ursachen des Umbruchs in der ehemaligen DDR* (Wiesbaden, 1991).

Klaus Liedtke (ed.), *Vier Tage im November. STERN-Buch* (Hamburg, 1989).

Konrad Löw (ed.), *Ursachen und Verlauf der deutschen Revolution 1989* (Berlin, 1990).

— 'Die bundesdeutsche politikwissenschaftliche DDR-Forschung und die Revolution in der DDR', *Zeitschrift für Politik*, 38,3 (1991), 237–54.

Christa Luft, *Zwischen Wende und Ende. Eindrücke, Erlebnisse, Erfahrungen eines Mitglieds der Modrow-Regierung* (Berlin, 1991).

Hans-Joachim Maaz, *Der Gefühlsstau. Ein Psychogramm der DDR* (Berlin, 1990).

Marlies Menge, *'Ohne uns läuft nichts mehr': Die Revolution in der DDR* (Stuttgart, 1990).

Sigrid Meuschel, 'Wandel durch Auflehnung. Thesen zum Verfall bürokratischer Herrschaft in der DDR', *Berliner Journal für Soziologie, Sonderheft* (1991), 15–27.

Hans Modrow, *Aufbruch und Ende* (Hamburg, 1991).

Harm Mögenburg, *Die Revolution in der DDR – Freiheit, Einheit und soziale Gerechtigkeit?* (Frankfurt/Main, 1990).

Günter Mittag, *Um jeden Preis: Im Spannungsfeld zweier Systeme* (Berlin, Weimar, 1991).

Armin Mitter and Stefan Wolle (eds.), *Ich liebe euch doch alle! Befehle und Lageberichte des MfS Januar-November 1989* (Berlin, 1990).

Jens Motschmann, 'Evangelische Kirche und Wiedervereinigung', *Ursachen und Verlauf der deutschen Revolution*, ed. Konrad Löw, 1990, 65–84.

Hans-Peter Müller, 'Die "Oktoberrevolution" und das Ende der FDGB', *Ursachen und Verlauf der deutschen Revolution*, ed. Konrad Löw, 1991, 85–104.

Heiner Müller, *Zur Lage der Nation* (Berlin, 1990).

Helmut Müller-Enbergs *et al.* (eds.), *Von der Illegalität ins Parlament. Werdegang und Konzept der neuen Bürgerbewegungen* (Berlin, 1991).

Erhard Neubert, 'Protestantische Kultur und DDR-Revolution', *Aus Politik und Zeitgeschichte*, 19 (1991), 21–9.

Neues Forum Leipzig (ed.), *Jetzt oder nie – Demokratie! Leipziger Herbst '89* (Leipzig, 1989).

Peter Neumann (ed.), *Träumen Verboten. Aktuelle Stellungnahmen aus der DDR* (Göttingen, 1990).

Fred Oldenburg, 'Vom realen Sozialismus zur freiheitlichen Demokratie in der DDR', *Zeitschrift für politische Bildung und Information*, 1 (1990), 28–44.

Karl-Dieter Opp, 'DDR '89. Zu den Ursachen einer spontanen Revolution', *Kölner Zeitschrift für Soziologie und Sozialpsychologie*, 43 (1991), 302–21.

August Pradetto, 'Der Zusammenbruch der DDR – ökonomische und politische Konsequenzen aus der Sicht mittel-osteuropäischer Länder', *Das Ende eines Experiments: Umbruch in der DDR und deutsche Einheit*, ed. Rolf Reißig and Gert-Joachim Glaeßner, 75–98.

Lothar Probst, 'Bürgerbewegungen, politische Kultur und Zivilgesellschaft', *Aus Politik und Zeitgeschichte*, 19 (1991), 30–5.

Bernard Prosch and Martin Abraham, 'Die Revolution in der DDR. Eine strukturell-individualistische Erklärungsskizze', *Kölner Zeitschrift für Soziologie und Sozialpsychologie*, 2, 43. Jg. (1991), 291–301.

Gerhard Rein (ed.), *Die Opposition in der DDR. Entwürfe für einen anderen Sozialismus* (Berlin, 1989).

Rolf Reißig, 'Vom Niedergang zum Untergang des realen Sozialismus', *Zeitschrift für das vereinigte Deutschland*, 4 24. Jg. (April 1991), 395–402.

Rolf Reißig and Gert-Joachim Glaeßner (eds.), *Das Ende eines Experiments: Umbruch in der DDR und deutsche Einheit* (Berlin, 1991).

Volker Ronge, 'Loyalty, Voice or Exit? Die Fluchtbewegung als Anstoß und Problem der Erneuerung in der DDR', *DDR – Von der friedlichen Revolution zur deutschen Vereinigung*, ed. G. Wewer, SH6, 1 (1990), 29–46.

T. Rosenlöchner, *Die verkauften Steine. Dresdener Tagebuch* (Frankfurt/Main, 1990).

Adam D. Rotfeld and Walther Stützle (eds.), *Germany and Europe in Transition (London, 1991).*

Bernd Rudolph, *'Der Massenexodus der Deutschen. Anmerkungen zur öffentlichen Stimmungslage', Materialien zur politischen Bildung*, 1 (1990), 14–18.

Günter Schabowski, *Das Politbüro. Ende eines Mythos* (Reinbek, 1990).

Hanning Schierholz and Hans-Joachim Tschicke, 'Wir sind das Volk – aber wer sind wir? Zur Veränderungsdynamik des politischen Bewußtseins in der DDR', *Materialien zur politischen Bildung*, 1 (1990), 9–14.

Thomas Schmid, *Staatsbegräbnis. Von ziviler Gesellschaft* (Berlin, 1990).

Michael Schneider, *Die abgetriebene Revolution. Von der Staatsfirma in die DM-Kolonie* (Berlin, 1990).

Rolf Schneider, *Frühling im Herbst. Notizen vom Untergang der DDR* (Göttingen, 1991).

Friedrich Schorlemmer, *Bis alle Mauern fallen. Texte aus einem verschwundenen Land* (Berlin, 1991).

Charles Schüddekopf (ed.), *'Wir sind das Volk!' Flugschriften, Aufrufe und Texte einer deutschen Revolution* (Reinbek, 1990).

SPIEGEL Spezial, *162 Tage deutsche Geschichte. Das halbe Jahr der gewaltlosen Revolution* (Hamburg, 1990).

Ilse Spittmann and Gisela Helwig (eds.), *Chronik der Ereignisse in der DDR* (Cologne, 1989).

Walter Süß, 'Revolution und Öffentlichkeit in der DDR', *Deutschland Archiv*, 23,6 (1990), 907–21.

TAZ (Die Tageszeitung), *DDR Journal. Zur Novemberrevolution. August bis Dezember 1989. Vom Ausreisen bis zum Einreißen der Mauer* (Frankfurt/Main, 1990).

TAZ (Die Tageszeitung), *DDR Journal 2, Die Wende der Wende. Januar bis März 1990. Von der Öffnung des Brandenburger Tores zur Öffnung der Wahlurnen* (Frankfurt/Main, 1990).

Reiner Tetzner, *Leipziger Ring. Aufzeichnungen eines Montagsdemonstranten, Oktober 1989 bis 1. Mai 1990* (Frankfurt/Main, 1990).

Uwe Thaysen. *Der runde Tisch. Oder: Wo blieb das Volk? Der Weg der DDR in die Demokratie* (Opladen, 1990).

Manfred Tietzel *et al.*, *Die Logik der sanften Revolution. Eine ökonomische Analyse* (Tübingen, 1991).

Frank Unger, 'Discourses of Unity and Some Reflections about their Aftermath', *German History*, 9,2 (1991), 173–83.

Hans-Joachim Veen *et al.* (eds.), *Deutschland-Report 8. Parteien im Aufbruch. Nichtkommunistische Parteien und politische Vereinigungen in der DDR vor den Volkskammerwahlen am 18. März 1990* (Melle, 1990).

Herbert Wagner, 'Die Novemberrevolution 1989 in Dresden. Ein Erlebnisbericht', *Ursachen und Verlauf der deutschen Revolution*, ed. Konrad Löw (1989), 9–16.

Gregor Walter, 'Der Kollaps der zentralen Machtstruktur der DDR', *Sozialwissenschaftliche Informationen*, 3 (1990), 158–69.

Christian Weber, *Alltag einer friedlichen Revolution* (Stuttgart, 1990).

Severin Weiland *et al.*, *9. November. Das Jahr danach. Vom Fall der Mauer bis zur ersten gesamtdeutschen Wahl* (Munich, 1990).

Micha Wimmer *et al.*, *Wir sind das Volk. Die DDR im Aufbruch. Eine Chronik in Dokumenten und Bildern* (Munich, 1990).

II. The GDR

Autorenkollektiv unter Leitung von Rolf Badstübner, *Geschichte der Deutschen Demokratischen Republik* (East Berlin, 1981).

Horst Barthel, *Die wirtschaftlichen Ausgangsbedingungen der DDR* (East Berlin, 1979).

Klaus von Beyme and Hartmut Zimmermann (eds.), *Policymaking in the German Democratic Republic* (Aldershot, 1984).

Bärbel Bohley *et al.*, *40 Jahre DDR ... und die Bürger melden sich zu Wort* (Frankfurt/Main, 1989).

Bundesministerium für innerdeutsche Beziehungen (ed.), *DDR Handbuch* (Cologne, 1985).

Bürgerkomitee Leipzig (ed.), *Stasi intern. Macht und Banalität* (Leipzig, 1991).

David Childs, *The GDR: Moscow's German Ally* (London, 1983).

David Childs (ed.), *Honecker's Germany* (London, 1985).

Karl Cordell, 'The Role of the Evangelical Church in the GDR', *Government and Opposition*, 25,1 (winter 1990), 48–59.

Mike Dennis, *German Democratic Republic. Politics, Economics and Society* (London and New York, 1988).

European Nuclear Disarmament. German–German Working Group. *Voices from the GDR: Documents on Peace, Human Rights and Ecology* (London, 1978).

Günter Fischbach (ed.), *DDR-Almanach '90. Daten-Informationen-Zahlen* (Stuttgart, 1990).

Forschungsstelle für gesamtdeutsche wirtschaftliche und soziale Fragen (ed.), *Glasnost und Perestroika auch in der DDR?* (Berlin, 1988).

Günter Gaus, *Deutsche Zwischentöne. Gesprächsportraits aus der DDR* (Hamburg, 1990).

Gert-Joachim Glaeßner (ed.), *Die DDR in der Ära Honecker. Politik – Kultur – Gesellschaft* (Opladen, 1988).

— *Die andere Republik. Gesellschaft und Politik in der DDR* (Opladen, 1988).

David Gill and Ulrich Schröter, *Das Ministerium für Staatssicherheit. Anatomie des Mielke-Imperiums* (Frankfurt/Main, 1991).

Antonia Grunenberg, *Aufbruch der inneren Mauer. Politik und Kultur in der DDR 1971–1990* (Bremen, 1990).

Gisela Helwig (ed.), *Die letzten Jahre der DDR. Texte zum Alltagsleben* (Cologne, 1990).

Hubertus Knabe, 'Neue soziale Bewegungen im Sozialismus. Zur Genesis alternativer politischer Orientierungen in der DDR', *Kölner Zeitschrift für Soziologie und Sozialpsychologie*, 3 (1988), 551–69.

— 'Politische Opposition in der DDR. Ursprünge, Programmatik, Perspektive', *Aus Politik und Zeitgeschichte*, 1/2 (1990), 21–32.

Henry Krisch, *The German Democratic Republic. The Search for Identity* (Boulder and London, 1985).

Ferdinand Kroh (ed.), *'Freiheit ist immer Freiheit …' Die Andersdenkenden in der DDR* (Frankfurt/Main, Berlin, 1988).

A. James McAdams, *East Germany and Détente. Building Authority after the Wall* (Cambridge, 1988).

Thomas Neumann, *Die Maßnahme. Eine Herrschaftsgeschichte der SED* (Reinbek, 1991).

Peter Przybylski, *Tatort Politbüro. Die Akte Honecker* (Berlin, 1991).

John Sandford, 'The Church, the State and the Peace Movement in the GDR', *GDR Monitor*, 16 (1989), 27–54,

Renate Schwärzel, 'Zum ökonomischen Vorfeld der Herbstereignisse 1989 in der DDR. Zur wirtschaftlichen Entwicklung der 70er und 80er Jahre', *Deutsche Studien*, Heft 112, 27. Jg. (Dezember 1990), 386–94.

Ilse Spittmann (ed.), *Die SED in Geschichte und Gegenwart* (Cologne, 1987).

— *Die DDR unter Honecker* (Cologne, 1990).

Dietrich Staritz, *Geschichte der DDR 1949–1985* (Frankfurt/Main, 1985).

John M. Starrel and Anita M. Mallinckrodt, *Politics in the German Democratic Republic* (New York, Washington and London, 1975).

Jonathan Steele, *Socialism with a German Face. The State that Came in from the Cold* (London, 1977).

Vladimir Tismaneanu, 'Nascent Civil Society in the GDR', *Problems of Communism*, 38 (March–June 1989), 90–120.

Henry Ashby Turner, jun., *The Two Germanies since 1945* (New Haven and London, 1987).

Ulrich Voskamp and Volker Wittke, 'Fordismus in einem Land – Das Produktions-modell der DDR', *Sozialwissenschaftliche Informationen*, Heft 3/90.

Hermann Weber, *Geschichte der DDR* (Munich, 1985).

— *Aufbau und Fall einer Diktatur. Kritische Beiträge zur Geschichte der DDR* (Cologne, 1991).

Werner Weidenfeld and Hartmut Zimmermann (eds.), *Deutschland-Handbuch. Eine doppelte Bilanz 1949–1989* (Bonn, 1989).

Roger Woods, *Opposition in the GDR under Honecker 1971–85* (Basingstoke, London, 1986).

III. German unification

Ronald D. Asmus, 'A United Germany', *Foreign Affairs* (spring 1990), 63–76.

Rudolf Augstein and Günter Grass, *Deutschland, einig Vaterland: ein Streit-gespräch* (Göttingen, 1990).

Christoph Bertram, 'The German Question', *Foreign Affairs* (spring 1990), 45–62.

Klaus von Beyme, 'Transition to Democracy – or Anschluß? The Two Germanies and Europe', *Government and Opposition*, 25,2 (spring 1990), 170–90.

Dieter Blumenwith, 'Europäische Integration und deutsche Wiedervereinigung', *Zeitschrift für Politik*, Jg. 37, H. 1 (1990), 1–19.

Stephen Brockmann, 'The Reunification Debate', *New German Critique*, 52 (winter 1991), 3–30.

Wilhelm Bürklin, 'Changing Political and Social Attitudes in the United Germany', *Politics and Society in Germany, Austria and Switzerland*, 4,1 (autumn 1991).

Deutscher Bundestag (ed.), *Auf dem Weg zur deutschen Einheit. Deutschland-politische Debatten im Deutschen Bundestag*, 5 vols. (Bonn, 1990).

Klaus von Dohnanyi, *Das deutsche Wagnis* (Munich, 1990).

Freibeuter. Vierteljahreszeitschrift für Kultur und Politik. *Thema Neues Deutsch-land*, 43 (1990).

Karl Wilhelm Fricke, *MfS intern. Macht, Strukturen, Auflösung der DDR-Staatssicherheit* (Cologne, 1991).

Hans-Dietrich Genscher, *Unterwegs zur Einheit. Reden und Dokumente aus bewegter Zeit* (Berlin, 1991).

Walter Göbel, *Deutschlandpolitik im internationalen Rahmen. Stundenblätter* (Stuttgart, 1990).

Martin Gorholt and Norbert W. Kunz (eds.), *Deutsche Einheit – Deutsche Linke. Reflexionen der politischen und gesellschaftlichen Entwicklung* (Cologne, 1991).

Volker Gransow and Konrad H. Jarausch (eds.), *Die deutsche Vereinigung. Dokumente zu Bewegung, Annäherung and Beitritt* (Cologne, 1991).

Günter Grass, *Ein Schnäppchen namens DDR. Letzte Reden vorm Glockengeläut (Frankfurt/Main, 1990).*

— *Two States – one Nation? The Case against German Reunification* (London, 1990).

Jens Hacker, 'The Dissolving of Germany's Dual Statehood and the USSR', *Politics and Society in Germany, Austria and Switzerland*, 4,1 (autumn 1991).

Horst Haitzinger, *Deutschland, Deutschland* (Munich, 1991).

221

Wolfgang Heisenberg (ed.), *German Unification in European Perspective* (London, 1991).

Wolfgang Herles, *Nationalrausch: Szenen aus dem gesamtdeutschen Machtkampf* (Munich, 1990).

Klaus Humann (ed.), *Wir sind das Geld: Wie die Westdeutschen die DDR aufkaufen* (Reinbek, 1990).

Eckhard Jesse and Armin Mitte, *Die Gestaltung der deutschen Einheit* (Bonn, Berlin, 1991).

Michael Jungblut, *Wirtschaftswunder ohne Grenzen. Wohlstand diesseits und jenseits der Elbe* (Stuttgart, 1990).

Karl Kaiser, *Deutschlands Vereinigung. Die internationalen Aspekte* (Bergisch Gladbach, 1991).

Erich Kuby, *Der Preis der Freiheit. Ein deutsches Europa formt sein Gesicht* (Hamburg, 1990).

Beate Kohler-Koch, 'Deutsche Einigung im Spannungsfeld internationaler Umbrüche', *Politische Vierteljahresschrift*, 32. Jg., H4 (Dezember 1991), 605–20.

Rainer Land (ed.), *Das Umbaupapier (DDR). Argumente gegen die Wiedervereinigung* (Berlin, 1990).

Gerhard Lehmbruch, 'Die deutsche Vereinigung: Strukturen und Strategien', *Politische Vierteljahresschrift*, 32. Jg., H.4 (Dezember 1991), 585–604.

— 'Die improvisierte Vereinigung: Die dritte deutsche Republik', *Leviathan*, 18 (1990), 462–86.

Ulrike Liebert and Wolfgang Merkel (eds.), *Die Politik zur deutschen Einheit. Probleme – Strategien – Kontroversen* (Leverkusen, 1991).

Leslie Lipschitz and Donagh McDonald (eds.), *German Unification. Economic Issues* (Washington, 1990).

D. Marsh, *The New Germany at the Crossroads* (London, 1990).

A. James McAdams, 'Towards a New Germany? Problems of Unification', *Government and Opposition*, 25,3 (summer 1990), 304–16.

Ingo von Münch (ed.), *Die Verträge zur Einheit Deutschlands* (Munich, 1990).

Helmut Peitsch, 'Wider den Topos vom "Schweigen". Westdeutsche Schriftsteller zur "Einheit"', *Das Argument*, 190 (1991), 893–902.

Presse- und Informationsamt der Bundesregierung (ed.), 'Vertrag über die Schaffung einer Währungs-, Wirtschafts- und Sozialunion zwischen der Bundesrepublik Deutschland und der Deutschen Demokratischen Republik', *Bulletin*, 63 (1990).

Presse- und Informationsamt der Bundesregierung (ed.), 'Vertrag zwischen der Bundesrepublik Deutschland und der Deutschen Demokratischen Republik über die Herstellung der Einheit Deutschlands – Einigungsvertrag', *Bulletin*, 104 (1990).

Jan Priewe and Rudolf Hickel, *Der Preis der Einheit. Bilanz und Perspektiven der deutschen Vereinigung* (Frankfurt/Main, 1991).

Jens Reich, 'Germany – a Binary Poison', *New Left Review*, 179, 120–4.

Wolfgang Schäuble, *Der Vertrag. Wie ich über die deutsche Einheit verhandelte* (Stuttgart, 1991).

Bruno Schoch (ed.), *Deutschlands Einheit und Europas Zukunft* (Frankfurt/Main, 1991).

Brigitte Seebacher-Brandt, *Die Linke und die Einheit* (Berlin, 1991).

Manfred Stolpe, *Aufbruch. Vom Vorgestern ins Übermorgen* (Berlin, 1992).

Horst Teltschik, *329 Tage. Innenansichten der Einigung* (Berlin, 1991).

Dan van der Vat, *Freedom Was Never Like This. A Winter's Journey in East Germany* (London, 1991).

Werner Weidenfeld and Karl-Rudolf Korte (eds.), *Handwörterbuch zur deutschen Einheit* (Frankfurt/Main, 1991).

Ulrich Wickert (ed.), *Angst vor Deutschland* (Hamburg, 1990).

Eberhard Wilms and Gunhild Wilms (eds.), *Die deutsche Frage* (Frankfurt/Main, 1990).

Anne Worst, *Das Ende eines Geheimdienstes. Oder: Wie lebendig ist die Stasi?* (Berlin, 1991).

Benno Zanetti, *Der Weg zur deutschen Einheit* (Munich, 1991).

IV. International aspects

Timothy Garton Ash, *We the People. The Revolutions of '89* (Harmondsworth, 1990).

Robin Blackburn (ed.), *After the Fall. The Failure of Communisms and the Future of Socialism* (London, 1991).

J.F. Brown, *The Surge to Freedom. The End of Communist Rule in Eastern Europe* (Oxford, 1991).

Alex Callinicos, *The Revenge of History. Marxism and The East European Revolutions* (Oxford, 1991).

David Carlton and H.M. Levin, *The Cold War Debated* (New York, 1988).

Robert Cox, ' "Real Socialism" in Historical Perspective', *The Socialist Register*, ed. Ralph Miliband and Leo Panitch (London, 1991).

Bogdan Denitch, *The End of the Cold War* (London, 1990).

Robert East, *Revolutions in Eastern Europe* (London, 1992).

D.F. Fleming, *The Cold War and its Origins 1917–1960*, 2 vols. (New York, 1961).

Mark Frankland, *The Patriots' Revolution. How East Europe Won its Freedom* (London, 1990).

Mary Kaldor, *The Imaginary War. Understanding the East-West Conflict* (Oxford, 1990).

The *Observer*, *Tearing Down the Curtain. The People's Revolutions in Eastern Europe* (London, 1990).

Gwyn Prins (ed.), *Spring in Winter. The 1989 Revolutions* (Manchester, 1990).

David Selbourne, *Death of the Dark Hero. Eastern Europe 1987–1990* (London, 1990).

Videos

Das Jahr der Deutschen   no. 004   Spiegel-Verlag
Teil 1: Fünf Wochen im Herbst 1989
Teil 2: Deutschland im Frühling 1990
Teil 3: Die letzten Tage bis zur Einheit

Jahresrückblick 1990   no. 005   Spiegel-Verlag

Die Stasi-Rolle   no. 015   Spiegel-Verlag

Learning Resources
Centre